The Pig and I

The Pig and I

Why It's So Easy to Love an Animal, and So Hard to Live with a Man

RACHEL TOOR

HUDSON
STREET
PRESS

HUDSON STREET PRESS
Published by Penguin Group
Penguin Group (USA) Inc., 375 Hudson Street, New York, New York 10014, U.S.A.
Penguin Group (Canada), 10 Alcorn Avenue, Toronto, Ontario, Canada M4V 3B2
(a division of Pearson Penguin Canada Inc.)
Penguin Books Ltd, 80 Strand, London WC2R 0RL, England
Penguin Ireland, 25 St Stephen's Green, Dublin 2, Ireland (a division of Penguin Books Ltd)
Penguin Group (Australia), 250 Camberwell Road, Camberwell, Victoria 3124, Australia
(a division of Pearson Australia Group Pty Ltd)
Penguin Books India Pvt Ltd, 11 Community Centre, Panchsheel Park,
New Delhi – 110 017, India
Penguin Books (NZ), cnr Airborne and Rosedale Roads, Albany, Auckland 1310, New Zealand
(a division of Pearson New Zealand Ltd)
Penguin Books (South Africa) (Pty) Ltd, 24 Sturdee Avenue, Rosebank,
Johannesburg 2196, South Africa

Penguin Books Ltd, Registered Offices: 80 Strand, London WC2R 0RL, England

First published by Hudson Street Press, a member of Penguin Group (USA) Inc.

First Printing, February 2005
10   9   8   7   6   5   4   3   2   1

REGISTERED TRADEMARK — MARCA REGISTRADA
HUDSON
STREET
PRESS

CIP data is available.
ISBN 1-59463-008-9

All photos courtesy Rachel Toor, with the following exceptions: Page 1, girl and dog, courtesy Harry Lapow. Page 7, mouse in martini glass, courtesy E. V. Noechel. Page 183, courtesy Theresa Flynn. Page 247, author photo, courtesy Erin Turner.

Printed in the United States of America
Set in Goudy
Designed by Eve L. Kirch

AUTHOR'S NOTE
Names and characteristics of many of the individuals mentioned herein have been changed to protect their privacy.

This book is printed on acid-free paper. ♾

For the REBs
with love, in friendship

Introduction

When I was a little kid and was asked about my siblings, I always responded that I had two: Mark, a brother, two years younger than me, and Barkus, a sister, exactly five years and one day my junior. I made no distinction between the human and canine; I could no more imagine my childhood without Barkus than I could envision sending my brother Mark to the kennel. The notion of family, to me, always included a dog.

I had named her. My five-year-old imagination came up with "Barkus," to the delight of my English professor father: the new member of our nuclear unit shared a name with a famous Dickens character, defined by the line "Barkis is willin'."

And Barkus was willing.

She was fifty pounds of shepherd–collie mix. We were sure about the German shepherd part, having taken her, at age eight weeks, from her mother. Her long, thick fur and the ruff around her neck gave credence to the collie speculation. Her coat was a harlequin of black and brown and tan. She had a fluffy and expressive tail, and penetrating eyes with dark eyebrows that made her appear as wise as she in fact was.

Barkus's patience was unbounded. She played with my brother and me, tolerating games of my invention, the purpose of which was to allow her to prove, repeatedly, that she was the best dog in the world. We'd play Which Hand? and, to challenge her acute sense of smell, I'd rub her beloved Milk-Bones on both my hands before holding them out and asking her to guess which held the treat. She'd guess, in good faith and spirit. I'd stage games with my friends, faux fights in which they tackled me so that I could see if Barkus would step in to protect me. She'd bark in complicity, feigning a spirited defense but knowing, as she always knew things, that the games were a sham. When my brother and I would fight, however, as we did frequently, often physically, she would stubbornly insert herself between us. She did not like conflict.

Barkus was good. She was also canny and clever. One night, garbage night, she wanted to go out. Out she went and made straight for the big metal trash cans at the end of our driveway. She smelled something appetizing and created a cyclone of refuse getting to it. She knew this was unacceptable. Caught in the act by my father, she slunk back into the house.

Just as he opened his mouth to express righteous indignation, Barkus began to limp, favoring her right forefoot. Anger turned quickly to concern. She was examined, but no wound was found. She soaked up sympathy and wolfed down consolation Milk-Bones.

After a while, Barkus wanted to go out again. She limped to the door, and we watched her from the window. We watched as she went straight back to the garbage, back to whatever she had found so irresistible before. My father barked out an order to return, and she did. Limping. This time favoring the other foot.

I grew up believing that intense interspecies relationships were as natural and as quotidian as bike riding and brushing your teeth. We had a dark gray tabby cat, Ishtar, who loved to go on family walks—until she'd get tired and sit down meowing, complaining for someone to pick her up to carry her home. Daedalus, named by me as a girl after James Joyce's artistic young man, was a yellow tiger cat who had six toes and loved Doritos. Wilbur's nominal home was a cage in the basement, but he was a free-range bunny, the color of honey, trained to pee in a kitty litter box. He loved Barkus. When she lay down, Wilbur would lie next to her, back legs flopped out straight behind him. Occasionally he would become overly and inappropriately amorous with her tail, at which times I would try to refocus his energies by teaching him tricks. I'd deal cards to him, and he'd take them in his mouth, separating the deck into two discrete piles. Then he'd shuffle them. Wilbur became quite the card shark.

It was on these beloved critters that I cut my teeth of love and care. Living with pets can encourage a little girl to think beyond herself, to break from the narcissism of childhood and extend a focus outward. Responsibility for the life of another no doubt fosters growth and develops character. There are plenty of good reasons for children to be raised with pets. Not the least is that animals make life that much more fun.

Growing up, I spent so much time with animals that I began to associate the people I knew with certain species. It was a habit of mind, unexamined and unexplained. In college I casually mentioned this practice to my friend Amy. She was surprised. And intrigued. She asked me the obvious question, one for which I was not prepared.

"I don't want to tell you," I said.

"Come on, Rach. What kind of animal am I?"

I didn't want my good friend to be offended. I didn't know if she'd understand when I told her that every single thing about her, from the way she moved to the way she ate and slept and groomed herself all screamed out one thing: gerbil. There was no value judgment; to me, it was like saying she had brown hair.

I wasn't confident she'd see it that way.

I was equally unprepared for her next, also obvious, question: "Well then, what kind of animal are you?"

I couldn't answer.

I saw myself in the behaviors of lots of different animals and saw, too, the ways they reflected me. But when pushed to name one with whom I had the same kind of clear, palpable connection that was so evident to me in other people, I was stuck. I didn't know what kind of animal I was. It was many years before the answer came to me: oinking and insistent, with hooves trotting clunkily across hardwood floors.

Barkus was never a pet. She was my first love. From her I learned about tolerance and patience, acceptance and loyalty. To her I gave unqualified, unfettered love. Sharing was a lesson that came easily to me, when taught by Barkus. For many years I've sought a man whom I could love as freely, as generously, as unequivocally, as I loved her.

The uninitiated might joke that it's easy to love a pet, because it can't talk back. (They will say *it* rather than *he* or *she*.) They'll say that loving an animal is about projection, about control, about never having to compromise. Those who haven't lived with pets tend to flatten the rough terrain of individuality into broad and often unfair generalizations. ("Dogs are unthinking followers," they will pronounce. "Cats are mercurial," they'll posit.) These people, lacking in their understanding of other beings, have missed the boat. Or perhaps, the ark.

Those of us who love animals know the vast and various ways in which you come to resemble your pets. I can think of nothing more heartwarming than the sight of an old man hobbling down a street dogged by an equally ancient nonhuman companion, both weathered, both grown lighter in hair and heavier in bulk with age, shuffling the same shuffle they do every day, performing a ritual that is as profound for them as churchgoing. Slim young women walk whippet-thin dogs dressed in matching Burberry coats up and down the streets of New York. Framed photos of pets—cats, dogs, horses, birds—peer out from desktops everywhere. Either you can see yourself across species or you can't. Either you get it or you don't.

In college I bummed dogs like cigarettes. Without a pack of my own, I had to beg and borrow to get my fix of canine company. Having been addicted to animals my whole life, leaving for school meant going cold turkey on the pet front. I learned to comfort myself with the next best thing: men.

I have had a long string of men in my life. Sometimes my lovers coincided nicely with my pets; other times there was conflict. Sometimes the men I was attracted to resembled the animals already in my life. At times the unconstrained qualities of my love for my pets painfully exposed the insufficiencies of my human relationships. If I hadn't lived with vermin at certain lonely times, it's possible that I could have gone whole days without hearing my own voice. Without another being—hooved, clawed, or pawed—whole days could have passed, too, where I did not feel the tug of connection, the enveloping warmth of being with someone I loved.

I used to joke that animals disappoint you by dying, men by living. As with all attempts at humor, there's some underlying truth here. When you love critters whose life cycles are naturally much shorter than your own, you know that you will outlive the critter, if not the love. Your heart breaks more often than you think you can stand. And when you love a man, even the best of men, you take on having to see yourself, facing yourself, all your insecurities and inadequacies and, if that's not enough to deal with, you also take on facing his. With love comes hope, but hope is too frequently followed by heartbreak. They go together, hopefulness and heartbreak, like macaroni and cheese, like chocolate and peanut butter, like girls and horses.

In my messy world, the quality of love is not strained. No matter where it is directed, the love is the same. The feeling that you get, fullness to the point of overflowing in your heart, the sense that your own small body cannot possibly contain so much emotion—whether it is provoked by having a miniature donkey lean his long-eared head against you or from having a transcendent tête-à-tête with a fascinating and handsome man—the experience of loving another creature feels the same to me. Different flavors, same treat.

Many women think that finding a man, a husband, a partner, will bring them a sense of fulfillment. I know the limits of men. I know, too, some of my own limits, and every day I seem to learn more. It's easier to love a pig, or a mouse, than to love a man. All that talking that comes with human relationships. All that Sturm und Drang. The mess. Conversations with long silences. The irritation of the way another person chews. The bathroom wars: toilet seat, toothpaste, the way the paper rolls—over or under. Believe me, it's simpler to train a pig.

And yet, and yet. As much as my animals have thrilled and fulfilled me, I must confess: Even, or perhaps especially, after all these years, I cannot, nor do I want to, resist the many and multifaceted charms of men.

Animals and men. I love them both.

One

But Mousie, you are not alone,
In proving foresight may be vain;
The best-laid schemes of mice and men
often go askew,
And leave us nothing but grief and pain,
For what was promised joy.

—Robert Burns

In the fall of 1980, multicolored leg warmers pulled over Chic jeans, long Farrah Fawcett hair blow-dried into wings, I sauntered onto the campus of a fancy-pants New England college. It could have been any of a number of ivy-encumbered, institutionally self-satisfied universities; it just happened to be the one that admitted me. I arrived to the strains of the Clash, the Ramones, the Pretenders, and Blondie—*"We live for love, we live for love"*—blasting from panes of leaded glass cranked wide. I came trailing a faint scent of Windsong with a top note of equal parts bravado and insecurity. I'd left behind a set of less motivated friends who thought it odd I spent so much time reading what was not required; a mother with whom I shared clothes and secrets; a cold and calculating father; the pesky presence that was my younger brother; two cats, Ishtar and Daedalus; and Barkus—governess, playmate, sibling. It was hardest to leave Barkus.

She had been the shelter in my stormy adolescence. To her alone I'd confessed my unspeakable fears—not smart enough, not pretty enough, wrong clothes, bad hair, oily skin, too loud, too harsh, too judgmental. I measured myself against the standards of teenaged perfection and, like most girls my age, found myself lacking in every single realm. But no matter how hard I was on myself, Barkus was always right there by my side.

Along with many of my fellow students, my guidance counselor had told me that I didn't have a chance of getting into the college I was now attending. I left my rural public high school in upstate New York, a place where football players were gods, to go to a college where the big men on campus sang a cappella in groups with silly names and the pigskin throwers were spurned and scorned. I put away my childish things—blue eye shadow, curling iron, artfully ripped off-the-shoulder sweatshirt and the Top-Siders I'd bought before going off to school (on the advice of the just-published *Preppy Handbook*)—when I discovered that real preppies eschewed makeup and wore legitimately ripped and torn Levi's, ancient hole-ridden cashmere sweaters, and their grandfather's overcoats.

Like a medieval cathedral, our college was designed to make you feel small. When you're eighteen years old and standing among vaulted arches, pointy towers, and ancient-looking gray stone, and you think you're there because someone made a mistake in accepting your application, and that everyone is smarter and more sophisticated than you, and you're positive they could and would be happy to point out exactly the ways in which you are deficient, well, you end up feeling kind of small. You step onto those ivied, ivory grounds, drink in the culture, and, like Alice down the rabbit hole, you "shut up like a telescope," folding in on yourself, getting smaller and smaller.

But what a place to learn. My new friends and I pored over the course catalog and salivated, tempted by the smorgasbord of classes we could take. We were Intellectuals. Or at least, we were intellectual groupies. And now, here, accepted, admitted, it was, unlike high school, finally cool to be smart. We reveled in sharing newfound knowledge, loved learning from each other as much as we lionized our professors.

My world opened and expanded in ways that would have shocked—and thrilled—my high-school self. One day I'm hanging out at the Dairy Queen with a mouth-breathing wrestler I've known since second grade, and the next I'm taking a course on a topic whose name I can't pronounce with people from countries I've never heard of. Talking about the vagaries of gnosticism would be unthinkable with the kids in my twelfth-grade homeroom; less than a year later I found myself in a late-night dorm huddle, discussing with glee the "ineluctable modality of the visible" and sharing a collective fantasy of turning *Paradise Lost* into a Saturday morning cartoon. We may have been dorks, but we were dorking out together. To be in a place where you recognize others of your ilk is a gift.

One of the best things about college is that you have an unheralded chance to log hours getting to know your friends. At no other time are you so intimately involved in the lives of people you meet; in college you live, work, play, eat, drink, and sleep together. Without the responsibilities and obligations that come later in adult life, you have the capital to invest in friendship, an investment that grows and pays dividends over time. Your friends' stories become your stories; what shapes them, shapes you. The act of telling these stories creates intimacy and knowledge: it is how you get to know each other and yourself.

My female friends were my touchstones. We intimidated each other in various, mostly unacknowledged ways, but we also found succor in being together. We learned each other's quirks and habits and, for the most part, accepted them. I found a core group of easy friends—good kids from stable middle-class families—who to this day provide me with solace and support, intellectual stim and the ability to send me into fits of pants-wetting giggles.

College also gave me a chance to flex newly emerging muscles of sexuality. In high school I'd had my share of boyfriends—earnest, kind young lads who would grow up to take over their father's farm, work in a factory, be a manager at the grocery store. I didn't like the geeky smart boys, so I let my eyes be my guide in picking men. Not wanting to go off to college a virgin, I gave it up to a power-lifting community-college student whose biceps were bigger than my waist and who was forever asking me the meaning of words I used. The whole thing took about three minutes. Is that all there is, I wanted to know?

No, I soon found out. College parties presented a veritable buffet of boys. They were attractive and smart, handpicked by the admissions office. We'd dance hot and sweaty into the night and retire to stiff and narrow dorm-room beds. I hooked up with the alcoholic son of a famous writer; a computer science major from Long Island; a prepster who told me that his father had shot himself to death the year before; a juggling, tai chi–practicing physicist; a coke-dealing coxswain; my "little brother," one year younger, assigned to me by the college so that I could show him the ropes (oh boy, did I show him); and plenty of others whose minds and bodies I vigorously embraced at the time and now cannot recall. Sometimes there was sex, though not always. Always, though, I'd leave their beds accompanied by the strains of the dawn chorus.

I didn't want a relationship; I didn't want to slumber with these boys or worse, wake up with them—that was too close. Relationships lasted from early morning until just before the sun rose. I wanted to take what I wanted and not apologize for it. I wanted to rewrite the rules of high school "good" conduct. I didn't want to give up any of the freedom I'd gained by leaving home. A brief physical connection provided an illusion of intimacy and that, absent a dog, was enough.

Sunday afternoons, my friends and I would meet up, stealing hours from our work, complaining about how much we had to do, and we'd rehash the night before. We'd tell each other that we would take only a fifteen-minute study break and would crouch in the manicured beauty of the school's courtyards, basking in the sun, recreating who had danced with whom, who went back to whose rooms, and how much we ate, drank, ingested. Two hours later, we'd get back to our books.

Conversations over dining hall dinners rippled from Faulkner and the Enlightenment to the soccer player with blond ringlets and beautiful calves. We ate boxes of yellow marshmallow Peeps while perusing *The Federalist Papers*, drank gallons of Tab over Janson's *History of Art*. In the tranquillity of friendship, we recollected the hurricane of emotions experienced the night before. Then we wrote papers on Wordsworth and the romantic poets.

What you don't get in college is to spend a lot of time with children, old people, or animals. You recognize what you took for granted back at home, and you start to miss it like crazy. You begin to feel atomized, intimidated, and in need of comfort. Kids who pined for formerly unappreciated younger siblings offered to babysit for professors. Those who longed for a dose of grandparently contact volunteered in nearby nursing homes. Me, I borrowed dogs.

I missed Barkus as soon as I got to college, missed having her lie with me on my bed, giving a better sense of security than a security blanket, more comfort than a comforter. Not long after I had settled in, I got a phone call from home. My father said he'd taken Barkus to the vet, and they'd discovered that her body was riddled with cancer. She was put to sleep that afternoon, he said. There was nothing to be done, he said. I didn't sleep or eat for days after that call.

A faculty member—a funny little Englishman—lived in our dorm, and with him lived his funny little dog, Sadie. She was some kind of terrier, a smaller dog than my fifty-pounder at home, but her whole body wagged when she greeted me, and she was as eager to go on walks with me as her owner was happy to have me take her. She pranced around campus on tiny paws, nails clicking crisply on the flagstone walkways. We dodged Frisbee games and students charging head-down to the library and walked and walked for hours.

For a while, I dated a graduate student named Kirk. I used him, brazenly, shamelessly, for canine contact: it was love at first sight. His dog, Bono, was an Akita, a showstopper. I would walk over to Kirk's off-campus apartment, give the man a perfunctory kiss hello, and then fall to the floor, on level with Bono, who'd run in circles, wagging his curled-up nubbin of a tail, and lick my face. Kirk would sit on the couch and watch. My amorous reunions with Bono would often go on for minutes, with Kirk no doubt wondering when his turn would come.

Borrowed finery helped, but it wasn't for daily wear. I valued my time with Sadie and Bono and had some brief—but emotion-packed—encounters with anyone who walked by with a wagging tail, but it wasn't like having a dog of my own.

By senior year, I was worn out. College life had lost its luster. I was ready for a change. I felt like I would never—could never—know enough. When you get to campus, you're told that you're the cream of the crop; after a couple of years, you end up feeling like skim milk. I was exhausted from studying so hard just to keep up. I was exhausted from being evaluated on the quickness and cleverness of dinner repartee, of talking cynically about books I hadn't read. And I was exhausted from trying always to be the best, smartest version of my-self. Living for the first time in a single room, with no roommates to come home to, I wanted company. I wanted to feel less small.

A dog would help, but was logistically out of the question. I needed . . . what? I needed a pet. But what? Who could live with me in a tiny dorm room? Who wouldn't get me kicked out of school just prior to earning a degree? Who could be quiet . . . quiet as . . . as a mouse! A mouse. Growing up, my little brother had a pet mouse, Moosie, who loved having her cheek rubbed and hated men. She was a tiny, fierce creature, sweet and loving, at least to those with two X chromosomes. Small, quiet, easy to care for but with more personal-ity than, say, a snake—the perfect dorm pet.

During winter break I went to the biology department of my town's local college and had a choice of about a bezillion white mice.

The professor who brought me there, a friend of the family, offered up the rodent booty and wondered if I wanted, perhaps, a handful of mice. No. Just one. He reached into a cage, pulled out one mouse by the tail, and put her in a box. I bought her a cage at the pet store that was probably in exactly the same scale to her as my dorm room was to me; instead of a long narrow bed, her space included an exercise wheel.

Naming was important. What was I to call this small creature? I tossed around various literary possibilities. I considered Virginia, after the divine Woolf, and Jane and Charlotte and Emily, whose novels rested in a nineteenth-century stack on my desk. I thought about calling her George—after Eliot, not Orwell, but it was 1984, and in our freshman "face book" anyone who didn't send in a photo was replaced by a picture of the dystopian author. I didn't want to burden my mouse with gender confusion. So, no, not George.

I settled on Prudence. It shouldn't count as a virtue (though in terms of choosing a pet for my current living situation, she was a prudent choice and this was, of course, a virtue). As virtues go, though, prudence is a mousely one, just as gluttony is a silly sin. According to Blake's proverbs, "Prudence is a rich ugly old maid courted by Incapacity." In my world, Prudence was a tiny, lovely mouse courted by one who felt indeed like Incapacity incarnate. Plus, I liked that her name was longer than she.

I brought her back to school, and her cage fit nicely on my desk, in the right hand corner, nearest the bed, beside my typewriter. She could, if she wanted to, look out the window, but I was never sure how far those little eyes could see.

Prudence's fur was soft as baby powder, talcy white. Her eyes were red beads, not unlike precious round rubies. Her ears were thin to the point of translucence, mapped lightly with delicate spidery veins. She had exquisitely tiny nails and long elegant whiskers. She was a fine-looking mouse. I thought she was beautiful. I'd wondered if a mouse could stand in for a dog, if she would satisfy my profound need for company. I didn't wonder for long.

I'm sure there were rules against keeping pets in the dorm. But people kept far less innocuous things in their rooms—hot plates, bongs, other non-studenty people. One group of resourceful and well-heeled hedonistic frat-boy types even installed a mail-order sauna. A pet mouse was small potatoes in terms of regulatory transgression. And besides, no one knew she was there, except for me and the people I invited into our room.

Most of my friends reacted with benign indifference to the fact that I kept a mouse as a pet; they already thought I was quirky and found this merely a confirmation. Betsy, who lived downstairs and always had food around, saved little treats for Prudence—pieces of stale bagel with traces of peanut butter, oatmeal raisin cookie crumbs, an apple core. Betsy wasn't entirely convinced that I could take care of myself, let alone another being, and she kindly wanted to make sure that my mouse didn't suffer from my lack of domesticity.

Prudence slept during the day, being nocturnal and all. She had busy nights, and I often fell asleep to the lullaby of her movements. She would spin on her wheel, running with such determination, such vigor, that it was hard to imagine what was going through her mind. Did she believe she was going to get somewhere else? Was she—oh, banish the thought—trying to escape? Maybe she was just getting her ya-yas out, running for the sheer joy of being in a physical body. Perhaps it was a game she played, changing her pace, varying the tempo. She'd often stop and sit while the wheel swayed gently back and forth. Was that reminiscent of returning to a mousely maternal womb? Was she comforted by the cradle, endlessly rocking?

With equal fervor and aimlessness, I jumped on wheels of my own. I cranked out papers on Shakespeare, Whitman, Truffaut, the teleological suspension of the ethical, the categorical imperative, Communist Five-Year Plans, the Krebs cycle, the Venus of Willendorf, the temple of Luxor—I wrote at night in my room, preferring that cramped space to the hivelike scene of the library. While Prudence ran in place, my mind whirred, trying to keep up, trying to be smart enough, quick enough, good enough.

Tramping through the dark hallways, up entryways whose steps were worn down by generations of worn-down students, I would get to the door of my single room, take out my hefty key, and exhale loudly.

Once I entered the room I would breathe deeply and sing out: "Dear Prudence, won't you come out to play?"

My darling mouse would, of course, be sleeping and not particularly interested in coming out to play. I could rouse her, though. She'd unfurl from the little rodent ball she had made of herself. She'd look up, blinking beady red eyes, maybe use a tiny paw to clean the immaculate fur on her head, licking it first, then pulling it over her ear. Her whiskers, fine filigrees, twitching, sensing, her nose animated, agile. She'd look at me, and I'd think, Okay, it may be silly, but I cannot but love this mouse. "It's beautiful, and so are you," I would sing to my dear, dear Prudence, holding her close to my face. She'd sniff me, whiff my breath, nose twitching, sometimes kissing me on the lips, sometimes investigating my nostrils. I'd let her explore. I found it delightful.

She was a clean and tidy mouse, never peeing or pooping except in her cage. Whenever I was in my dorm room, I would prop open her door and let her come out to explore, or stay in, as she pleased.

I would sit at my desk, and she would run around it, checking out messy sheaves of paper, climbing alpine piles of books. "She walks in beauty like the night," I said of her, to her. I read from Milton while she patrolled the expanse of my desk, occasionally peeking into my coffee cup or craning her neck to look down to the floor. "Space may produce new worlds," I told her. She'd sit back, use a hind leg to scratch her neck, and then carry on about her business, whiskers twitching.

As I wrote on a cheap plastic portable Smith-Corona, Prudence liked to crawl onto the keys, chasing after my fingers as they flew quickly in fits and starts. She'd climb onto the tops of my hands, and I would stop, turning them over to palm her, at the same time looking down at the sentences peeking from the top of my typewriter and finding them wanting. I loved it when she'd interrupt my work like this. I loved that she would seek me out.

I stroked her cheek, and she would lean, exposing so much of it to my finger that eventually she'd keel over onto her side, one front paw near her face, a back foot stretched out like a ballet dancer's.

As soon as I stopped, she'd right herself and get busy again. Prudence became my life that last semester. My biggest love affair in college was with a mouse.

It was as much a relief to leave my fancy-pants university as it had been an affirmation to be admitted. It had not been an easy four years. I was ready to go. But to where?

I had taken a seminar first semester of senior year, taught by Jane Randall, an editor from Oxford University Press, on the "art" of editing serious nonfiction. Jane was more open and accessible than any faculty member I had encountered, and she generated in me a desire and recognition of the need for guidance. I made an appointment to meet with her after class.

In the privacy of my teacher's office, I let down the veneer of arrogant self-confidence I'd worked so hard to cultivate and revealed myself to her, asked what I should do. Not one to shy away from giving advice, she suggested I try out publishing.

Second semester, I tried it. I commuted one day a week to New York City to type letters for the economics editor at Oxford. I Xeroxed. I filed. I typed. A lot. It meant getting up before the sun, when Prudence was still wheeling in her cage. Unable to afford cab fare, I tramped a large number of more-than-slightly-iffy blocks to the station, training it into Grand Central with the other working stiffs. I liked the atmosphere of the office, and I was intrigued by the idea of an industry where you read books all day. So, when, a week or two after graduation, a job opened up as assistant to Jane Randall herself, I jumped at the opportunity and accepted the position.

I arranged to sublet a spacious one-bedroom apartment in Queens. I had wanted to find a place in the middle of all the action—in the city—but everything was too expensive for someone who was yet to be making an income. Queens isn't that far from Manhattan, I reasoned.

Before embarking on my new career, my new life, I decided to treat myself, and Prudence, of course, to a week in the country. We took a trip to Maine to help my cousins on their farm during haying season. Never particularly outdoorsy, I had spent my younger years loving all things having to do with horses. While my cousins had no mounts of their own, they did have access and extended it to me: I thrilled to ride through the lush, wooded countryside. And I embraced the notion of toiling under the summer sun; I embraced the concreteness, the discreetness, of cutting and bailing. After a week of hard and gratifying work, sweaty, physical, depleting, and honest labor, Prudence and I flew back to our new urban home. We landed in Newark amidst horrors of cancelled flights and scores of tired, cranky people waiting in crowds for buses back to the city.

While I was standing in line, a short, handsome, ginger-haired young man—about my age, with Popeye's forearms and a ready smile—noticed that I was talking to my tote bag. I had carried Prudence on, cage and all, in a canvas L.L. Bean bag. She was like Gulliver, carried in his traveling box by Glumdalclitch, the Brobdingnagian giantess girl. Thinking of Swift and Gulliver's descriptions of the disconcerting experience of being carried in his little house caused me to periodically stick my hand in Prudence's cage, allowing her to climb into it and feel comforted.

"What's in there?" he asked, with a smile and the quivering excitement of a puppy.

"You can't tell," I said, whispering, bringing him closer, bringing him into my conspiracy: I'd had to conceal Prudence during the flight. The airline, I was told, did not transport animals.

"Swear," he said, raising a hand and looking like a Boy Scout, eyebrows raised, eyes wide.

"Prudence. Mouse." I opened the top of the bag to allow him a peek.

"Why do you have a mouse with you?"

"Because she is my love."

"Ah. I see."

We sat together on the bus back into the city, our legs sometimes touching. I planned to take a cab from the Port Authority Bus Terminal, where the bus would drop us off, to my apartment in Queens.

He had an elastic face and spoke quickly, using accents and his hands.

His name was Charlie, he said. He was, he said, an actor.

I asked what he'd done—had I seen him in anything?

"No," he said, "I'm studying."

He named a famous acting teacher whose name was foreign to me. Then he reeled off a litany of actors whose names I did recognize— anyone would—and said, without arrogance, that they were his thespian siblings.

"So," I said, my hand in Prudence's cage, watching as she climbed on it, glancing back at him from lowered eyes. "Do you wait tables? Drive a cab? Do nocturnal legal proofreading?" If I didn't know all the famous acting teachers, I did know something of the lives of fledging actors.

He laughed. A big laugh for a small guy. An honest, open laugh. "No, I work for my father," and he explained the nature of his father's company—something vaguely technical. "I do whatever he needs me to do."

The bus arrived at Port Authority, and there were some awkward moments.

I thought about it.

Briefly.

Then we got into a cab that brought us to his place on the Upper West Side. It was only marginally larger than my dorm room. Charlie shared it with another actor who was out of town for a few months.

"A job," he explained, with only a soupçon of envy.

We settled Prudence's cage on a coffee table and spent the next forty-eight hours in the tiny, windowless space. He asked me lots of questions and seemed impressed by my answers, by me. It was strange and unfamiliar to feel impressive. We talked for hours, slept a little, made out a lot, and woke each other up when some new thought crept in, something that had to be shared, just then.

Finally Prudence and I went home to Queens. But we came back to Charlie's frequently. Spending time with him in the glamour and bustle of upper Manhattan made me soon hate taking the subway over the river to my outer-borough home. True, it was spacious and cheap, but I may as well have been in outer space, so far away from everything did it seem.

The city was enchanting. While a youngster, I forcefully and naively defended the clean, open spaces of my rural home against my Greenwich Village Grandpa Harry's unabashed cheerleading for the Isle of the Manhattoes. Over time I learned to see the grime and dirt and neon and squalor through his loving eyes, saw the ways the world could change in one city block, understood that the pace of merely walking down the street—speedy, impatient, directed—could make your mind work faster, harder. I'd emerged from the chrysalis of college to alight on the flower of the world's greatest, biggest, brashest, noisiest town. I didn't want to be living in the weeds.

Charlie offered good looks, unstinting enthusiasm and praise, a big heart, a hard body, and an insider's ability to negotiate New York. It was impossible not to like him. He was the kind of guy you'd stop on the street to ask directions. He would be able to tell you how to go where you wanted to go, and then he'd take you there. On the way, he'd never stop talking, joking, gesticulating.

Through a friend, Charlie snagged a great SoHo studio apartment. It was great in the three most important features of real estate: location, location, and location.

Two months after we met, Charlie asked Prudence and me to move in with him. I said yes.

It was a lovely space—cozy, though, for two people and a mouse. Into the first section of the apartment, over the kitchen—just a short row of appliances—Charlie and a handy friend built a loft. It made the kitchen area cavernous, but gave us a place to sleep.

Just as our space improved and became multileveled, so, too, did Prudence's. We got her a new cage. From her single square room, she moved into a three-story luxury suite, with ladders, hiding spaces, and an even bigger wheel. Her favorite thing, though, was still cardboard toilet paper rolls. Forget about the fancy mouse house, with its door and peepholes—what she wanted most was a plain old toilet paper roll whose ends she could fray, making confetti with which to line the inside. Easy to please, my Prudence. All in all, she was a happy mouse. Except for one thing. She hated Charlie.

Prudence hated Charlie with a vehemence that was startling. He was so innocuous, so easygoing, so willing to please. And yet, any time he came near her cage, she would grab the bars with her tiny paws and shake them, like some crazed and outraged prisoner. She would gnash her teeth, this gentle mouse, who had never bitten me and had often, when I held her up to kiss her, softly kissed me back.

Charlie tried so hard. When I was at home, I let her run free on the coffee table. Charlie would lay his hand on the table, palm up, in a gesture of friendship, and Prudence would come running, charging the length of the table. She'd stop short near his hand, crane her neck while keeping her body at a distance, and viciously sink her sharp teeth into his index finger. Then she'd zoom away in speedy retreat. He fell for it every time, like Charlie Brown going to kick the football and landing on his back, yet again, as Lucy pulled it out at the last minute.

Charlie worked hard on himself. He studied acting with his famous teacher. He learned the Alexander technique to improve his body carriage. He took voice lessons. But he never auditioned. He always came up with a good excuse for why he didn't, but I guessed it was because he feared rejection. Charlie instead worked full-time for his father's company. Still, after many months, what he did, exactly, was never entirely clear to me.

I thought that what I was doing, on the other hand, was completely clear. I was a young publishing professional. I loved my job, whizzing through piles of clerical work, quick and dirty, and then sitting with my boss while she explained to authors, many of them established academics, what was wrong with their books—and their ideas—and how to fix them. No one was better than she at getting to the heart of a problem and extracting it for clinical examination. The notion of telling someone what was wrong with them appealed and came easily to me. I practiced on Charlie.

I became increasingly critical of him, and the more critical I got, the more eager and desperate he was to please me. Charlie never got angry with me; he only tried harder. If I stormed off in the morning, upset about his forgetting to set the alarm, that he hadn't made the coffee, that he took too long shaving—whatever irrational peeve I could muster—later in the day he would send me flowers at work. I amassed a collection of florist shop vases that lined the bookcases in my office and then began to pile up on the floor. I grew to dread the phone call from the receptionist who singsonged, "I have something for you at the front desk." The silly woman thought I'd be happy to get flowers. The more I stepped on Charlie, the more he groveled, and the more I resented him. I didn't like the person I was becoming.

Charlie was loving; he was considerate. He was generous, funny, and eager to please. We'd have dinner at trendy restaurants, where he'd mimic the snooty waiters. He'd stop off after work at Charivari, an upscale boutique, and come home with a coat for me that cost more than my biweekly paycheck. Weekends he would rent a car, and we'd take off for the Hamptons. He had money, and he shared it freely. But even as he found ways to accommodate me, buying me jewelry and taking me on more elaborate and elegant trips, I felt trapped.

Had I picked him because of his real estate? Had I chosen to be with him because he so clearly worshipped me? Did his loving me so much—despite my incessant demands, my belittling complaints— mean that he just wasn't discerning, that he was desperate? Was it because he was short? Did he have to be with a small woman, and was I the best he could find? More than merely the Groucho Marx club-joining issue, I felt my edges getting so hard that I worried whether I would ever be able to soften. Like Prudence, I gnashed my teeth at poor Charlie whenever he came near.

I loved the homey comfort of getting back first from work, taking Prudence out of her cage, and sitting on the couch reading a novel as she scurried about, stopping often to sniff the air for a sign of Charlie's arrival home. I loved being alone. I fantasized about business trips where I could sleep by myself diagonally across a hotel-room bed.

When we went away for the weekend, I would leave Prudence

plenty of food and water. Coming home, I would rush to her cage before taking off my coat, anxious to make sure she was okay, wanting
to take her out for a romp around the coffee table. Charlie was tolerant and understanding of my relationship with her, though I suspect
it wounded him that he never saw a fraction of the affection I lav-
ished on Prudence.

Charlie's childhood had been replete with abandonments and
crazy, bitchy women. Anyone who's ever read *Cosmo* knows that some
relationships exist or continue because they feed complementary
pathologies. Ours chugged along for a year. I needed to feel big and in
control; Charlie's experience of love was being treated like shit. Charlie never stopped trying, but I did. Perhaps I never started. He was too
small a man for me. He brought out all my own smallness and petti-
ness. We were eager to try out grown-up life; in our haste, we got ourselves into the kind of stunting relationship that takes most couples
years to get stuck in.

My own small mouse continued as a source of delight and pleasure.
As she grew older she, like all of us, became more like herself. Her irrational rage at Charlie seemed only to increase.

One morning, after a few days of unusual lethargy, I found Prudence lying unnaturally still in her cage.

She'd died in the night.

Animals had always been a part of my life. But Prudence was the
first creature that I was solely responsible for. The being who had only
me. I experienced the burden of caring for her as a gift. When I looked
at her, into her ruby red eyes, touched her impossibly soft white fur,
stroked her transparent ears with my fingers which scaled to hugeness
by the fact of her, my heart felt full to eruption. I am, I told myself, in
love with someone who weighs less than a Snickers bar.

My love for Prudence was as real as any I would feel. I joked about
it. How serious a person could you be if you are in love with a mouse?
I hoped it would save me from impulses toward intellectual pretension, from taking myself too seriously. But my love for Prudence—
feeding her and cleaning up after her and delighting in watching her
sleep—was not a joke. She had been with me through lonely times in

college and had helped me start to make the transition into adulthood. That she hated Charlie was at first funny. That she continued to hate him and treat him badly even as he did everything he could to make her life better showed me she was her mother's mouse. She loved me, she reflected me. And then she died.

It was the same day I had scheduled an interview for another job at Oxford, with a fearsome vice president who, even though his office was no more than fifty yards from mine, never spoke to me. It was a job I wanted badly. I didn't bother to show up at the appointed time, kept my office door shut and cried, remembering Prudence sitting on my fingers as I typed, thinking about the softness of her fur.

His secretary had heard about my loss—news traveled quickly in my office—and called me to reschedule.

When I finally did meet with my future boss, the first thing this powerful and scary man said to me was, "I heard you had a pet that passed away. I'm so sorry."

He went on, at length and with surprising humanity, to talk about the recent death of his dog. His face changed when he talked. His eyes were always a bit rheumy, but now they were rheumy and soft. The dog was a corgi, the same kind owned by the Queen of England, he was quick to point out.

"They think they're big dogs," he said. I smiled.

I was hired. He never knew that my pet had been a mouse.

Charlie and I broke up.

I moved out.

Two

Anything like the sound of a rat
Makes my heart go pit-a-pat.

—Robert Browning

The difference between solitude and loneliness is that one sucks.

I moved out of the apartment I shared with Charlie and into the only place I found that I could afford. For more than half my monthly earnings, I got digs in the East Twenties. In a converted hotel, my "apartment" was exactly nine feet by twelve. Plenty big for an area rug, not big enough for a kitchen. The previous occupant had left a loft bed, under which I could fit a chair and a small desk. The bathroom was smaller than a closet. When you sat on the toilet, your knees touched the door. Showering involved yoga moves, especially if you dropped the soap.

25

It wasn't much, but it was mine. Mine, mine, mine, I chanted as I stomped around the place. I now had a room of my own.

I missed Prudence. Memories of losing her were painfully fresh and could still make me tear up. It tore me up. I was happy not to be living with Charlie anymore, but coming home at the end of the day to my empty place was more of a sorrow than a relief—no one, not even a mouse, stirred there. I had no one to whom I could announce that, at the end of the day, I was home.

For us epic heroes, us working folk, it's always about the journey to get back home. It's the place you leave from, and the reason you fight temptation and battles to get back. It's the telos, the goal. It's about who and what you've left behind, mostly who. Baseball players know about getting back home—they run to rejoin their teammates. Odysseus had Penelope and his dog Argos waiting for him. What's the point of trying to return if there's no one there to greet you, to recognize you, even, or perhaps especially, if you are changed from your travels?

I had a Prudence-shaped space missing from my life. For the first time since high school I watched TV, needing the sounds of other sentient—if not necessarily thinking—beings. I was lonely, and it sucked.

I spoke on the phone with Joan, an old family friend, about how much I missed my rodent companion. Not everyone could understand how the world had grown gray for me when I lost my white mouse, but I knew I could turn to Joan, a technician at Brookhaven National Labs in nearby Long Island, who had long worked with lab animals. She listened to me grieve for Prudence and began to tell me about the rats she worked with.

"They are so cute, so sweet," she said, "And so smart and interested." Had I considered a rat as a pet?

I had not. I didn't want to replace Prudence; the idea of "supersizing" her held no appeal.

"So sweet," she said. "So smart."

Rats are the welfare mothers of the animal world. Everything gets blamed on them, including things for which they bear no responsibility. And I was lonely. So I thought about it. Maybe I was ready for a little edginess, something a little more challenging.

I called Joan back. "Okay," I said. "Would you bring me a rat, please?"

I still had Prudence's cage, her three-story, deluxe luxury apartment. I took the train out to Long Island, got dinner and a rat from Joan, and toted my new pet in a shoe box back to the city with me. I decided to name her Hester, after Hawthorne's stigmatized woman, unfairly branded. If you're a rat, I reasoned, you don't need a scarlet letter hanging around your neck—you are a scarlet letter.

The cage was ready, clean, made comfortable with fresh cedar shavings, a big water bottle, and some pellets of rat food. I reached into the shoe box to remove the newly christened Hester. Fast as you could say "welfare mother of the animal world," she bit me. She whipped her head around and sank her ratty teeth into my hand.

I yelped and cursed. ("Fucking bitch!") I put my hand back in, again wanting only to transfer her to the cage, and she bit me again. The bitch. The evil, rotten, stinking, thick-tailed, beady-eyed, ugly, plague-spreading, corpse-nibbling, tenement-living, dirty subway-scurrying bitch bit me again. She may have looked like a bigger version of Prudence—white, with red eyes, and a tail longer than her body—but this rat was no mouse.

For the next few weeks, it was a relief to go to work, to get away from her. I was still working happily, unalienated in my labor, as an editorial assistant at one of the world's oldest and most prestigious publishing houses. The vice president I was working with, Herman, was one of those smart, nerdy men who always seemed uncomfortable in his body, at odds with his physical self. His was a life of the mind. He loved his work and loved to talk about the books he was editing, to describe the arguments and what made them important. He also loved his authors. He would wine and dine them. The three-martini lunch era was ending, but you wouldn't have known it from dining with Herman; each day he'd spend the afternoon sleeping at this desk, head back, mouth open, snoring softly.

On the rare occasions he took me with him to lunch, I was careful not to drink, afraid of saying the wrong thing in front of an author, and later passing out at my desk and drooling on a manuscript. Eventually Herman began to assign me books to edit, and eventually I began to have authors of my own.

Herman never wanted to be a mentor, but he taught me unintentionally. From him I learned to love my authors. To become a fan, an enthusiastic reader. Editing is like love. You need to see these authors for who they are and need to see, too, who they want to become, where they want to go. You help them become their best, truest, smartest selves. You do it by being critical and supportive at the same time.

Because of Herman's special position in the company—he was a kind of institution, having published not only Big, Important books, but also books that made money—I became special. Because of his pull, he was able, after some prodding, to promote me. He even began to champion me, though it was still against his nature to do so. I didn't wear my success lightly—I wrapped myself in it like a cloak. I was puffed up and full of myself, and it didn't help that other editors made "young Turk" comments about me.

Every so often, when I got too obstreperous, my sanguine officemate Terry would say something like: "Well aren't we just little Miss Smarty-Pants today?"

"That's little Ms. Smarty-Pants to you," I'd answer, prancing around our small space.

She'd shake her head, smiling furtively into a manuscript.

I played on the company softball team, even though I am not a person who should ever play ball sports. I am afraid of projectiles, especially when they are directed at me. In one game we played the team from a glossy men's magazine. It was the geeks against the Greek gods. They wore cleats.

Someone who obviously didn't know about my inability to catch anything except the occasional cold had sent me to left field. Do you know how many balls are hit to left field? A lot, at least that day. I was mortified to learn that the opponents were playing to our weakness: me. My team quickly made me Catcher for Life (the pitcher ran in to cover home when necessary), and I was grateful for this accommodation of my inability to play the field.

After the games we'd go to the Dublin House, a pub on the Upper West Side, and share pitchers of beer. We were a bunch of twenty- and a few scattered thirty-somethings, living in the most vibrant city in the world and scraping by doing what we loved. Like most fresh-out-of-college kids, I assumed that I'd always have access to a peer group that shared my interests and lifestyle; in the world of publishing, I still did. The lower ranks were filled with people who loved books and wanted to talk about them. Some were taking a pit stop on the way to graduate school, some trying to make their own way as writers, and a few assiduous folk were determined to climb and claw up the editorial—or marketing, or copywriting, or production—publishing ladder.

Taking advantage of my access to smart, attractive male coworkers, I had a few desultory office affairs. Nothing too serious, at least not serious for me. I was enjoying my freedom, enjoying living alone. I was not enjoying the company of the bitch rat, however. Telling myself that maybe she was freaked out from the move—leaving the comforting fluorescent lighting of the lab, the scent of hundreds of other experiment-bound rodents—I tried again to connect with her one Saturday afternoon, making a peace offering of some peanut butter (a rodent fave) slathered on a cracker. She ignored the food but wasted no time chomping on my skin. Then she withdrew.

Bitch.

She ran to a corner of her cage and cowered. I retreated to a corner of mine and sat at my desk, head in hands, wondering what I had done to deserve this. I'd always been able to connect with animals. Squirrels in parks followed me around, regardless of whether I had food to offer them. Strange dogs stopped barking when I neared, wagging their tails in delight to the sound of my voice. What was wrong with Hester? Or, more disturbingly, what was wrong with me?

I figured it might be good to get out of the apartment for a little while. I knew there was a party that night at the Brooklyn home of one of the publicity assistants. I decided to go, hoping to find some comfort there, to smooth balm on the wound of existence, not to mention the rat bites on my hand. The rejection from the rat had left me dejected. With the animal world failing me, I'd have to turn to the next best thing.

I needed a new boy.

The party was filled with the usual suspects—other publishing assistants, their friends, roommates, significant others, and so on. It was the eighties, and we were down-market yuppies, not making enough money to truly participate in the decade of greed but still able to enjoy an occasional baked Brie or sun-dried tomato. We loved our eighties music. We danced. And sang. I was enjoying myself. I'd already had a wee affair with one of the guys there, a sweet, smart copywriter named Bob. He gave me tapes of the Talking Heads and the B-52's and left home-baked brownies on my desk and was so obliging, so like Charlie, that I had to dump him. I never told him that I was dumping him, though; I just avoided him and refused to take his calls. After Charlie, I'd had enough of sweet. I was ready for a challenge.

He was standing with his back to me. Tall, thin, with dark hair. He was talking to a woman, also tall, thin, and dark haired. They were looking at a piece of art on the wall of the apartment, and I could see that she was talking. I watched as he bent his head to her, tilted it to attend to her. From that gesture I decided, It'll be him. There is balm in Gilead.

Then he turned. Never mind.

He wasn't exactly ugly. Well, yes, he was. His face was long and thin, his was a Modigliani head. His nose was off center. He had two big rabbitlike front teeth. His eyes were pale, but less so than his skin, which shone with the pallor of someone who was never awake during daylight, someone who maybe drank a lot of thick red liquid.

I moved on. There were plenty of people to talk with at the party, and so I did: talked, laughed, and drank strong, homemade vodka concoctions. It was fun. Then it was late, and I was sitting on the couch.

He sat down next to me. "Vince," he said.

He began to speak about the downtown clubs.

"Not for me," I responded without enthusiasm, looking around the room for someone more interesting, someone less hideous.

"Oh yeah?" he said, his head pulling back while his shoulders remained still.

"What's your bag?"

"My bag?" It was 1985. He might as well have asked me my sign. Who talked like this?

"Yeah." He simpered.

"Books," I said. "Books are my bag."

He told me that he had just finished reading Joyce's short story "The Dead." "I read it every year," he said.

"No way," I said, shocked, and for the first time interested, for the first time looking him in the eye.

"So do I." So do I. It was one of my annual rituals, along with watching *Harold and Maude* on New Year's Eve and eating myself sick on candy corn the day after Halloween.

We started to talk. He had gone to MIT. I looked at him again. MIT? This odd-looking man in corduroy Levi's, high-top basketball shoes, and a flannel shirt? He had studied physics? Yes, of course he had, and literature. Literature! He read Joyce. Annually! A geek who knew things I didn't and shared with me a love of things I loved. His face now looked intriguing, not deformed as I had initially thought.

He asked about my work. I told him about a book I was editing, a history of a forgotten incident, a lynching. He asked about the author, how old he was (young, the book had been his PhD dissertation), whether or not he was married (he wasn't). He then opined that my author probably wanted to nail me.

This, from the guy with a melting face who spoke in seventies-era clichés? Maybe I was wrong about him.

"Excuse me?" I said.

"Come on," he said. "You know how attractive you are. You know he wants you."

I laughed. Since we'd never even met in person, just spoken on the phone, I was sure, I told him, that my author wanted no such thing. Just good editing and lots of editorial attention.

"Yeah, right," Vince said, smiling as if he knew something I didn't.

I had to pee. I asked if he'd excuse me.

"Come back, okay?" he said with an insistence that surprised and flattered me. "Okay?" he said softly, and took my hand, turning it over and looking, tracing the lines of my palm with his other hand, gently. He looked back at me, and his eyes went soft.

Could it be that I had misjudged? He was handsome, looking at me like that, my hand in his, his eyes on mine. "Yes, I said, yes, I will, yes."

Vince smiled broadly, recognizing the last line of *Ulysses*. His teeth really weren't that bad. Just big. With a gap.

I made my way to the bathroom, but coming back, Bob the copy-writer stopped me.

He put his hand on my shoulder and stopped me in my tracks. He wanted to talk. "I guess it's time to throw some dirt on this thing," he said. "Bury it."

Sigh.

I'd wanted to get out of it without ever having to talk about it. Not honorable, I knew. Bob wasn't going to belabor a conversation, but he did want closure. I owed him at least that.

"I'm sorry, Bob," I said. And I was. I really was.

"Okay, then," he said, and hugged me. I held him and felt sorry, sorry about not being able to be in a relationship with this sweet man, or with sweet Charlie. Sorry that I was such a bitch.

I went back to the couch where Vince was waiting. I sat down, and when he looked at me, his eyes flashed. I'd always wondered what that looked like, when you say someone's eyes flash. But I saw it. Anger, disappointment, betrayal, longing, excitement—a whole host of emotions I couldn't place were visible, if for only a second, in his eyes.

"Who was that?" he asked with a scowl and a pointed point of his long head in the direction of Bob.

"Oh." I let my voice trail off. "History. Now."

It looked like he was going to say something else, and I waited, but he didn't. Instead he asked if he could call me, asked for my number. He had a pen, but no paper. So I wrote my phone number on the back of his hand.

Once I finished, he took my hand, looked it over. "You have beautiful hands," he said. "Nobody, not even the rain, has such small hands."

"Cummings," I replied, with a smile.

He kissed my hand, not noticing the rat bites.

When I got back home and turned on the light, I looked into her cage. She was standing up, sniffing the air. I came over to her and she watched me with those beady little eyes.

"Hester the Molester," I said to her.

I opened the cage to put some more pellets in, and she came charging over. Her teeth were bared, no doubt ready to find more flesh. I dropped the food and withdrew the hand. She stood defiant, paws on the bars of the cage's door, just as Prudence used to do whenever Charlie walked by. She feels about me the way Prudence felt about Charlie, I thought, as I got ready for bed, feeling a sick twinge in my stomach. As I walked by her cage a final time she watched me, still, whiskers twitching. She is a nasty piece of work, I thought. No wonder people hate rats.

"Good night moon," I said, looking out my sole, dirty window. "Good night, bitch," I said, glancing into her cage.

* * *

The next day, I told Terry, my officemate, about him. "Physics and literature! He reads Joyce and quotes Cummings!"

"Yeah, yeah," she said, older, wiser, married. "Does he have a job?"

Later that day, Vince called. I agreed to meet him for a drink at King Tut's Wawa Hut, a downtown dive bar. "I'm smitten," I told my officemate as I put down the phone.

"So what else is new?" she asked. "You were smitten with Bob."

"Was not."

"Was so."

"WAS NOT."

"Every time he dropped by, you got all fluttery and started to babble."

"That was only for the first week."

"Yeah, sure."

"This is different," I assured the doubting Terry.

"Yeah, sure."

All afternoon, I could hardly concentrate on my work. I fidgeted in my seat, got up for coffee too many times, replayed our phone conversation in my mind over and over again.

I wore a short, black flouncy skirt, a plain white T-shirt, a lei of fake pearl necklaces, and multiple bangles on my wrists. It was the age of Madonna (the first age of Madonna).

I was looking forward to this date.

Until I walked into the bar and saw him. I'd forgotten about the way his face seemed to be melting, the nose sliding off to one side, the odd paleness of his eyes. The physicality of him made me want to turn and walk right back out.

He asked what I wanted to drink. A lot, I thought. I ordered a scotch and soda, downed it quickly, and then got another one. While I slugged away, he spoke. He told me about his work—he had venture capital money to design and build a machine that could compose and record music electronically. He told me about the composers he worshipped: Karlheinz Stockhausen, Pierre Boulez, Steve Reich. (I'd never heard of them.) He talked about math. Math and music. Talked about the connections, the patterns between them. (What was I thinking? He wasn't ugly at all.)

We ended up back at my apartment. As we walked in, Hester began running around her cage. She seemed agitated, more so than usual. She frantically sniffed the air, sitting up, head high.

"Oh," he said, a little surprised, when he saw her.

"Ignore her," I warned. "She bites. She was a mistake."

"I'd rather concentrate on you," he said, and somehow, it didn't sound that smarmy. He held me by both shoulders and looked at me like he was appraising a piece of artwork.

"You are so—" I didn't let him finish. I didn't want to hear his appraisal, so I kissed him. He kissed back. We sank to the floor, right there, right under Hester's cage as she ran back and forth, and kissed until our lips were swollen and sore.

A pattern was established. Vince would spend the night in my small apartment and then, in the morning, walk me to work. Since he didn't have a regular job, I became his vocation. He'd call me during the day, two or three times, just to let me know he was thinking about me. Often he'd tell me, graphically—sometimes pornographically—exactly what he was thinking. He needed reassurance. When we were in bed, he prompted talk. What he wanted—needed—to hear were things along the lines of "Oh baby baby you're so good oh baby baby yes yes yes it's so big baby baby you're the best the best the best." At first I thought he was joking. Who says stuff like this? Apparently the women who slept with him, once he told them what they were supposed to say. I couldn't help but laugh. Then I realized it wasn't a joke, at least for him. So I learned my lines and told him what he needed to hear.

It was worth it. I loved being with him, loved talking to him. His knowledge was broad and deep. By his bed he kept a copy of Boswell's *Life of Samuel Johnson*, a guitar, and a bong. On weekend mornings at his place, he'd bring me breakfast in bed—a stale bagel—and he'd "noodle" around on his guitar, playing naked, the wood grain shiny against his pale white skin.

Whenever I'd come home to my rat-infested apartment, Hester would be alert from the moment I walked in. Each time I opened the door to give her food, she'd scamper over, a sinister look in her eye. She wanted blood, I could tell. So I learned to be very quick.

A few weeks after I got her, I could no longer put off cleaning her cage. This meant taking her out. I was less than eager to risk another close encounter and less than concerned about catering to her every whim—but it would've been inhumane to let it go any longer. I opened the door and, after some tentative air sniffing and poking about, she climbed out. I was able to guide her to the floor, where she could safely hang around while I was cage-cleaning. In such a small space, it wasn't likely that she could get lost.

I got busy dumping cedar shavings into the garbage and getting fresh ones, scrubbing clean her water bottle over the bathroom sink. Once the cage was newly fresh, I looked around for her—but I didn't see her. Where had she gone? Could she have gotten out?

As I scanned the room for her length of tail, I wondered, does the world shift if you lose an enemy? Do you lose a piece of yourself? I didn't have much time to contemplate this before I looked down at the floor to see the cords to my answering machine and telephone gnawed to bite-size bits and pieces.

I still couldn't find the despicable rodent. I looked and looked and finally saw her in the corner where I piled my shoes, perched atop a pair of Italian leather Joan & David oxfords that Charlie had bought for me. She had chewed a hole right through the top of the left shoe. I screamed. She looked up at me. Smug? Was that a smug look on her ratty mug? I plucked her up by the tail and swung her into the cage. No, I thought, I would not miss my mortal enemy.

Later that night I found a pile. She had collected things from around my apartment and secreted them away in a corner. She'd stashed a red button, a gum wrapper, a used tissue, and a plastic hula girl—from a memorable night filled with frou frou drinks—and piled them up. Sneaky little rat.

*   *   *

I continued to play—or attempt to play—softball and hang out with my friends from work. One of the women I'd become close to had jumped from our ship to the Land of Lost Boys—Marvel Comics. I began to call her "Marvel" and took to stopping by their offices on my way home from work. The men—it was mostly men—who worked in comics were exactly what you'd expect: boys. The editors tended to come in late, often hungover, and worked late. They were funny and immature, witty and weird. After six, there were always people around, working, playing, or some combination that brought them loads of fun, and unimaginable—at least in the publishing industry—amounts of money. People were always throwing things, launching ambushes, hitting each other with fancy and expensive toys. Marvel, my sweet and lovely friend, was a surprising entry into this testosterone-filled cadre: a small, prim woman from Ireland with stereotypical red hair and freckles. She was a few years older than me and was married to an Italian cabdriver. I often went to her apartment in Queens, where she would fix me a cup of Horlick's, a sugary British malt mix that you combine with hot milk. "It's calming," she'd say. And it was. She was. I relied on her for stability; she liked that I lightened things up.

I wanted to introduce Marvel to Vince, to get her take on him, her approval, so we three arranged to meet at Le Figaro Café in the Village. Marvel and I got there first, and sat chattering away, sipping our cappuccinos amid walls covered by pages of the French newspaper from which the café took its name.

"Why did you pick this place?" Vince asked as he strode in, sitting down next to me, not even acknowledging my friend. "Café Reggio is much better."

For the next few minutes, he stared past my head and looked out the window, a tired, bored expression on his face. When asked questions, he responded curtly, as if it were a chore to converse.

When Marvel mentioned a mutual acquaintance of ours, a man she worked with, Vince sprang to attention. "I've never heard you mention that guy before," he snapped.

I hadn't mentioned him because I didn't know him that well and didn't have any reason to bring him up.

After that, Vince sat close to me and kept a hand on my arm. I could see Marvel looking from his hand to my arm and back again. After a short time, she excused herself, said she had to be somewhere, she said, and left. I knew that there was nowhere she had to be. She just hadn't wanted to be there. I didn't blame her.

When I questioned her about it later, she asked, "Do you think he's, um, the right kind of person for you?"

"What do you mean?"

She hesitated.

I filled in the silence. "He was tired when you saw him. He's usually much more, well, engaging."

Was he? I was feeling defensive.

"Okay, then," she said, smiling, but looking sad.

On a rare night home alone, I was reading in bed, missing the sweet fullness of loving Prudence. I looked up and saw Hester in her cage, standing at the door. As much as I disliked and resented her, I hated the idea of losing the war. She had ruined my perfect record of being able to connect with animals. With a sigh, I decided I'd try just once more.

Carefully, carefully, I let her out and then swung her by the tail up onto the loft bed. Company. I just wanted company. While I read, she explored the hills and dales made by the comforter, staying mostly near my feet. I could see her occasionally looking in my direction, watching my hands each time they turned the page. As nervous as I was, it kind of helped, having her there. The way she sat, ears alert, whiskers twitching, she almost looked cute, in a ratty bitch kind of way.

Suddenly she came charging, right toward the hand lying idle on my stomach. I flashed back to tiny pointy teeth and just as she got to my hand, I used it to shoo her away. She went flying to the foot of the bed.

"Get away bitch rat," I said.

She shook herself off, looked me dead in the eye, and came galloping back. Again I flung her to the foot of the bed. Again she charged, once more into the breach.

I looked at her. She didn't look angry or frightened. She was alert—and interested. Could it be? Maybe, just maybe, what I had taken for aggression was actually play. Maybe what I thought was hostility was in fact interest. Had I so profoundly misread her? Slowly I moved my hand in front of her. She watched, thought about it, and then gave chase. I stopped and held my hand still. I braced myself as her mouth came near to my finger. I froze, waiting for pain. She sniffed, sniffed, and, gently, with her nose, nudged it. I moved my hand in circles and in circles she followed. Hester wanted to play.

I lay my hand down, flat, palm up. She crawled slowly onto it. I brought her up to my face, eye to eye. Finally, we saw each other. Until that night, I had seen only what I'd wanted to see. I was shocked by my own ignorance, by my inability to recognize her for who and what she was: playful, curious, and engaged.

My heart swelled, and I felt that euphoric sense of completeness that I had not experienced since before Prudence's death. This, I felt, was the beginning of a beautiful relationship.

Outside my little cubby of an apartment, the decade of decadence was in full swing, and New York was a hopping town of clubs and drugs and excess. Vince got "put on the list" at a lot of the hot clubs—Area, the Tunnel, Limelight. He would ask me to go, and I would say no. I had to get up early to work. These places didn't even get going until two in the morning. "You go," I'd tell him. "I don't mind." And I didn't.

He minded, however, when I went out with my friends for post–softball game drinks. He minded when I had dinner with out-of-town authors who came in to meet me, men with whom I'd worked and had gotten to know on the phone, and through reading their manuscripts. Men I'd never met in person. Whether they were married or single, straight or gay, young or old, he always said they wanted to sleep with me.

"You know I'm right," Vince would say smugly, about everything. Sometimes I'd love him for that, because sometimes he was right. I didn't mind being proved wrong, when I was. But I wasn't always wrong. Vince, on the other hand, was always right.

I stopped playing softball, stopped going to bars. I even stopped stopping by Marvel Comics on the way home from work. The more time Vince and I spent together, the lonelier I began to feel. The closer we became, the more distanced I felt from the type of person I aspired to be. But I cared about Vince and admired his intellect. I felt a connection with him that was important to me. I believed that he needed me, that I saw through to the core of what was good and special about him, that, through my creative act of seeing, I apprehended something others missed.

Like Hester, Vince stashed things. Notes I'd written him in haste I'd find squirreled away in his apartment. I became more careful about what I committed to paper, wanting to compose things that he'd want to keep. He kept track of who paid for what. He made fun of my nine-to-five job, but was happy to have me use my meager salary for dinners out. He'd hold things I'd said in reserve, using them against me when necessary; sometimes they'd be words spoken in moments of tenderness and affection. He would pull them out during a fight, offer them up as argument, and sully them in the process.

Every night, as soon as I got home, I'd let Hester out of her cage and put her back only when it was time for sleep. She still had a predilection for chewing on important wires and leather shoes, so I learned to keep them out of her way. If you are going to love a rat, you can't be too attached to material possessions. You also have to be stalwart against friends and acquaintances who tell you to find a more appropriate object of affection.

I found out what she loved. Her mother's rat, she loved sweets. She became hyperalert to the crinkling sound of candy-bar wrappers. She loved to cuddle up close, to nest into small spaces. She didn't like open expanses—tiny niches, say, armpits, were what made her feel safe. She was interested in everything. She would follow my fingers anywhere, climbing up the chair, over the desk, doing all she could to keep up. But she wasn't just a follower; she was an explorer, my Hester, fearlessly looking into every nook and cranny of our apartment. Like most explorers, she got dirty.

So I'd wash her. I'd fill up the bathroom sink with warm water, made sudsy by a few drops of nice-smelling Suave shampoo. I'd hold her tight so she wouldn't be scared during the initial dunking, and let her swim around while gently scrubbing her white fur—she had a beautiful coat of thick white hair. She was an exquisitely hygienic creature, constantly grooming herself and, like Prudence, never, ever peeing or pooping outside her cage.

When she was clean and fragrant, I'd towel her off with a washcloth. She liked the rubbing and lengthened herself to help out. I'd get her as dry as I could, and then I'd take out the hair dryer and, on the lowest setting, I'd blow-dry her to soft and fluffy whiteness. Queen Hester, I'd call her, holding her up to my face and breathing her in.

The hardest part of loving Hester was learning to say no. At night, she didn't want to go back in her cage—she wanted to stay out and play. Every single night, we'd go through the same painful ritual: I'd lift her to her cage, and she'd stretch her arms and legs out wide, making herself huge, trying to keep from fitting through the door.

When I told Joan, the family friend who had convinced me to adopt Hester, about this behavior, she laughed and said that my difficulty in dealing with Hester stemmed from the fact that I'd never been a parent. No child wants to go to bed, she said. But as a parent, you have to know what's good for them. Hester is smart enough to understand that at night she goes back into her cage. You just have to get over it.

So it became a game. I let her grab onto the sides of the cage to keep herself from being put inside, and then I held firm. Bedtime is bedtime—in you go. I'll take you out again in the morning. That's the deal.

It was equally hard to say no to Vince. When I couldn't—or wouldn't—accede to his wishes, he, too, stretched himself out, long and firm. I didn't want to lose him, so I continued to try to deal.

It was April, my mother's birthday, and I wanted to spend it with her at her new home, upstate. My parents had divorced a few years before, soon after my brother had left for college. My mother moved into an apartment about fifteen minutes from where I'd grown up, but miles away in terms of culture and ethos. Now living in a community of artists, she was thriving, and I wanted to celebrate her forty-eighth birthday with her. I asked Vince if he wanted to drive up with me, and he volunteered to go and rent a car, with my credit card.

We arrived after a four-hour drive, and my mother and I squealed our welcomes. (We can be squealers, my mother and I.) When I turned to introduce Vince, he was already walking around the apartment, looking at her paintings.

"Hmmmmm," he said, appraising, weighing, assessing.

My mother met her grandrat instead.

I took her out of her travel cage and showed her off.

"She's beautiful," my mother said, holding out her hands to Hester, who bravely came forward to accept grandmotherly praise.

My mother tried to draw Vince out, but he was characteristically dismissive and clingy. That night, in the guest bedroom of my mother's new place, Vince whispered over and over that he loved me. I muttered a reply but knew that this relationship wasn't right; I was finally starting to admit this to myself. He was controlling and demanding, insecure and impatient—perhaps not unlike my father, to whom, soon after, we paid an obligatory visit. When he learned that Vince had gone to MIT, my father asked him to fix the VCR. Vince tried, and failed.

"That's what an MIT education gets you?" my father joked, with a characteristic edge.

"Yeah, well, you wanna talk about quantum electrodynamics?"

I heard Vince mutter "asshole" under his breath.

And then we left.

I've suffered from migraine headaches since I was a child. Chronic illness is a drag. You have to deal with the illness itself, but it also comes packaged in a host of social problems. First, you have this problem, and that's a problem. Then you don't know when you're going to be incapacitated, and thus you are fearful about making plans. Finally, if you do have to bail out, which sucks in and of itself, you pile guilt onto your growing heap of troubles.

Like many sufferers of chronic illness, I became an expert on myself: good at adapting, figuring out which drugs I needed to take to be able to get through whatever I needed to do. There were four of us headache people in the office. On certain days, with certain weather conditions, we were all out sick.

Marvel could tell within fifteen seconds of looking at my face if I had a headache. I loved her for that. I now have a permanent vertical crease in my forehead, etched there from years of pain.

Vince could never tell when I had a headache. When I told him I did, he didn't seem to notice, or care. Except when I told him I had one at night—then he accused me of making up excuses to get out of having sex with him.

Soon our fights were more frequent than the times between. I'd lie awake in bed wondering if it was him or me. Was he crazy and volatile, or was he passionate and fiery? Was I difficult to please, or was he not interested in pleasing me? I was, I had to admit, rather self-assured; okay, I was downright arrogant. I was doing well in my job and felt buoyed by Vince's intense attentions. Perhaps

I'd mentioned that one of the handsome male editors had been praising my work. Perhaps I'd told him that one of my authors had called me his angel. Perhaps I'd been trying to make him jealous. Was I trying to keep him off guard, attempting to prevent him from getting too close? I had a hard time gauging my own complicity in our troubles. How do you know if it's him, you, or the dynamic? How do you know?

After a night of fighting, Vince would call me the next morning, contrite and apologetic. He'd tell me something funny, quote a line of poetry, or use an analogy from physics that made me soften, and I'd agree to see him again that night. Yeah, I'd think. It was probably me. My friends and family didn't like him because they didn't see him for who he really was.

One thing that wasn't open for interpretation was that Vince did not appreciate Hester. He didn't say so. But I knew it. He pretended to like her. He paid lip service attention to her, nodding in her direction when he entered the apartment, saying a limp hello. Vince wore black leather pants in the days between when they were cool and when they became cool once more. He was a rocker, he said, and "rockers wear leather pants." One morning Vince was sitting in the chair under the loft when Hester climbed up and landed on his lap. Maria Shriver was on the TV, all glossy hair and chipmunk cheeks. Vince was talking, and I was in the bathroom. Over the roar of my hair dryer, I heard a shout, and a squeak.

"What happened?" I stepped out to find Vince standing, fuming, holding his crotch. Hester was cowering in the corner, near her cage.

"What happened?" I shouted.

Hester had been sitting in Vince's lap, and she had nibbled a hole right through his prized leather pants, down to bare skin. (Which is not quite as amazing as it might seem: I'd marveled from the beginning that Vince didn't wear underwear and thought it was odd, even a little gross. Now it seemed dangerous, as well.)

"What did you do to her?" I asked, scooping Hester up, kissing her head, checking her over to make sure she was okay, and then putting her safely back in her cage. She appeared fine, but I wasn't clear on how she had gotten from his lap to the corner. He was seething, glowering at her, and refusing even to look at me.

"I hit the little bitch," he said. "Okay? She ate a hole through my pants. They're expensive, dammit. Fuckin' A," he said.

"Not okay," I said, slowly, clearly. "Don't you ever hit her again. Ever."

I looked at Vince. Through the hole in the black leather I could see the pasty pale flesh of or near his genitals. I began to laugh, then couldn't stop. I could tell he was angry, but he was trying to contain it. He chuckled weakly. "Maybe I can get them fixed," he said. It was one of the few lighthearted moments we had shared in too long.

Although I'd have thought it was impossible just weeks before, Vince became even more jealous and controlling. He sensed that he was losing me, and he was right. He wanted to know where I was every moment I wasn't with him. I became resentful and didn't want to tell him. I was getting sick of this crap when, one night, a bunch of people from the office were going downtown to CBGB to hear Cyndi Lauper, and I decided to go. Since I'd been seeing Vince, I hadn't seen much of anyone else.

It was fun. I began to realize how cut off from my friends I'd been, how isolated. It struck me that maybe it was time to end things with Vince, that maybe he really wasn't the right person for me. I couldn't love him into being a better—or a different—man.

When I got back to the apartment it was around 4:00 a.m. The message light on my answering machine was flashing angrily. There were eight messages, all from Vince, wanting to know, in increasingly hostile tones, where I was. Where the fuck I was.

I'd been home long enough to take Hester out of her cage and to change into a sleeping T-shirt. There was a knock at the door. It could only be him.

He strode into the apartment demanding to know where I'd been and, more important, who I'd been with.

I told him it was none of his business.

He asked what I was trying to hide.

"Nothing," I said. "I'm not hiding anything. It's none of your business."

"You are my business," he said.

"Jesus," I said, and then I capitulated. "Friends from work."

Who, he wanted to know. Which friends?

"No one you know. You don't like my friends, remember?"

"Tell me their names."

I did, and then I got to Bob's name.

"Bob from the party?"

"Yes."

And then he hit me. The rat bastard hit me.

I stumbled backwards across the length of the apartment and landed against the window.

"Bitch," he said, and slammed the door behind him.

I knew, of course, that there were women who were abused by men. But I wasn't one of them. I was too strong, too smart, too self-aware. I went to a fancy-pants college. I was a successful young professional. How could this have happened to me? I should have known, I told myself. His anger, his jealousy—I should have known. I blamed myself for letting it get so far. I knew he'd call after that night. And I knew that I would tell him that it was over. It was finally over.

I lay on the bed, Hester nestled into the cave under my arm. There she was, the smartest, sweetest, bravest, most loving rat I'd ever known. This nocturnal noise-making, phone cord–chewing, Italian leather shoe–gnawing, finger-chasing, candy-hounding, chair-climbing sweet, sweet rat: my love. It was my own misreading that kept us apart initially. Until I saw Hester for what and who she was, we couldn't connect. She wasn't who I wanted her to be—Prudence. She was and could only be herself. Until I saw Vince for who he really was, I was going to keep getting hurt. Like most of us, I saw what I wanted to see. Love can be an imaginative act of seeing not only what is there, but also what isn't.

Looking down at my rat, nestled into my armpit, I felt mostly lucky in love.

Three

Some of my best leading men have been dogs and horses.

—Elizabeth Taylor

The bright lights of the big city were beginning to get on my nerves.

I was sick of living in a cage. I was twenty-four years old, and I wanted a normal life. Normal people didn't live in apartments the size of area rugs. Normal people didn't subsist solely on white rice and soy sauce. Normal people didn't have ugly jealous boyfriends who hit them. Normal people may not, I thought to myself, be in love with vermin, but that part wasn't about to change.

So Hester and I moved to Brooklyn, into two floors of a gorgeous brownstone in the choicest part, on the choicest street, of Park Slope, through an ad I'd seen in the *Village Voice*. The only problem was that we had to share this space with two other early twenty-somethings. I came to refer to them as Frat Boy and Pencil Dick. Frat Boy had been one, and Pencil Dick probably had one, not that I ever saw it, but sometimes you don't have to see it to know.

We'd get back from our jobs—Frat Boy was, naturally, a stockbroker, and Pencil Dick did something technical—make some food, and then go out. We'd come back late and stay up later, munching chips and swilling beer, talking about girls and boys. Frat Boy went most places on Rollerblades; PD was working on a screenplay. It was easy to live with them. These guys, conventional, unsubtle, loud, didn't take much personally, and little seriously. No slights, real or perceived, would have perturbed them.

We had a neighborhood bar, The Gaslight, a dark, smoky place, which, after being open for decades, was now closing. The boys and I attended the swan song bash at the bar. It was crowded with people like us—same age, same mentality. Good hunting grounds for a normal boyfriend. I'd had enough of edgy and challenging. I was ready to go back to nice.

I saw him. He was big and solid, a handsome big-headed man like you find in adventure films. Like Harrison Ford, Jeff Bridges, Kurt Russell, the romantic leading men of the day—he was a big man with a big face. Substantial, hardy, hearty. First he was across the bar; then he was sitting next to me. Then we were talking, conversational volleys lobbed lightly back and forth. His hair was dark and full, his face flushed pink. He was movie-star handsome, soft-spoken, and warm. He wore jeans and a worn, soft, pink Brooks Brothers button-down shirt. No man had ever looked so good in pink.

Patrick, he said his name was, Patrick O'Malley.

"A nice Jewish boy," I said. "My mother will be so pleased."

He threw his head back and laughed, his eyes, heavily lidded, becoming little slits.

He bought me a drink and had himself another. He bought me a bunch of drinks, actually. He outdrank me by about two to one, which didn't strike me as strange since he was easily twice my size.

He offered to drive me home. I offered that I lived two and a half blocks away.

He drove me home.

We sat in the car and talked for another two hours. He had a mellifluous voice, a voice like a movie star, like William Hurt. He walked me to my door and kissed me good night. He asked for my phone number and repeated it ten times while standing on one leg and tapping himself on the head. A goofy movie star. He said he'd call.

He didn't call the next day. We'd had so much fun, toying with words, swatting images back and forth, I wasn't worried.

The next day I began to worry. Surely he had liked me as much as I liked him. Or was I wrong? Maybe he was busy. Maybe the phone was broken. All night I checked it, making sure there was a dial tone. Then I hated myself for being a woman who checked a perfectly functioning phone for a dial tone. But still I checked, just in case.

Frat Boy and Pencil Dick were in the living room, watching TV. They tried to comfort me in their lame-ass way, saying, in unison, "Don't worry—he'll call."

"I don't know what you're talking about," I shot back, and went up to my room.

I put Hester on the bed for a romp and told her that he'd call. I put her back in her cage, checked the phone four more times, and then went to bed.

On the third day I came home from work pissed. Screw him, I thought. He wasn't so great—just a regular guy. Who needed a regular guy when I had my rat?

Then he called, blissfully ignorant of the three days of agony I'd just endured. He was upbeat and enthusiastic and wanting to know if I wanted to go out to dinner with him.

"Come on, Rachel," he said, when I responded coolly. "Have dinner with me. Please? Please please please?"

I guess he did like me after all.

Patrick didn't have a lot of anxiety. He made a lot of jokes. He listened more than he talked. He played music—drums—in what would have been a garage band, if Brooklyn had garages. He lived a few neighborhoods away in Sunset Park, in a brownstone that he owned. He'd grown up in posh Brooklyn Heights, had gone to Columbia; he'd lived in New York City his whole life. He was eight years older than me, then in his early thirties. He drove like a man. When he put his arm around my seat while backing up, I felt cared for.

His mildness took me by surprise. I was used to the maniacal obsession of Vince, the dull devotedness of Charlie. The fact that Patrick would wait three days after seeing me to call, which he did, every time for the first few months, drove me nuts. He had a life and wasn't prepared to drop it all, all at once, just for me. For the first time, I had to fit in, and it made me crazy. I could have called him, of course. But I didn't. I was comfortable being brazen only if I was sure that I wouldn't be rejected. His casualness kept me uncertain.

He liked Hester. While Vince had, at best, tolerated her, Patrick seemed genuinely fond of the little rat. One night, he brought over a camera and took some glamour shots of Hester, laid out on a fluffy green towel, posing in a fetching, come-hither fashion. He had them developed and gave one to me, framed. He got her. He got it.

We slipped into an easy pattern, getting together a few nights a week, having dinner, sharing a couple of bottles of wine, maybe seeing a movie. Patrick cried at movies, even if they weren't sad. He cried hardest at happy endings. He got dehydrated when we went to see *Moonstruck*.

One day we were sitting on the stoop of his brownstone. Patrick pointed out a sign across the street and said that when he'd first read it, he thought it had said, "This area is patrolled by uninformed police." (Of course, it really read "uniformed police.") I laughed and laughed, and he laughed with me and then started to cry. "I didn't think anyone else would find that funny," he said. That I did, he said, meant the world to him.

I wasn't used to a man who cried so easily, who was so undemanding and self-contained, who loved to laugh and seemed not to need to impress me or try hard to get me to like him. He was who he was. He was a good man.

I gave Patrick the keys to my apartment, a big step. He came over every night to my place after work instead of asking me to ride the RR train farther out to his Sunset Park brownstone. He had his own typesetting business in Manhattan, but he wanted to close it down, seeing that his industry was going to go the way of Betamax. Computers, he posited—which were then mostly clunky beige boxes with black screens and green type—were going to make his expensive typesetting equipment obsolete.

Two and a half years after she'd come into my life, Hester started to ail. When you live with someone, you know when he or she is sick—she was slower, less alert. I also could feel a lump on her belly, which I tried to ignore. I didn't know how old she'd been when I adopted her, but I did know that rats generally live a thousand days. A whole lifetime in a thousand days. I knew, too, that they are prone to mammary tumors.

Patrick and I brought her to the vet, who delivered news I knew but couldn't bear to hear. Patrick held me while I held Hester, and the vet administered the shot.

She had been my playmate, my friend. She had listened to me, nose twitching, eyes alert, as I had rattled off my hopes and dreams, had carped and complained. She'd made me laugh more times than I can remember, but now I cried. I cried and cried.

Patrick buried her in his backyard, under the rosebush he'd planted over his mother's ashes. He held me while I cried. He made every effort not to pass Hester Street when we drove back to Brooklyn from Manhattan. He listened as I talked about her, listened, for the fiftieth time, about the night I saw her for the first time, the battle on the bed that had called a détente to all hostilities.

We began to spend more time in the privacy of Patrick's house. He asked me to move in, but the memory of being a victim of the New York housing market, of growing to resent Charlie after being stuck in the apartment with him, was still too fresh. I liked our easy living situation, being together and apart, having a choice. I said no.

After Vince, I was eager to introduce Patrick to my friends. I sought validation; I wanted to make sure I had chosen better this time.

Marvel had recently left her cab-driving husband, whom she'd married too young and eventually grown apart from, and I volunteered to help her paint her new apartment in Greenpoint, a slightly seedy area, also in Brooklyn. Patrick volunteered to help me help her.

"He's wonderful," she said when he left to get a pizza. "A big improvement."

My friend Sarah, a former coworker who had just left Oxford to go to law school, said, "He's really handsome."

"Yeah," I replied.

"No," she said. "I mean he's really handsome."

My mother came to visit and stayed with us at Patrick's house. She said, "The way he looks at you. I can't get over the way he looks at you. He shoots love at you with his eyes."

I loved being with him—the way he smelled, the way he threw his head back when he laughed, the worn spots on the collars of his Brooks Brothers shirts. When he was sitting down, I'd curl up in his lap like a kitten. I reached for his hand when we walked down the street and held on as if for life. Until we came to a dog. Then I dropped it like a hot potato—I had to pet, had to talk to, the dog.

We'd go to the park and see people playing with puppies. I'd look at them eagerly, the way Hester used to look out from her cage when she heard a candy bar wrapper crinkling, the way some women look at other people's babies in their strollers. Ever since I'd left Barkus for college, I'd longed for a dog of my own.

We were not entirely without pet: Patrick shared his house with Willy, an elderly longhaired black cat he'd inherited from his mother. Willy had had a sister named Emily, who had committed suicide by jumping out the window in Patrick's mother's house, the same open window she'd sat by every day of her life. One afternoon she'd had enough and jumped. Willy wouldn't come if you called him—unless you called him Emily, and then he'd come running. I wondered if Willy thought that Emily was his name, or if he missed his sister and was hoping for an opportunity to see her again. It was hard to know what went through Willy's mind.

On a crisp spring Saturday, Patrick and I were walking down the street, somewhere in Brooklyn, and passed a pet store window. It was filled with guinea pigs, rabbits, some turtles, and a parrot.

"I want to live in a window like that," I said to Patrick. "All those species, peaceably kingdoming. I want a window of my own."

Patrick laughed, his big-head-thrown-back-eyes-like-slits laugh.

"I want a window," I said again.

"If you move in with me," he said, "you can have a window. And a door and a closet and . . ."

"And?" I asked.

"And a dog." He smiled.

"No kidding?"

"No kidding."

The week I moved into Patrick's brownstone we went to the North Shore Animal League on Long Island, where every New Yorker who wants to adopt a pet goes. We spotted a three-month-old Rottweiler who looked promising, except that he was a he, and I wanted a she.

Then the vet tech brought in a new cage. The puppy had just passed her medical check and was now entering the adoption phase. She was nine weeks old. Blond. Quiet. The vet tech said she was a shepherd cross, which is what they always say when they don't want to call a mutt a mutt. She had enormous ears and a pointy face. I picked her up, and she settled comfortably into my arms.

We continued to look around for a less pointy dog, and I continued to hold on to her. Another couple had their eye on her, and I knew that if I put her down, the choice might no longer be ours. I held fast, even though I worried she was perhaps too quiet, too dull, maybe even a little dumb. I wanted a big smart dog, not a small dumb one. The other couple kept eyeing her from across the room, the way I'd looked at Patrick when I first spied him at The Gaslight. In the face of competition, I refused to put her down. Patrick and I huddled, speaking over her head. We decided we'd take her, perhaps caving in to mimetic desire: that they wanted her made us more confident in our decision.

She was supposed to be named Sophie. Patrick had not only asked me to move in with him, he'd given me a typeset invitation that read

The Hound of Forty-seventh Street
cordially invites
Sophie and Rachel
to an open door party
Saturday, May 9, 1987
Sniffing and Pawing—Bring Your Own Bones
Garden Apartment
Live Cat (Come early!)
Attire Optional

And, in small print at the bottom—*We welcome overnight guests. Extended stay accommodation available. Inquire.*

Looking at our new puppy in the clear light of day, out of the shelter, away from the sterile fluorescence of the animal hospital, she was no more a Sophie than I was a Brittany or a Tiffany.

We settled on Hannah, after Hannah Arendt, the philosopher, writer, thinker, the author of *Eichmann in Jerusalem: A Report on the Banality of Evil*, her subtitle coining a beautiful and apt, if counterintuitive, phrase. Hannah was a good and serious name. I liked that. Patrick liked the name because it was a palindrome. Hannah, our philosophical, same-backwards-as-forwards, dog.

The three of us became a unit. We lived together, played together, slept together, and ate together. Well, Hannah, actually, didn't eat with us. She had food issues, right from the start. She didn't like to be seen eating and would wait until we had gone to bed. Then we'd hear her in the kitchen, slowly crunch, crunch, crunching through her food. As long as she's eating and healthy, I thought, she's entitled to some privacy.

Willy the cat kept to himself—except when someone was on the telephone, and then he'd come running, jump into your lap, and knead your belly like dough with his clawless paws. He couldn't really meow; when he opened his mouth to speak, he just kind of quacked. Patrick said he'd always been like that. Hannah chased Willy around the house. He was mostly too fast for her, but his lush, long-haired tail eventually began to look like a pine tree that had barely survived a fire.

On weekends we'd take Hannah to the park. We'd separate, and she would gallop between us, shuttling with delight to get from me to Patrick, from Patrick back to me. I'd stretch out my arms like an airplane and she'd put her big ears flat against her head and come charging—to me, then past me—circling around, and then zipping back to Patrick.

I still hoped that Hannah would become a big dog. Occasionally I'd look down at her and command her to grow. She'd cock her head, like Nipper, the RCA dog, and look at me, wondering what, exactly, I expected her to do. "Grow," I said. "Grow."

Hannah's oversize ears pricked up into disproportionately large triangles, and her snout, though not collie-long, protruded to create a pointy effect. When I came home from business trips, having not seen her for a few days, she always seemed pointier.

Over time, Hannah's pointiness grew on me. It became cute, adorable. Her quirks and imperfections—if there were any—became part of who she was, which was who I loved. I realized that at some level, like a doting parent, I had lost all objectivity. As she grew and I grew to know her, she became more and more beautiful to me.

Hannah matured into sixty solid pounds, with a barrel chest and thin, elegant legs; she was a thinking dog, perfectly capable of kicking up her heels and having fun, but, from her earliest days, fundamentally serious. Like Barkus, she had eyebrows that stood out dark and expressive against her otherwise light-haired face; these contributed to the gravity of her countenance. She was so earnest, so serious, it was hard not to tease her.

"Oh, look," I'd say as we were driving along in Patrick's car, "a dog!" I'd look out the window in the front, and she'd sit up in the backseat and look, too. She'd look and look, ears huge and pricked alert, frantically casting about. Where's that dog? I don't see a dog.

"Oh," I'd say. "Oops. It was a fire hydrant."

She took it in good humor, but she'd always fall for it again.

I never used a leash when I walked her. She usually stuck to my heel. But sometimes youthful enthusiasm would get the best of her, and she'd dash ahead. At that point Patrick and I would hide—behind a tree, ducked into a doorway—and watch. She'd soon realize that we weren't close behind and would begin to look around. You could see her recalling: When and where did I last see them? What could have happened? Shit, I shouldn't have been running up here without them. Then concern would show itself in her eyes, and she'd come charging back to find us. After a couple of rounds, she knew it was a game, and she'd check behind every tree, look into every doorway, until she found us. Then she'd glue herself to my lower leg for the rest of the walk.

I adored Prudence and Hester, came to know and love their rodent ways, but Hannah and I were different. I could read Hannah's mind. One midsummer's night we were sitting on the stoop, and I watched her as she watched a man walking up the street toward us. His build was similar to Patrick's, and he was wearing the same kind of clothes: jeans and a button-down shirt with an unstructured blazer over it. He was carrying a briefcase, as Patrick often did. I knew before she began to get excited, big ears pricked forward, tail straight up, that she thought the guy was Patrick, and I knew the fact that he was African-American, about sixty, and dressed entirely in green made no difference.

Hannah waited patiently each morning until there were signs

of life coming from our bed. Then she'd pop up and settle herself between us, lying lengthwise, like a person, head on the pillow. She'd greet the dawn and greet us, with a howl all her own. She would sing for a long time, and we'd join her, each of us yodeling at seven o'clock in the morning. Patrick would grind her ears, and she'd coo. She never licked. Instead, she snuggled her head, sometimes her whole body, into us. Willy would come onto the bed and sit at the foot, looking at us, blinking, quacking. I'd wrap my arms around my sweet, smart, pointy dog and my big, smart, gentle boyfriend and think that this was the life I'd always wanted.

In addition to being the perfect companion in so many other ways, Hannah was also an easy and avid traveler. We took her with us whenever we went on road trips. She always wanted to go, though it turned out she was more fond of getting in the car than being in it— for her, as for so many of us, anticipation often surpassed reality. When we went on vacations that involved flying, though, I couldn't bear the idea of stowing her like luggage in the hold of the plane, so we left Hannah in the care of a canine professional, a woman we called the Dog Lady.

The Dog Lady lived right on Prospect Park. She had two dogs of her own and took into her cramped apartment between five and seven boarders. She'd come highly recommended, but the first time we left Hannah with her, it was torture. We were going on a weeklong ski trip to Davos, Switzerland, and even as the Dog Lady reassured me that Hannah would be fine, I felt tears wetting my face.

"Really," she said. "She'll be fine. You're making her more upset. Just go."

Patrick took me gently by the arm and led me away so that we wouldn't miss our flight.

I worried about Hannah the entire time we were away. When I found myself having too much fun, I flashed back to the look of betrayal on Hannah's face when we left her behind in the Dog Lady's apartment. I was convinced that in our absence, something horrible, unthinkable, had happened. Or, that the Dog Lady simply wouldn't get her, wouldn't be able to see her and would treat her as a, well, dog. I marveled to think that every day, mothers everywhere dropped their children off at day care centers. How did they do it?

"Do you think the Dog Lady will contact us here if . . . if she needs to?" I asked Patrick over dinner the second night we were away.

He reached across the table, took my face in both hands, and looked me sweetly in the eye. "Stop worrying." He kissed me on the head.

The second we got back to our apartment, I zoomed to the phone to call the Dog Lady. I did not help Patrick bring in the skis, did not take off my jacket. Instead I dialed frantically.

"How is she?"

"Rachel?"

"Yes, yes, how is Hannah?"

She was holding back. I knew it. She had bad news, and she was afraid to tell me.

"Well," she said, slowly, too slowly, "if you ever want to get rid of her, I'll take her."

Get rid of her? What was she talking about?

"She is an amazing dog. I've met a lot of dogs, but Hannah is special."

My racing heart began to slow.

"Listen to this," the Dog Lady said. "One day I was walking the other dogs. I left Hannah at home because I wanted to take her out alone—she seems to prefer the company of people to that of dogs."

My maternal heart swelled.

"When I got back, Hannah had dragged the boots I'd been wearing to walk her into the middle of the floor, right in front of the door. On top of the boots she had placed her leash—a leash that was hanging up with a dozen other leashes. She'd had to sort through them, but she wanted to make sure I got the message."

I was not surprised.

"Do you want to pick her up tomorrow? I won't charge you for another day."

"No. I want her back now."

"Okay, but I'm serious. I'd really like to have her if you ever decide—"

"No. Thank you. No."

One of the great things about living with a gentile was Christmas. Growing up, I'd had a lot of Christmas envy. My father's take on being Jewish was to be vigilantly alert for anti-semitism. My relationship to religion and ethnicity was framed in the negative: no celebrations, only an awareness of the possibility of hate. When I lived with Patrick, we had a Christmas tree, which I ornamented with the enthusiasm of the newly initiated. Low-hanging candy canes were quickly disposed of by Hannah, who ate them, plastic wrappers and all, and Willy, who batted them around the house. On the upper reaches, I hung a plastic dinosaur, some extra big, fluorescent pink earrings, a string of paper clips, strands of multicolored yarn, and an origami bull. You know, the usual.

Patrick hung stockings for all of us. Willy's had catnip in the toe, and he'd sit under it, staring blankly with the desperate expression of a crack addict. Hannah's had toys, which she played with from Christmas until New Year's, and then lost interest in. Mine was filled to the brim with candy, and unlike my patient dog, I simply couldn't wait.

Patrick came home from work one day about a week before Christmas to find me with my hand in the stocking. That hand had already been making frequent trips from stocking to mouth.

"Hey," he said. "Get out of there. You're supposed to wait."

"Oh." Innocent, naive, Jewish little me. "I had no idea."

He nailed the stocking higher up the wall.

The next day he came home to find me on a chair, stretching high to reach in.

He grabbed me by the legs and carried me away from the stocking and into the bedroom. Smothering me with kisses, he declared that Santa knows who's been naughty and who's been nice, and that I had been a very naughty girl.

The punishment was better than the crime.

* * *

Because of my own transgressions, it was hard to be mad at Hannah for hers. Long before the Christmas stockings were hung, we'd become accustomed to returning from work and discovering that our lovely girl had gone on a rampage in our absence. She would get into the garbage and strew it all over the floor like rice at a wedding. She would chew—books, shoes, pieces of furniture—whatever she could find. She knew that this wasn't a Good Thing. We'd open the door to find a house decorated with the shredded remains of our belongings and no dog. Hannah would be quaking in the bathroom, in the bathtub (she hated taking baths), punishing herself for being bad.

She had an overdeveloped moral sense. It was one of the many things I appreciated about her.

Our lives were filled with love, fun, and weekend getaways. One October Friday, the three of us piled into the car and left the hustle of the city during the height of the autumn colors to visit my mother upstate.

Being in the car for four hours gave us a chance to talk. Patrick was generally a laconic sort, but on this trip, he had something that he wanted to discuss. He wanted, he said, to talk about Us, the status of our relationship. We determined that we were both happy with the way things were, but discovered—to my surprise—we were both ready for more of a commitment. We decided to become engaged.

I didn't think I'd ever get to this point. Throughout my adolescence, I'd studied the real-life marriage of my parents and thought no. Marriage looked to me like servitude, a relationship of unequals, a house filled with screaming anger and slamming doors. I didn't want to be mother to anyone but a dog—or a mouse or a rat—and I certainly didn't want to be a wife.

But with Patrick, I believed things might be different. He was eight years older, and he was ready to be married. I knew I would never be trapped with him the way my mother had been jailed by my father. He would never try to dominate, intimidate, or torture me. This was a man who cried at movies, even happy movies. He spoke little, and when he did, it was softly. We'd go to dinner with my friends, and he'd say almost nothing, sitting, smiling, looking handsome and pleasant. After, I'd get the call: "That Patrick. What a great guy." He made punning jokes at no one's expense and came off as sweet and clever. He was smart like Hannah, and, like her, serious and good.

Who wouldn't want to marry such a man? I'd already moved in with him—that was the hard part. Getting married was what normal people did, and I wanted a normal life.

We arrived at my mother's house. We'd giggled about what we'd say when we got there, how we'd tell her. When my mother opened the door to us, Patrick said, "I'd like to ask for your daughter's hand in marriage."

"Why are you asking me?" My mother grinned. "It's her hand."

I loved being engaged. I loved everything about it—from the practical implications and what that said to the outside world (no, we're not just roommates—thank God I don't have to use the word *boyfriend* anymore) to the linguistic richness of the term: engaged. We were engaged in each other's lives. We were engaged in our relationship, not just riding a wave.

What I didn't like was the question that followed as surely as a person's eyes glanced from my finger, which sported my grandmother's diamond ring, to my face: "So, have you set a date?"

A date for what?

I hadn't been aware how tired a question that is. And how annoying it is when you haven't.

We thought about various ways to do it. I called the Swiss embassy to find out about getting married in an alpine town, since many of our vacations involved skiing. The nice woman told me to spare myself the trouble: Get married in the United States, honey, and honeymoon in Switzerland. It'd be a lot easier.

One of the big stories of the year had been the fact that a garbage barge had been floating around the country, looking for a place to land its trash. It ended up in the filthy New York Harbor, naturally, and the epic journey was all over the papers. At one point, we were so sick of trying to figure out how and where to do the deed, we considered getting married on the garbage barge. Eventually we were persuaded to dump the idea.

Neither of us wanted a big wedding. We were happy living together and didn't feel a need to rush. So we were engaged for a couple of years. There was no reason to force the issue. No reason, that is, until Patrick finally shut down his typesetting business and began to work freelance. We realized that if we were an official couple in the eyes of the state, he could go on my health insurance at Oxford. That seemed like a darned good reason to tie the knot.

Three months of planning. Three hellish, horrible months. Quarreling with me over every detail, my mother was transmogrified into someone I didn't recognize. The blessed event was to be in her house, and my mother, despite her artsy, somewhat bohemian ways, has always liked things to be "just so." I found myself arguing with her over the color of napkins. She went nuts.

I myself stayed completely calm. Except for a few, minor screaming fits over the guest list. ("No, you may not invite crazy Cousin Cookie to my wedding.") Except for a few anxiety-filled days and nights thinking about what to wear. ("No I am not going to wear a stupid fucking white fucking wedding dress.") Except for a few endless conversations about food. ("Okay, we can have the goddamn Thai satay. Fine. Fine. I'm not talking about this anymore.")

The fun part was ring shopping. I wanted a plain gold band. Patrick wanted to get the rings from Tiffany. His mother had been an elegant lady. After her husband left her and she was fired from her advertising job and left with four kids and they had to go on food stamps, she still managed to take the family to the opera and the ballet. She had always loved the magisterial jewelry store on Fifth Avenue.

The rings came in blue suede boxes. Those boxes were nestled inside the robin's egg blue Tiffany box, tied with a white satin ribbon. It frightened me to see the plain gold band out of the box and on my finger. It looked like my hand had been abducted and was no longer mine, no longer attached to me. It looked like the hand of some old married person.

Clearly, we needed practice. Every few days I'd shout out, "Ring practice!" I'd race to the drawer where we kept the rings, take them out, and put them on our hands. Patrick was typically tolerant of this. We'd wear them around the house for about fifteen minutes, or until I could no longer stand it.

It was a small wedding in my mother's small house, in the dead of winter, in upstate New York. We'd decided to invite no more than fifty people—almost all family—and not ask our friends to make the journey. We planned a party in our own house in Brooklyn for our friends. We were all crammed into the living room, and the judge, who we'd never met before but was the friend of a friend of my mother's, first tried to marry Patrick's friend John to my friend Sarah.

"No, no," Sarah said.

"No, no," we said.

No one was wearing white. It was an honest mistake.

Flustered, excited, tired, Patrick said, when asked, "With this thing I thee wed." With this thing? This thing?!

That was it. I started laughing, and I couldn't stop. You know, the kind of fit where, as soon as you try to stop, it just makes it worse and you laugh harder until your stomach hurts, your eyes water, your face gets tired, and you have to pee.

The impatient judge waited for me to stop laughing. Patrick had tears in eyes, happy-movie tears. He laughed a little, but as soon as I was able to wrest the vows from my hysterical mouth, he stopped me with a kiss. And then we were married. Just like that.

Hannah, the flower dog, wore a festive bow and found the whole endeavor less than entertaining. We were making her legitimate, and she was having none of it. She'd never liked parties, and this one was no exception. It wasn't that she lacked in social graces; those she had in abundance. She was just extremely discriminating. There were people she liked and those she didn't, and rather than dodge the latter, she preferred to hide under a piece of furniture or in another room.

It was clear that Hannah did not like my father, and she tried to steer clear. Oblivious and insensate, my father pursued her. Walking after her, seeking her attention and affection with an outstretched hand, he persisted until Hannah took refuge under the couch.

After being single for about five years, my mother had met a man, George, who was, like her, an artist. And as wacky as she. Before I ever met him, I knew he was wonderful—I'd seen his work in the Port Authority Bus Terminal that first night I went home with Charlie, and several times after. And I'd seen another of his pieces in a shopping mall near my college. He made audiokinetic sculptures, gigantic Rube Goldberg–like contraptions where metal balls zoom and career in a brightly colored enclosed space, whirling around and landing in woks, bouncing up and being caught and sent through a roller coaster. You watch and believe that metal balls have never had so much fun.

George looked like Henry Fonda and was playful and silly. Unlike my father, he never tried to control my mother; he encouraged her independence and her art. After three years together, he moved into her house—coincidentally, the same weekend as my wedding to Patrick.

They both loved their granddog. They discovered that, when asked the question, "Did you get into the garbage?" Hannah would turn her head to one side, unable to make eye contact. She responded the same way to "What did you do?"

The day before our wedding, I walked into the house to shrieks of laughter. My mother, George, and Hannah were sitting in a row on the couch. My mother, in mock anger, would say, "What did you do?" and then, in perfect synchrony, the three of them would turn their heads to the side, all in the same direction. The humans giggled maniacally, Hannah looked guilty, and then my mother would ask the question again.

I liked being married, though I was apt to stumble sometimes over referring to Patrick as my husband. I wasn't comfortable with the word until I thought of its other usages; then I loved the image of him cultivating and nurturing me as if I were a crop, raising me and feeding me as if I were a barnyard animal. I was careful always to refer to him by name, rather than in relation to me. It disturbed me when women used "my husband" to start every sentence, especially if I knew the names of their husbands, knew the men. I didn't like erasing the individual to privilege the position.

I kept scrambling up the rickety publishing career ladder, becoming at a tender age a full editor at a venerable publishing house. Patrick closed his business and got a good-paying job as the manager of the in-house typesetting arm of an advertising agency. It was the late eighties. We did late eighties things. We never cooked—we either ordered in or went out. We skied and went to the beach at the appropriate seasons. We shopped. We shopped. We shopped.

Patrick's hours grew longer. He was running a department and had yet to master that most important of managerial skills: delegating. He preferred to do everything himself. He'd get home late, we'd have a late dinner, and then he'd spend the next few hours in front of his computer. I'd read for a while and then go to bed. He'd come to bed, late.

Patrick loved his job; the higher I got up the publishing ladder, the less I loved mine. He loved New York; I missed being able to walk out a front door and be outside. We loved each other. We talked about daily life. What did you have for lunch? How's your coworker/sister/aunt doing? We didn't talk about much else—not the content of our work, not the ideas shaking loose in our brains. I'd thought that marriage would be like an extension of the late-night conversations I'd had in college—where you throw ideas back and forth, push and challenge each other to think harder, talk about the books you'd read. At the end of the day, we'd come home tired, worn down. Patrick liked to make jokes, play with language, and relax. He was good at relaxing.

It was an easy life, a normal life, but I heard deep in my being a low hum of dissatisfaction that I refused to acknowledge, like when you pretend not to notice the mosquito in your tent, and you lie there hoping it will decide to buzz off. Life was easy, normal, and perhaps normal was supposed to be, well, if not boring, at least not exciting. I did have Hannah.

We moved into Manhattan, and Hannah became an Upper West Side dog. We had our favorite spots—she loved going into Laytner's Linens, the hardware store, and to her favorite, the Pet Bowl. The dog food and treat store was one block from our apartment. Once we crossed the street onto the Pet Bowl block (she sat at every curb until given the signal to cross), she'd dart ahead into the always-open door of the Pet Bowl, march up to the cash register, and patiently wait for a treat. It wasn't even that was so enamored of the treats; she just liked the ritual, liked having her own store.

We took long walks in Riverside Park. Hannah would glance over at other dogs, but mostly she paid attention to me, chasing an occasional squirrel because she was, after all, a dog.

One day I watched as she bolted across the park in search of a squirrel. I watched as she fell and yelped in pain. She had galloped onto an unseen drainage grate—it had been covered with leaves—and her front leg went down between the bars. I got to her, and she was crying. I looked at her leg and saw that the fur had been scraped off, leaving a raw wound. She cried and cried. She was hurting; I started crying. I knew—I could tell—that her leg wasn't broken, and that this would heal over. But seeing her in pain, crying and looking at me and begging me to make it stop, was almost more than I could take.

Since the time Hannah was a tiny baby, I have lived every moment of every day anxiously aware that if something happened to her, it would be more than I could bear. I do not know how mothers of children are able to sleep.

Saturday nights, my friend Sarah, who left publishing for law school, would come over, tired from a week of difficult classes, and we'd look out the window across the streets into the windows of Zabar's, our upscale New York deli. When the lines got short enough, we'd dash over, and I'd buy us some cheese, tofu spread, crackers, and a gargantuan hunk of Russian coffee cake. We'd go back to my apartment and wait until it was late enough to get the Sunday *New York*

Times and then we'd read it, sipping wine. Patrick would be at the computer, working. He didn't mind that Sarah came over so frequently, that she ate with us often and went to the movies with me.

Soon, though, I was spending more time with Sarah than I was with Patrick.

I couldn't, wouldn't admit it. We were married. This was the happily-ever-after time, the part you don't read about, because it comes after "The End," the part when it all works out. But it didn't feel like it was working out. I hadn't realized that marriage was a continuation, not a sea change. We didn't all of a sudden start talking about books and ideas; we didn't connect more deeply. We talked about what we had for lunch and where we'd ski next winter. I don't know what I had expected, but it wasn't this. I felt stuck.

It was hard to reconcile stuckness with the sense that it was still fun to be with Patrick, still easy. He was in some ways indeed like the perfect college roommate—easy to live with but not someone you'd necessarily keep in touch with after graduation. We never argued, dividing the chores and the goodies evenly and naturally. We appreciated each other's sense of humor. But I didn't know what he thought about—if he thought about anything other than work—if he had dreams that he didn't speak of, if he dreamed at all.

With Hannah, though, I could watch her sleep and believe I knew her dreams. I could tell the difference between the times when she was chasing rabbits, and when she had nightmares about watching the door close as we went off to work, leaving her alone for the day. I knew if she wanted to go out for a walk. (That was easy—she always wanted to go out for a walk.) I knew if she was waiting for Patrick to come home; I knew that she was upset when I was in bed with a migraine. Hannah and I communicated in silent and profound ways.

One afternoon I went to lunch with a colleague, a woman like me, on the cusp of thirty, who looked at me from under expertly plucked eyebrows, put down her fork, and said, "Sometimes I could just hate you. Everything comes to you. You've had it so easy."

I put down my own fork and gaped at her.

"You have the perfect job," she said, "the perfect husband, the perfect apartment. The perfect fucking life." She was smiling, and while I knew she meant it as a compliment, there was also an edge to her words. She thought I was living the life she thought she wanted.

I looked over my shoulder to see if there was someone else she could be describing.

I pointed out that all I really had was the perfect dog.

She waved her hand dismissively and continued. "You've never had to work for anything. You've never had to struggle."

She couldn't see how much of a challenge it was just to get up each morning and to wonder if I was giving authors the right advice on how to fix their manuscripts; every day I struggled with the guilt of being married to a good and kind man and yet constantly questioning whether the relationship was enough, believing that as much as I loved him, fearing that he was not The One. Every day I struggled to find some meaning in life. Who was she talking about?

We droned on, Patrick and I. He worked, came home, and worked some more. I spent my Saturday nights with Sarah and the *New York Times*. He never minded—or perhaps he simply didn't notice—when I went out at night, had dinner with authors, or took off on long business trips. He was content, happy.

We'd been married for about a year and were, once again, driving up for a ski weekend in Vermont. Whenever we went on vacation he brought with him manuals about learning Quark Xpress and other computer programs. I brought a whole lot of warm clothes and a big stack of books. I was prattling on about a novel I'd just read. I turned and looked at him. He was smiling.

"Are you even listening to me?"

"Yes," he said.

"It doesn't seem like it."

"Well"—he smiled—"it's kind of like listening to birds chirping in the trees. It's very pleasant to listen to you."

Engagement had led to marriage, which had resulted in less engagement. We shared less, laughed less. We didn't argue, but then, we never argued—not over politics, religion, how to raise Hannah, what color to paint the bedroom, what to have for dinner. It was effortless, unchanging. Like death.

We skied a lot. We planned a weeklong vacation in Colorado after which I'd go on to an academic conference in San Francisco, and Patrick would stay and ski more. Ski vacations were for me much like going to work. You get up early to catch the first lift. You ski until lunch. You ski after lunch until you catch the last lift. You finally get to quit, and then you gamely—if you're me—manage to heave food into your mouth at dinner, and—if you're Patrick—you drink a lot of wine. Patrick loved to ski. I loved watching him ski. His big body was transformed into that of a graceful dancer. He seemed most at home on the slopes.

I went to San Francisco at the end of the week while Patrick stayed on. I called him when I got to California. He didn't answer the phone in the hotel room. He's at the bar, I reckoned. Whatever. I kept calling. It got later and later. No answer. Maybe he'd fallen asleep. The next morning I called early, well before the first lift. No answer. Maybe he'd gone for breakfast. That night I continued to call and continued to hear only ringing. I left messages. I was getting anxious. The next morning, still no answer. I called the hotel manager and asked her to check the room. She calmly reported that his things seemed still to be there, and that the bed had not been slept in.

I quickly moved beyond anxious. I thought about those runs at the end of the day, the difficulty of skiing when your legs are like rubber. I thought about Patrick's fondness for a drink or two at lunch. I called all the hospitals in the area. I called the police. Nothing. I couldn't do the work I had to do at the conference, didn't want to hear about manuscripts on ancient Roman law, couldn't spend another nanosecond listening to a description of another book about Sappho. Couldn't eat, couldn't sleep. I was three thousand miles from home with a husband who was MIA.

Just as I was ready to go to the emergency room myself and ask to be sedated, Patrick called.

"What's up?"

He'd decided to go to Aspen and check out the scene there for a couple of days. Wasn't a big deal, he said. What was I so worried about—why had I gotten the hotel involved?

He didn't understand that I was worried about him, worried sick.

Loving someone means coming to terms with the fact of his or her mortality. Every moment I looked at Hannah, even when she was still plump with puppy fat, I told myself that someday she was going to die. I could feel my heart already starting to break, even as she was right here, beside me, shooting love at me with her eyes. Patrick didn't understand my worries. He didn't share them. His emotional life was muted, the way Hannah had seemed when we first saw her in the shelter. Over time my connection to Hannah had deepened as she opened up to share her life with me. My connection to Patrick seemed ever more tenuous.

When we both got home, I said that I wanted more. I didn't know what it was. Maybe I was a meaning-in-life overachiever, bringing my perfectionist tendencies to everything, wanting to have the life my colleague thought she saw me living.

In December 1991, the country went to war, and Patrick and I decided to split. We'd been together for five years, married for two. Patrick didn't argue with me. He understood, he said. He put his head down and worked even harder.

In keeping with my quest for deeper meaning, I decided to quit my job and leave Manhattan. I'd heard that outside of death, the most traumatic events in a person's life are divorce, starting a new job, and moving. I figured I'd consolidate my troubles and get them all over at once. I had fallen into publishing, rather than having chosen it as a field. I wanted to think hard about what I wanted to do next, where I wanted to live. Patrick had never been receptive to the idea of leaving New York City. Now that I was to be on my own, the world opened for me. I could go anywhere, do anything. While I was trying to figure it all out, though, I needed to make some money.

Patrick arranged for me to have an interview with a firm he had done some work for. I was hired to oversee the process of translating Time Warner's Annual Report into five languages, acting as liaison between Time Warner, the design firm, and the translation agency that had hired me. I worked longer hours than I ever had in publishing and was paid three times as much.

The night that I took off my wedding ring, I went with Sarah to a party of her fellow law students. They were smart, interesting people, and I ended up talking with a guy named Scott. He had a wiry body, a sharp wit, and an impressive knowledge of film. He'd read a lot. I flirted with him, remembering how much fun it was to flirt.

Sarah called the next day to say that Scott had asked for my phone number. She was reluctant to give it to him, she said. He was a good guy, and she wasn't sure she could trust me not to hurt him. She'd seen me with Charlie. She knew poor Bob. She liked Patrick. Scott was a friend.

"He's a nice guy," she said. "You're just going to dump him. Why don't you find someone else?"

"He's a grown-up. A big boy. Give him my number."

I could hear her rolling her eyes. She gave him my number. She did, however, take it upon herself to explain to him the facts of my life. When she told him I was married, she said that he brought both hands to his neck in an act of mock self-strangulation. She said, much to her dismay, that he also looked intrigued.

I began to spend time with Scott, who paid a lot of attention to me.

The translation firm where I now worked was way downtown. After a long day, I'd walk to up New York University law school and meet Sarah or Scott—sometimes both. Often Sarah and I walked the four or five miles to the Upper West Side, talking through the city blocks. "What will become of me," I'd wail. "Maybe I could go work on a dude ranch in Wyoming?"

"Yeah, right," she said, eyes rolling.

We continued to live together, Patrick and I, though separately, in the way that people do when they're breaking up. I thought it was fine. He worked late and on the weekends went solo to Vermont to ski. We loved each other, but just couldn't make it work. We were good friends, but didn't have enough to say to each other. It was so hard to know if it was the right thing to do, to split up. How do you know when it's time to give up? How do you know how much is enough? How do you know if you should try to work harder, work differently, or cut your losses and move on? It would have been easier if there'd been some definite, some tangible reason to decide to call it quits. To know with certainty that we were doing the right thing. But how do you ever know what the right thing to do is?

I was clear about one thing: I didn't want to drag anyone else unwitting into my messy life. When I first started seeing Scott, I made sure he fully understood the situation he was getting into.

"I am leaving my husband," I explained. "I should have a big flashing red light that says 'Danger! Do not enter' affixed to me. I am not someone you want to get attached to. We will be able to spend time together for a while, but I am ultimately trying to figure out what to do with my life, and I'm probably going to leave Manhattan. This is just a fling. Do you understand?"

"Understood," he said. He also said that he would be leaving for San Francisco when he graduated in a few months. It worked for him.

A few months after Patrick and I had decided to split, I was sitting outside our apartment building, in Scott's car, kissing him good night. I pulled away from him to see Hannah's snout pressed up against the window. She was standing on her hind legs, looking in, attached by a leash to Patrick. She was wagging and confused. Patrick was looking in the car window, and when he saw what he saw, he threw his head back and laughed.

"Busted," he said.

He simply laughed his big-headed laugh and took Hannah upstairs to our apartment. I felt sick. I hadn't ever wanted to hurt Patrick, and just as he cried at happy movies, I knew he laughed when he was sad.

There was never a question of who she'd go with. Hannah was first and always my dog. Willy stayed with Patrick. When, after six months of living like roommates, I decided to take a job in North Carolina, Patrick, generous to the end, said, You take the car. He also insisted I take the down comforter from the bed.

"You'll need it more than I do," he said, "even down South."

It was a joke. I was always cold, even when it wasn't. My body, Patrick said, had a hot spot, between my navel and my ribcage: it was like a furnace, he said, hot to the touch. I radiated my heat, couldn't keep it in. His skin remained cool, always cool. Just another difference between us.

A few months after I moved to North Carolina, I flew back up to New York for the weekend, needing to see the friends I'd left behind. I'd called Patrick, asking if he wanted to get together. Hearing his voice again—we'd not talked since I left—was like hearing on old song, a song I used to love. We met at an Indian restaurant we used to like. He brought a bottle of wine. Looking at him was like looking in the mirror; his face was more familiar to me than my own. We didn't dive into the wreck, didn't talk about what had gone wrong or why. That I had to figure out on my own. I fought against the idea that I had failed, that it was my fault that the marriage didn't work. It was a hard fight. Sometimes I felt like I had won, but most of the time I felt like I had lost—something. I wasn't sure what. Looking at him, I wondered why I couldn't just do it, couldn't live that life.

Four

*Dogs love their friends and bite their enemies, quite unlike people,
who are incapable of pure love and always have to mix love and hate.*

—Sigmund Freud

I hadn't exactly wanted to live in the South, and I wasn't sure I wanted to stay in publishing. But I was running out of ideas and needed to get out of Manhattan. So I agreed to be an editor at a real university press, Duke, a small regional upstart that was making scholarly waves. If I'd been a lesbian or more Jewish, I would have found a community waiting to welcome me with outstretched arms. These

pockets were well established in Durham. It was a surprisingly
progressive, culturally rich place. In the first year I lived in the South
I saw more dance, theater, music, and art than I ever did living on
the Upper West Side of Manhattan.

Durham, a city of nearly two hundred thousand people, felt in many
ways like a small town. It was a shock to move from the anonymity of
New York to a place where the wine guy at the local, upscale organic
foods market—someone to whom I'd never spoken—asked one day
why I no longer wore my black leather motorcycle jacket. I lived in a
neighborhood near Duke, populated mostly by people affiliated with
the university. I looked around and saw plenty of folks who looked
like people I'd want to know.

I made my friends at Dog Club, a loose and informal meeting of
people who brought their dogs to campus every day after work—from
around five to eight—so that they could run free on a part of Duke's
sprawling, gothic campus and socialize. You knew the names of all
the dogs. The people you knew as Tahoe's mother, or Marley's dad.

There was a social hierarchy within Dog Club that rivaled Bev-
erly Hills High: some dogs were popular and everyone followed them,
sniffing where they sniffed, peeing on their pee, while others were ignored or worse, picked on—the canine equivalent of the chess club.
There were special friendships, pairs who would go off together and
ignore the rest of the group. There were dogs you had to be aware of:
Moe, a scruffy Disney-star type, was a lovely guy. But if you were sitting on the grass, he was likely to come up and claim you as his own
in the inimitable way that dogs own fire hydrants. You didn't want to
be on the ground when Moe was on the prowl.

When we lived in Manhattan, Hannah rarely interacted with
other dogs—as the Dog Lady from Brooklyn so aptly pointed out,
Hannah, quite human herself, was more fond of people than dogs.
We'd occasionally run across a dog-club group in Riverside Park, but
she'd only watch from the sidelines, never wanting to join in. She
also rarely saw other people: Patrick and I had had a handful of frequent visitors, and Hannah always greeted them enthusiastically, but

mostly we got together with our friends outside of the apartment. Hannah's Manhattan life revolved around us.

Hannah grew to love Dog Club. While the other dogs raced around the grounds, barking and chasing and playing, Hannah stayed with the group of people who huddled together in winter, or sat on the grass (absent Moe) in warmer weather. She went to each person, poked her snout against their leg to announce herself, then turned and backed up until her rump was right there, right near their hand, and they could do nothing but pat and scratch until they found the spot, the right spot. If necessary, she would squirm and twist her body until they figured it out. She'd come to understand that some people needed guidance.

I became friends with a woman, Simon's mother, who was a graduate student. It was taking her a long time to finish her thesis, since she insisted on having a life outside of graduate school. She had a surfeit of friends, prepared elaborate dinner parties, and supported herself by cleaning other people's houses. She wasn't in a hurry to finish her degree. Her name was Mary, and she was deserving of John Irving's sobriquet: she was a gradual student.

Though Hannah and Simon—a lanky, shaggy, ball-obsessed dog—liked each other, theirs was no great love affair. But they were happy to go on walks with us, trotting off ahead, yoked together by invisible traces, moving in unison and finding the same things interesting, stopping at the same places. We spent a lot of time walking the dogs and then going back to Mary's not-yet-condemned rented house. It was falling apart, but oddly elegant, done up with a European flair. Mary was Dutch, had come to the United States for college a dozen or so years before, and never left. She was an elegant cook and an elegant woman. We spent hours hanging out on her porch, the best part of the house, drinking wine, smoking cigarettes, and talking, talking.

I'd been on my own for about eight months, perhaps the longest time I'd been without a boyfriend since high school. I was ready to meet a man.

"I have a lot of great male friends, Rach," she said.

"Good," I said.

"A number of them are doctors."

"Ick," I said.

"But they're nice. You'll like them. I like them, why shouldn't you?"

"You're a better person than I. I don't like doctors."

While my social experience with doctors had been limited, unlike many Jewish girls, I didn't subscribe to the notion that MDs were the ultimate marital prize.

"I think you'll like Jonathan," she said.

She brought us together in an easy, natural way: I got a panicked phone call one evening. Mary said that her good friend Jerry was trying to finish the final project for his architecture degree and needed magazines for a collage. Now. Right now. She knew I had lots of magazines and wanted to know if I would bring them to Jerry's house, not far from mine. She was planning to stay there all night, if necessary, to help him. Also helping him was their mutual friend, Jonathan.

I corralled the dust bunnies nibbling at my collection of old *New Yorkers*, *Harper's*, and some guilty issues of *People* (Madonna was on the cover—again), picked up a hefty stack of the glossies, and went over. I walked into a small space crammed with constructions of paper buildings, and three people: Jerry, Mary, and the man she'd wanted me to meet, Jonathan. We said our hellos, they showed me what I was supposed to do (cut out images), and I started in. I'd glanced at Jonathan quickly, but not again. He looked like a Jewish doctor: balding, glasses, with a mustache and no beard. A mustache and no beard is a look I detest, a look that generally works well only on cops and porn stars. He was wearing a tight T-shirt with the Coca-Cola logo in Hebrew. Not my type.

Jonathan had a lot to say. He asked me questions and when I answered, he built on my answers and twisted and turned the conversation to places that surprised—and, yes—delighted me. He was enthusiastic and expressive, commenting on how knowledgeable I was and exclaiming over it. His wit was ready and quick; he made deflecting, self-effacing jokes that gave him, I must say, a certain charm. We ended up talking more than working, while Jerry sweated and cursed at his project. It got late, and I left. Nice guy, not my type.

He called the next day. "Dinner?"

Hmmm. I wasn't sure.

"You have to eat," he said.

Jonathan showed up at my house fifteen minutes late. He wore pants that were at least two sizes too large, and I wondered if under all that fabric was a chubby, soft body. It was impossible to tell. He walked through the door talking about the case that had kept him late at the hospital, and while I'd been pissed off waiting, my pique abated as he drew me into his story, a good story, well told. This could be okay, I thought.

We got into his car, a smallish, silver thing whose paint was peeling off. There was a problem on the driver's side, Jonathan said, so he kept the window rolled down, stuck his arm out, and held onto the roof to keep the door shut. He drove to the restaurant so slowly that people behind him flashed their lights and whizzed by in disgust while he talked nonstop. When he spoke, he looked at me. Not at the road ahead, but at me. He turned his head fully ninety degrees to the right and looked at me. The more he talked—and he talked a lot—the slower he drove. I picked my cuticles until they bled.

After a lifetime, we got to the Japanese restaurant we'd agreed was the best in Durham. When we sat down and I could concentrate on what he was saying, ohmigod. Jonathan was a psychiatrist from a family of psychiatrists, but unlike his father, who worked the "talking cure," Jonathan was a scientist. He not only treated mental illness biologically, with drugs and other medical interventions, but he also did serious, published research. He had studied biomedical engineering and had a physicist's need to understand the natural world. He was a couple of years older than me, on the other side of thirty. He was smart, funny, and wildly, widely in command of a diverse range of information. He sparkled when he spoke. I forgot about the mustache and the too-big pants and the terrible driving and listened and talked and argued and wow—this was a different kind of date.

Until the food came. I began to eat, but he continued to talk. Our conversation had wandered erratic like a frog, changing direction, landing in unexpected places; he kept saying, "but I want to return to" and still, it couldn't be pinned down and couldn't be left to dangle. So he talked. I was happy to listen.

When he took a break and I began to speak, he bent his head low to the food, opened his mouth, and shoveled in great mounds of rice, not stopping between loads, just piling it in rapid-fire, stray grains escaping all over the table. He'd start talking again, and the overloaded and precarious chopsticks would make it partway to his mouth and hover. Threatening. He didn't notice when it spilled over, onto the table, onto his lap. Watching him eat was horrifying. Half his dinner was on his tie; giant splotches of teriyaki spotted the table. "Oops," he'd say as another big dollop fell. When the date ended, I was ambivalent about seeing him again.

But I realized that it was easy to find polite eaters—much harder to engage with someone whose mind set yours whirling. We sent each other things, after that, clippings mostly, in manila campus mail envelopes with long lists of names and departments crossed out. He shipped over articles he thought I'd find funny: a story about narcoleptic dogs, a news article about how dolphins extend their penises as a gesture of friendship, arcane medical trivia. I passed to him poems and short stories, things I suspected he'd missed in his quest of a scientific education and guessed he'd like.

I wanted to know what he knew. When we went out for dinner again, I asked him to explain quantum mechanics to me, briefly and without resorting to equations. He hesitated, arguing that it had been a long time since he'd studied it and that he'd have to go back to his books and brush up.

"No," I said, "give me the broad outlines of what you understand—that will suffice."

His description was general enough not to require a science back-

ground and detailed enough to demonstrate the oddity and beauty of
what happens when the world gets very, very small. It was like poetry, the universe in a grain of sand.

Jonathan had Charlie's sense of humor, Vince's intellect, and
Patrick's gentleness. If only he didn't shovel the food, wear the bad
pants, and drive so poorly. And if only he didn't stink—no one
had ever told him. When I mentioned to him the social utility of un-
derarm deodorant, he explained that each year at his college they had
to throw out all the furniture in the computer lab because of the eye-
searing odor that permeated it. He laughed hard at the memory, but
didn't quite get where I was going with the discussion, so I bought him
a stick of deodorant and told him it would be in his best interest—if he
wanted to keep seeing me—to start using it. I also went through his
closet and threw out every single button-down shirt with an ink stain
on the pocket, every tie with a bit of food stuck to it. It decimated his
wardrobe, but I was less embarrassed to be seen in public with him.

As much as I loved talking to Jonathan, these little things drove
me nuts. I still wasn't sure he was my type, whatever that was. I could
take the relationship only one day at a time. We spoke on the phone,
and he told me about patients with disorders so bizarre and so interesting, it was like talking to Oliver Sacks. Lying together in the dark, we'd
talk about ideas and things and he'd show me places on my own body
that I didn't know existed, with names that defied belief. (Can you
find your "anatomical snuffbox"?) I was there, right there with him,
wanting to be with him. But after a short drive, sitting down to a meal,
or waiting for him to show, anywhere from fifteen minutes to a half
hour late, I'd decide that I'd had enough. On a Wednesday he might
ask if I wanted to see a movie on the upcoming Saturday and I would
answer with a contingent yes: if we're still seeing each other by then. I
threatened to dump him every few days. I couldn't help it. I just wasn't
sure. And I couldn't manage to keep my uncertainty to myself.

Jonathan had grown up with a dog that his father called Juniper
and his mother called Jennifer. Jonathan had seen Jennifer/Juniper

get hit by a car and die, a trauma he still carried with him. After that, he didn't have much enthusiasm for dogs. Because he sensed that it was important to me, he paid desultory attention to Hannah, but no more. She was equally cool with him.

When my divorce became final, I decided I needed to go away, by myself, to the beach. I'd read Anne Morrow Lindbergh's *Gift from the Sea* and become inspired to venture to the water myself, to the North Carolina coast, as a final, symbolic tribute to my marriage, my former self. The transition had been quick, without too much real pain. I wanted to take some time to mark it, to honor the past and think back on my time with Patrick, what I'd learned, what I'd missed. I wanted to bring Hannah, but there was at the time a state law preventing hotels and motels from accommodating dogs. I couldn't face putting her into a kennel, and Jonathan offered to keep her. It was a dilemma, since I didn't know if I trusted this man to be able to dress himself each morning, let alone to take care of my baby. They didn't even seem to like each other. But Jonathan convinced me it would be okay.

I don't know exactly what went on that weekend. Maybe they were able to see each other for the first time, easier without the distraction of me. Hannah and Jonathan were both intensely focused on me while I was around; I took up a lot of psychic space and demanded undivided attention. In my absence, they found each other.

Now, when Jonathan would come over, he and Hannah greeted each other amorously. Jonathan spent time playing with Hannah. She'd never been a gamey kind of dog—no interest in balls, sticks, or toys. She didn't roughhouse, didn't tug-o'-war, rarely jumped around. I had taught her a few tricks, though. If asked, she'd give you a high five. She could crawl on her belly like G.I. Joe. And if you cocked a finger at her and said "Bang," she'd slowly fall to the ground and roll over on one side, head down, a lone paw stuck in the air.

This was the trick that Jonathan loved the most. He'd come up to her, both hands blazing with itchy trigger fingers. He'd fire off a series of bangs and down Hannah would go. Jonathan would crouch beside her and give her a long and vigorous belly-rub. He'd sing out a string of unspellable, only Jonathan-pronounceable terms of endearment, and Hannah would sing in response. Jonathan brought out all Hannah's silliness, and she reinforced his.

We shuttled back and forth between our homes. Jonathan was leasing a house from a medical school friend. It was one of those new-construction, all-the-mod-cons, wall-to-wall-carpeting starter homes in a neighbor with cul-de-sacs and without sidewalks. The house was clean but dark, so we called it the Dungeon. Hannah and I lived in a tatty old apartment complex, each unit motel-like in a row. It was two stories high and had two bedrooms upstairs, two bathrooms (one up one down), and a kitchen as big as the bedroom I'd left in Manhattan. It was spacious if not spiffy; it was worn-in, with character to spare. Cleanliness was conspicuously absent from my list of virtues. We called it the Sty.

When I went on business trips, Jonathan was always happy to spend quality time with my dog, though naturally I still worried about leaving the two of them together, unsupervised. When I'd call in from the road, Jonathan would tell me long, richly detailed stories about what he and Hannah had done, how many walks, which social activities. After a while, I started to feel like her life with him was more fun, more interesting, more exciting than her life with me.

Only once was there an incident.

Jonathan, as a joke, had given a friend who had come to visit a summer sausage, mostly, I think, because it was called a "Yard O' Beef." The friend gleefully received the present, but when he left, he didn't take it. The idea of a Yard O' Beef was better and funnier than the yard itself. For many months, maybe even years, the Yard O' Beef served as a kitschy objet d'art on Jonathan's kitchen counter.

I know that she hated herself for doing it. After Jonathan had gone to work, Hannah could resist no longer. She crept up, snagged the Yard, and ate it down to a few Inches O' Beef. Jonathan came home to those few inches and a dog with intestinal issues that had given way all over his spanking-new, wall-to-wall beige carpet.

He told me the story on the phone, giggling, referring frequently to the Yard O' Beef, while I tried to ascertain if Hannah was okay and if I should break up with him.

* * *

Jonathan was always game, always up to do things, always willing to go. He was also, it turned out, to my surprise, an athlete. One afternoon, I went with him to a pickup basketball game on Duke's campus. There were a bunch of cool, tall, black guys passing a ball around, getting ready to play. Jonathan approached them—all five feet nine inches of him, older, balding, with heavy black safety glasses, gym socks pulled up to his knees, too-short shorts, and a T-shirt with an equation on it. They picked sides. Jonathan was picked dead last. It didn't seem to bother him at all, though I winced for and at him.

Then they began to play. Jonathan moved with astonishing speed and grace. His shots never failed. Within minutes it became clear even to a neophyte sports watcher that he was far better than anyone out there. It wasn't until much later, until I learned more about basketball, that I understood how impressive it was that he could dunk.

In high school I'd been a gymnast, making the varsity team in ninth grade. Being a gymnast meant being at war with my body, willing it to do my bidding—to tuck, to roll, to flip, to stretch—and being frustrated when it would not comply. My body seemed outside of my self, something to be controlled and mastered by my mind.

The ultimate rebuff was when I started having problems with my knees, a treason of the body, an angry recalcitrance. I quit when I was fifteen, ending my relationship with sports. Small-boned and thin, people often mistook me for someone who was athletic. My response was always, "I am an intellectual, not an athlete."

Jonathan was an intellectual and an athlete. Both/and, rather than my reductive either/or. He loved basketball most, but he'd also run track. He logged a 4:30 mile in high school, and he high-jumped over six and a half feet in college. That, I learned, is pretty darned good. He skied and biked and canoed. When I met him, he was playing in an over-the-hill (over thirty) fast-pitch baseball league. I was impressed by his competence and his passion, but I shared neither.

For most of my life, my closest friends had been runners, the men doing it to stay in shape, the women driven mostly by fear of fat.

I had college friends who would get up at dawn every day and run miles and miles, regardless of weather. In New York, Sarah never neglected her daily slog around Central Park. After I'd moved to Durham, my college roommate Val; her boyfriend, Eric; Jonathan; and I went to the North Carolina Outer Banks for a weekend. The three of them went for a run on the beach. I stayed back, lying on the deck in my black bikini, reading a novel, eating Oreos, and smoking an occasional Camel Light. I thought they were crazy.

Hannah was a four-year-old Manhattan-reared couch potato. She needed exercise, and Jonathan began to take her for runs on the trails through the Duke forest. At first I was reluctant to let her go. (Would they get lost? Would she get hurt? Could she keep up?) But then I saw how excited she became when he asked if she wanted to go for a run—wagging and circling and occasionally even letting out a little whine—and I couldn't say no. I made him take her on a leash—though I never leashed her myself, even in New York—because, well-respected doctor or not, I still wasn't entirely comfortable with his relationship to responsibility.

I began to feel left out. When I asked if I could join them, they both gave an enthusiastic yes. We went on a three-mile loop around Duke's golf course that Hannah and I had walked many times with Mary and Simon. Running the course was a different story. Nowhere was it flat. The loop was littered with hills, and they all seemed to be going up.

Hannah ran ahead, coming back periodically to make sure we were still with her, and Jonathan ran by my shoulder, offering non-stop encouragement ("You're doing great!" "You have a beautiful stride!" "You're a natural runner!") and advice ("Slow down, there's a long way still to go!" "Use your arms!" "Relax your shoulders!") until I stopped, turned to him, and said, in less than dulcet tones, that if he didn't fucking shut the fuck up I was going home right now.

Running the course was a lot harder than I thought it would be, and I hated doing something that I wasn't good at. I hated that Jonathan saw me not being good, and I realized that my style is to want to figure something out myself and ask for help only when I need it.

Mostly I hated that I was such a bitch when he was only trying to help. After that first time out, I wasn't sure that running was for me.

A few weeks later, we tried again. It was raining, and we went to a trail in the forest owned by Duke. When we set out, I set down the ground rules. No coaching. No words of encouragement. Just shut up and run. Jonathan is good at many things, but shutting up is not one of them. While we ran, he began to talk about whatever he was thinking about. He was thinking about his work, about a patient, and he launched into a long story. I stopped thinking about how much it hurt to breathe and how heavy my legs were, and just listened to him. When we got to a point where we could either turn around or keep going, I surprised all of us by wanting to continue. It wasn't so bad.

After that he knew how to run with me. When we started up a hill, I'd bark out, "Tell me about schizophrenia!" And he would. A natural pedant, Jonathan could spin out a mini-lecture on almost anything. If I didn't suggest a topic, he'd go on about whatever came to mind. One cold morning, when I wanted to turn around after two minutes because I was freezing, he discoursed on thermodynamics and equilibration. Well before he finished, I was warm.

I learned to let Jonathan regulate the pace. Like most beginning runners, I started out too fast, went from uncomfortable to hurting, and then had to stop, hating every bit of the experience. He led the way at a pace so slow, it seemed silly. But when I realized at the end that I'd run three miles, not only without stopping, but without discomfort, it dawned on me that he knew what he was doing.

I became a runner.

My friend Deborah, a coworker from Duke Press, was a sharp and perspicacious woman who loved Hannah almost as much as I did. She was one of the few people I trusted to take care of her when both Jonathan and I went out of town. When we were in town, it was always fun to go out with Deborah and her boyfriend. She called us "The Rachel and Jonathan Show." She said that when we were together, it was fun for others to sit back and watch. I was often the straight man for Jonathan's jokes, but he could also prompt me to paroxysms of funniness that I didn't think could come from me. We bantered and played. We riffed and riled each other into frenzies of silliness and verbal gymnastics. Deborah said it was a delight to watch us, that she felt she saw me as most myself when I was with Jonathan.

When my mother and George came to visit us, we all stayed at Jonathan's house. It was more comfortable than my Sty. Jonathan was a gracious host and made them feel welcome and cared for. They felt so much at home that at one point, when he was trying to record a new message on his answering machine, my mother and I were chasing each other around the table with squirt guns, screaming and squealing. Each time someone called, they asked: "Did you record your answering machine message at the zoo?" He kept that message for a long time.

George took to Jonathan immediately. My mother saw how much fun we had together, but she said he seemed, well, absentminded. She wasn't sure how serious he was; she thought he was always joking around. I dismissed her concerns. She didn't see him talk about his work; she didn't see the way he could see right through me.

Jonathan never got pissy. He was never in a bad mood. I did and was often. I had always been terrible at hiding my feelings, and thoughtless about where I vented my frustration; Jonathan did everything he could to mitigate, alleviate, soothe. Jonathan the anodyne. I was picky about everything: where we ate, what movie we saw, how we dressed, where we went. We did things my way. Jonathan seemed to care less about all this; he seemed happy just to go along.

When I decided that I wanted to try camping, Jonathan was eager to go. (He was always eager. It was irritating.) I hadn't been camping since I was very young. But now that I was shucking off my urban shell and becoming more a part of the physical world, it seemed like a good idea. I liked the concept of camping. Jonathan had camped a lot and had—or could borrow—all the necessary gear. Not knowing what equipment was needed made it hard for me to know what he might have forgotten. (He did tend to forget things.) I was forced to put myself in his care, give up autonomy, and trust him. This did not come easily.

We'd gone to an outdoors store, and the staff there had suggested some lovely trails in the mountains, about a four-hour drive away. Jonathan seemed to know what they meant when they talked about "trailheads" and "mile markers." We made a plan.

We started out late, naturally. As we drove, as Jonathan drove, I began to get anxious. His driving always made me anxious, but now I was also generally anxious about the trip, worrying that it would be dark before we got there, wherever *there* was. A couple of hours after leaving Durham, the scenery got scenic and I tried to concentrate on that. Jonathan wasn't the least bit concerned, and, as was his wont, made a lot of jokes. Which served to make me more anxious, and a little pissy. It got dark, and we were driving on a deserted road in the middle of nowhere and we still had to hike in and put up the tent and do whatever else you have to do when you go camping, which I didn't know, because I didn't camp, and goddamn it I was pissed.

We couldn't find the trail the outdoorsy guys had mentioned. Jonathan was determined to find it. They'd said you could hike in to the waterfall, and he thought it would be great to see the waterfall, and I thought we were in for a night of—what? *Deliverance?* Sleeping in the car? I wasn't sure what frightened me so, but I was not happy, and when I am not happy, the world is not happy with me. I complained. Jonathan told me not to worry.

Finally he picked what he called a trailhead, parked the car, and out we got. It was very, very dark. Jonathan loaded himself up with stuff, leaving me only a little, though I complained that I was perfectly capable of carrying more. He led the way, and Hannah and I followed behind, sulky, a little scared. Okay, it was me that was sulky and scared; Hannah trotted along happily. We went for about ten minutes like this, in the dark.

"Here we go," he said, and put down the stuff.

I could barely see. Jonathan was wearing a headlamp, while I carried a feeble flashlight.

My childhood memories of camping involved a huge tent smelling of canvas and mildew that required screwing poles together and hammering big heavy stakes into the ground; flannel sleeping bags, also mildew-scented, in which you froze, even in the summer, and through which you felt every stick and stone and mound and missing divot of earth; and hours spent building a fire. I tried to forget that this was my idea.

It took Jonathan about five minutes to put up the tidy little tent, clean and light and airy. He then laid fluffy down sleeping bags out on inflated pads. Ten minutes later, there was a light- and heat-giving fire, and marshmallows, Hershey bars, and graham crackers all ready to go. He had apprehended the fact that a paramount reason for my wanting to go camping was to eat S'mores.

"See," Jonathan said. "It all worked out."

And it did.

Our spot was soft and mossy and somewhere, nearby, was a stream that we could hear tinkle in the night. The tent was cozy, and life was good. We talked until we nodded off. At least until the tinkling of the stream called to our own baser natures, and in the middle of the night, we both awoke, having to pee.

Hannah had settled herself in the tent. We had zipped the sleeping bags together, and she was on the empty space where my feet would have been if I were a lot taller. We got up and crawled out of the tent. Hannah stayed inside.

Looking around in the dark, I saw streams of light coming through the trees.

"Holy shit," I said to Jonathan, "those are moonbeams. Actual real-life moonbeams."

As when any unexamined phrase or idea or cliché is experienced unmediated, it was a revelation. (Corned beef is corned!) I called for Hannah to come out and look, to see that the moon actually has beams. She poked her nose through the open flaps of the tent, saw that we weren't going anywhere, and went back to sleep. Still a city dog, she was happy to romp and roam in daylit nature, but she liked her creature comforts in the dark.

Our camping trip was, in many ways, a turning point for me. I knew I had control-freak tendencies, but that weekend showed me how ridiculous it was to be unwilling to put myself in the care of someone who had more experience and knowledge than I, at least about finding trailheads and pitching tents. I realized that Jonathan's ways of doing things were different from mine, but that didn't make them wrong. I made a mental note to try to remember that.

After a year of dating, Jonathan and I decided to move in together. This decision was not made easily—well, not on my part, at least. I'd moved in with Charlie because he offered prime real estate—which then became a kind of prison. Similarly, I continued living with Patrick after we'd decided to split because it was so hard to snag another apartment in New York. With Jonathan, this would be less of a problem: Durham is not Manhattan. The real issue was whether I'd be able to make the commitment to him. Our relationship was moving forward, if in a jerky fashion. We decided that we were both ready to take the next step—though I pointed out pointedly that this was just a next step and didn't necessarily imply further steps. I was still hedging. But I was willing to try to move forward. We found a house to rent in the woods close to Duke, a big beautiful house on a beautiful lot. And though he worked in academia, rather than in a private practice, Jonathan's doctor's salary was still substantially more than mine. He generously suggested that we split the rent proportionately.

We prepared to move into what we came to call "the Love Nest." No more Dungeon for him, no more Sty for me. This was going to be something entirely new and different.

We hired a moving company. The movers were instructed to go first to my house, load up, move on to Jonathan's, load up, and then unload at our new place. Everything was packed and ready to go.

Except that they never showed. It got later and later, and finally when we called they had no record of our move.

There was a not small amount of potty-mouth language. Jonathan and I had both waited until the very end of our leases, and we both had to be out that night. At the latest possible moment, dangerously close to closing time, we rented a gigantic truck, and, with the help of Mary, our elegant mutual friend, and Mark, my less-than-athletic brother, we moved all the stuff ourselves. It took much of the night. In the wee hours, I made us take a break and eat some Oreos and drink some tequila. For some reason, I thought that would help.

The next morning, Jonathan and Mark took Hannah for a walk to survey the grounds. The Love Nest was nestled at the top of a long driveway. Not steep, but a definite incline. The moving truck was parked in the driveway, facing down.

They had been walking on the street and, for who knows what reason, had looked back, at just the right moment, to admire the house. I believe that my brother, when he closes his eyes at night, can still see it: the big truck was rolling down the driveway, headed toward the house across the street. Jonathan had forgotten to set the emergency brake.

My brother is a lawyer. He mentally ran through all possible outcomes.

"Oh shit," he said.

Jonathan is a doctor. And an athlete. And the person who forgot to set the emergency brake. He ran to the truck, which was gaining velocity by the second. Somehow, he opened the door. Jumped in. And, as it hit the street, was able to pull it to a stop.

Jonathanness. Through carelessness, inattention, sloppiness, or because there was simply something more interesting or fun to do, he'd bring a situation to the brink of disaster. And then, through quickness, agility, imagination, competence, and courage, he'd pull off a spectacular save.

The Love Nest was a huge house—much bigger than we needed or could use. There was a bonanza of bedrooms and bathrooms; we had living spaces that we never entered. We shared the upstairs bedroom, but we each also had rooms of our own. Jonathan had a home office, as well as a room just for his musical instruments, a panoply of stringed items—guitars, violins, lutes, and mandolins. I had a study, with a huge built-in desk, built-in bookshelves, and an embracing gold-velour armchair in which I could curl up and read. Hannah loved being with me in my study. She'd sleep under the desk. Sometimes I'd come home to find her in my armchair.

One of the great things about the Love Nest was that it provided easy access to trails. Running had become—still surprising to me and all who knew me—an important part of my life. Hannah's, too. As soon as she saw me reach for my running shoes, she got excited. Sometimes, if I took too long getting ready, she'd let out a sharp bark. We'd set off together, keeping pace, warming up, and then, when we reached the familiar trail, she'd bound ahead to give herself time to stop and sniff. She'd come back to me, check in, and then go off again. In the summer, when it was hot and humid, we'd stop at each stream.

"Go get a drink," I'd say, and she'd wade in, step by reluctant step. "Drink, please."

She'd drink.

"Now lie down," I'd tell her. "Get your chest wet."

She'd hesitate—just to make sure I wasn't kidding—and then she'd sit.

"All the way, dude."

Holding her head high, she would lie down and wait, looking miserable, waiting for me to say it was okay to sprint out of the water. Once Hannah was back by my side, the two of us would disappear into the woods, quietly moving forward on an invisible tether.

After a decade in scholarly publishing, I coasted as the learning curve flattened. I suspected it was time to leave when I heard phrases like, "The only good author is a dead author," fly unbidden out of my mouth, and I caught myself referring to the people whose books I was proudly publishing as BFWs: Big Fat Whiners.

I realized that like many people, I had fallen into a profession that came naturally to me: I was a critic. I was comfortable sitting in judgment of other people's work, saying whether or not it was good, or good enough. When I actually took the time to edit manuscripts, my job was creative only in the sense of understanding or imagining where the author wanted to go, and helping—or trying to help—her get there. Generally I did not edit. Generally I simply said yes or no—to ideas, to adjectives, to structures. Saying no was easy for me.

The same went for the manuscript submissions that I received from academics, from the distinguished men and women who hoped that I would publish their books.

"It's not like I'm saying the book shouldn't be published," I would tell myself, and others. "I'm just saying," I would say, "that I'm not going to be the one to publish it." I would wait for a manuscript to land on my desk that would either blow me away, or, more typically, that I knew was doing the job it was supposed to do: filling a gap in the existing literature, proffering a new way of thinking about something important, whatever. Yes, no. No was always easier, and less work.

I was only a traffic light. My role was to listen. To play handmaiden to knowledge, helpmeet to scholarship. A yes from me could lead to tenure, promotion, academic success. When the reviews came in, if the book was received well, it was my success for picking it, and if not, hey, they weren't my dumb ideas out there. My job was to listen, not to speak. To judge, to break down, to criticize. No one ever taught me how to do it; in publishing, you learn by apprenticeship. There were no rights and wrongs, no clearly defined markers. I knew that bad books could sometimes sell well and that too many great books went unread. It was a murky business, publishing.

Each night Jonathan would come home from work (late, always late) and say, "I had a really interesting case today."

He'd tell me about it, and he'd tell it well. I always had questions, some of which he could answer, others he hadn't thought about. I learned a lot about neuropharmacology, about brain disorders, about psychiatric illness and practice. I loved it when he told me about his cases. Sometimes they were hysterically, unintentionally, funny.

My favorite from his repertoire of stories was about a young guy who had been a wrestler and was suffering from homophobic panic. Jonathan quizzed him about his early sexual history. The guy

thought about it and said, "Well, you know, the usual stuff: toma-
toes, chickens . . ."

One of Jonathan's specialties was sleep medicine, and ironically,
for the first time, I began, for some inexplicable reason, to have trouble sleeping. I knew through Jonathan about all sorts of sleep med-
ications, prescription and herbal, traditional and alternative. I knew
about good "sleep hygiene," medical lingo for good bedtime behavior. I didn't want to take drugs, and I was reasonably hygienic in my
sleep habits. But I still couldn't get to sleep.

After a few weeks of insomnia, Jonathan came to the rescue. Bedtime would arrive. He'd lie next to me, gently rubbing my back. Then
he'd tell me a story. He'd use his special sleep story voice: low, soft, almost a mumble. The essence of a good sleep story is that it's boring.
Really boring. Really repetitive. Nothing exciting should happen in a
sleep story. And so my boyfriend the sleep doc would nightly trans-
form himself into the anti-Scheherezade, lulling me to sleep by boring
me. Often the stories were about a little girl (not a thirty-something-
year-old woman) who did not want to go to sleep. Dull dull dull. Off
to sleep I went.

One night he told me a different story. It was called "Boat, Noodle, Shoe."

Unfortunately, it was amazingly effective. I fell asleep right after
hearing the title. I assume I did, at least, since I can remember nothing else of the story. Jonathan claims that with "Boat, Noodle, Shoe,"
as with all his sleep stories, he told it all the way through to the finish, since he wanted to be sure that I was truly and soundly asleep. (I
did usually manage to complain during the boring little-girl-who-
wouldn't-sleep-stories that they weren't working, just before I nodded
off for the night.) But I remember nothing of the story. Except for the
title. "Boat, Noodle, Shoe."

He refused to tell the story again, or even what it was about.
With that title, I'm sure it was great.

* * *

"I had a really interesting case today. . . ."

He'd tell me about it, and I'd say, "I could do that."

He'd say, "You could do that."

We often become that which we most resist. I decided to apply to medical school. I was bored with my job and loved the idea of doing something entirely different, of being taught a new skill. It wasn't so much that I envisioned myself as doctor, rather that I looked forward to the journey, the process of becoming one.

Before I could apply, I would have to go back to school and take all the hard science classes I had studiously avoided in college. I thought it would mean quitting my job as an editor, but my boss at Duke Press suggested I stay on three-quarters time, which would allow me to keep my benefits; he said that he would schedule meetings around my classes. Jonathan was ecstatic to be in a position to help me with my homework, and was delighted by the prospect of reviewing elementary science concepts. I was excited to be taught—unlike in publishing, I wouldn't have to figure it all out on my own. I'd have a path clearly laid out before me. All I had to do was follow it.

When I wasn't working, I was in class, and when I wasn't in class, I was doing homework. Jonathan encouraged me in every way I could imagine. If I had a question about organic chemistry, I'd call him at work. If I couldn't find him, I'd page him, and patiently, calmly, while his patients waited or his assistant tried to pull him away, he'd take me through it. He helped me with lab reports, tried repeatedly to get me to understand the concept of standard deviation even as I kept forgetting. But what he did, most importantly, was to believe so strongly in my ability to do anything—and to do it well—that I started to believe it, too. Love is when someone sees you for who you are, understands what you want to be, and helps you get there. Before Jonathan, I'd never felt so truly loved.

And I'd never loved before, not like this.

* * *

But of course, being me, good old critical me, I found things to complain about. As much as I loved him, certain aspects of living with Jonathan drove me up the friggin' wall. I have never been accused of being a neat-freak, but Jonathan made me look like a (pre-conviction) Martha Stewart. He left dishes piled to Everest heights in the sink. It wasn't so much that he minded washing them. He just didn't see the precarious stacks—they didn't bother him. In his home office, teacups turned into petri dishes. Every time he opened a cabinet door, it remained open. If he put milk in his cereal, the milk stayed out. I stayed away from the kitchen. Not that either of us was interested in cooking. Jonathan was happy to have a peanut butter and jelly sandwich each night for dinner, and I ate breakfast cereal. But, if either of us had, hypothetically, wanted to cook, it would've required an hour-long kitchen-cleaning session before we could even start.

I tried to explain to Jonathan how awful it is to get up in the middle of the night, pad into the bathroom in the dark, the cold, sit down to relieve your aching bladder, and then fall into the toilet. He understood, he said. But still, the toilet seat remained up. Our bathroom wars were no different from those of other, normal, cohabiting people: the way the toilet paper rolls, over or under, is the way your mother had it rolling. That is the right way. The other way is wrong. Toothpaste-squeezing practices, hair in the drain, products on the sink—these are issues to be worked out, places where compromises need to be struck. I knew that. What I didn't understand is how Jonathan managed to make sticky yellow spots on the floor near the toilet.

"Why do you pee all over the floor?"

He knew exactly what I was talking about. "The stream bifurcates. You can't get both in at the same time."

He had an explanation, an answer, but never thought to do anything about the resulting mess.

I grew to resent his blithe-spiritedness, his passive, amiable disregard of all housekeeping matters. I found myself cleaning up after him in a rage—a familiar, feminist rage that I thought had stopped with my mother's generation. If I pointed out the problems, he would attend to them. But pointing them out felt a lot like nagging. No one likes to be a nag. Not even me.

And, in keeping with our first date, I was always waiting for him. I waited at restaurants, movie theaters, dinners, parties. I waited at home. I asked that he just let me know what his ETA was, so I didn't have to worry while I waited. Sometimes he remembered to call, but often he forgot. My impatience increased geometrically.

His untidiness; his eating; his sentences that went on for days, punctuated by long pauses and *ums*; his discourses (about things I may or may not have been interested in—he never seemed to notice); that he would interrupt my own speech to comment on how good the food was, or that there was a bird outside; his chronic, incessant joking whenever I brought up something that made him uncomfortable—all of this bothered me. And when I was bothered, I was expressive. I told him exactly what was wrong with him. He listened. He tried to change what he could. He catered to my desires.

I tried not to be bothered, but I couldn't get over the little things. I couldn't stop being a critic. It was too ingrained in me. I myself had been criticized by my father, and watched as he picked apart my mother and brother. I wanted to stop, to be more accepting, but I couldn't.

Then we'd have one of those conversations—over dinner, during a run, driving somewhere—that went on like a mighty river, far, wide, deep. We'd be carried away together, and I'd think, Yes, this is the way it's supposed to be. Never had I found anyone so interesting, so interested. There are plenty of smart people in the world, fascinating people, good people. To love the way someone's mind zigs and zags; to know that, as frustrated as you may get during the telling, every story is worth listening to; that after every movie you see together he will point out something you've missed; to have someone who can hold you when you cry, and say the things you need to hear to feel better—that is rare indeed.

At a certain point, I stopped thinking about dumping Jonathan and instead wanted to marry him. Suffering the little things was worth the big payoff. I'd met my match, the man who would push me to be the best person I could be. So he was irritating and messy. I'd learn to live with it. I wanted to live with it. I wanted to marry Jonathan. It would be different this time. This would be the marriage of two minds. I did not want to admit impediments. He clearly adored me, never ignored me.

I wanted to marry Jonathan and began to try to tell him.

Jonathan evaded—jokingly, lovingly, sweetly—the subject. He didn't want to talk about it. For the shy, having a good sense of humor, a quick wit, is a triumphant evolutionary attribute. For those who want to avoid confrontation, it is a handy tool. But in a relationship, when your partner wants to push up her sleeves and get into the dirt and grit of the future, and there you are, cracking jokes, derailing conversations with puns and silly patter, you should realize that you may incite a murderous rage.

Jonathan agreed that we needed to talk about The Future, but he never wanted to do it. We'd been living together for about a year when we decided that, for my spring break from pre-med classes, we would drive to New England. We'd go to Connecticut, where his brother and sister-in-law lived, to Boston, and then hang out in the Berkshires for a few days. Spring in New England is generally bleak, and this one was no different. We were in the car for hours, and it was in the car, cooped up, nowhere to run, harder to hide, that Jonathan finally spoke.

There are times when your own life turns into *Rashomon*, the same story made almost unrecognizable through the prism of another set of eyes. I never knew how little I knew about Jonathan's perspective on our relationship, on me. Withstanding my criticisms of him was like being pecked to death by chickens: individually they were not impressive, but cumulatively he had been broken down.

Jonathan and I rarely argued. I'd rail and decry and emote. He'd rationally, reasonably, agree. This was, after all, a man who, when told by an opposing player during a rough and physical three-on-three basketball tournament "If you fuckin' foul me one more time I'm gonna slam you up against the wall" responded, "That's reasonable." It's frustrating to scream at someone like that.

We knew a lot about my problems with Jonathan: he was too quick to praise me ("Wow, you look amazing in that [old ratty way-too-huge] sweatshirt"), he was scatterbrained, he was chronically late, he peed on the floor, he left the kitchen cabinets open, he worked too much, he was too interested—in me, in everything. But the biggest problem, it turned out, was that he didn't ever state his own needs. I was expert at expressing mine: it was easier for him to deal with fulfilling them than to think about his own. Our relationship was Rachel-centric. I may have realized this, but it didn't strike me as problematic.

Somehow, trapped in the car, driving through gray hills and dirty snow, Jonathan was able to say many of the things he'd been storing up for a couple of years, without rancor, without bitterness, but with percipient clarity into how this couldn't work for him any longer. We continued talking when we got home, and finally he said that he felt we needed to break up. It came as a shock. I'd been so focused on what was wrong with Jonathan that I'd ignored the big problem: me.

I'd never been dumped before. I never understood that when you say your heart is breaking, you feel it physically, in your body, right there, in the place where your heart lives.

Five

All animals are equal. But some animals are more equal than others.

—George Orwell

The heart is friable. It can crack, can crumble like hard cheese, in ragged chunks, bits falling here and there, making a mess on the floor and every little where. The heart is an obstinate asshole. You can tell it everything, explain why things are the way they are, but it will not relent. It will not stop. It will not shut the fuck up. The heart will not be silenced.

He was right. I knew that he was right. As good as Jonathan had been for me, I wasn't good for him. My judging and criticizing, my hectoring and haranguing, did not make for gracious Southern living. That he didn't tell me what he needed didn't mean, as I had vainly supposed, that he didn't need. I plowed over him, silenced him. I suppose I thought—if I'd bothered to think about it—that I was waiting for him to speak up, but he never did, waiting instead for me to come to the realization myself. And now my heart would not stop crying.

Breakups had always seemed both inevitable and evolutionary. What you learn from one relationship, you take with you and cash in on the next. Each one helps you become a better person, a better relationshipper. In retrospect you see the problems and why you needed to move on. It made sense. It had just never hurt so much before.

I was sitting in my armchair the day after we returned from our trip, sobbing, wondering, How did this happen? How could I have let this happen? Jonathan came in, touched my shoulder gently—set off a louder crying jag—listened to me, his eyes rimmed red, told me that he loved me—I sobbed harder now, my body shaking from hurt—but all he could say was that he just couldn't do it. He couldn't be with me. He tried to hug me; I shook him off.

"I'm sorry," he whispered. About a million times.

And then he left.

"Don't worry about the house," he said. "Stay as long as you need to. I'll keep paying the rent."

I couldn't afford to move, I couldn't afford the time to look for a new place. I couldn't keep up with my work and my pre-med courses. I stayed in the gold armchair and cried.

People would call for Jonathan, and I'd say that I didn't know where he was. I didn't. He'd gathered up a few things and left. I found out later that he sometimes stayed with friends, sometimes in a hotel, and more than a few nights he slept in his office.

I'd look at the kitchen sink bereft of dirty dishes, the cabinet doors shut tight, the pristine bathroom floor, and I would wail. I had never felt so alone.

Jonathan began to send me e-mails, quick notes. I'd see his name on my computer screen, and my heart would start to chatter. Maybe, maybe.

But no.

He was writing to ask if I was okay, did I need anything?

"You fucking asshole," I'd answer.

I blasted him for daring to ask if I was okay after what he'd done to me. After he'd broken my heart. *Broken* my heart. Broken *my* heart. No matter where you put the emphasis, it was almost inconceivable. Almost.

"I am so sorry," he said, in every exchange.

I knew he was. I was, too. But I was too hurt to say so.

Being the dumpee was a new sensation, and, as much as I was suffering, I wallowed in the unfamiliar status of having been dumped, a more sympathetic position than being the dumper. I celebrated my lack of agency, trumpeted the fact that this was done to me. I am victim, hear me roar. There was nothing for me to feel guilty about in terms of how or why the relationship ended. No one makes you talk about your own flaws and failures when you are the dumpee. You are unequivocally, categorically, tragically, heroically, the injured party. To the outside world, at least.

After the stream of tears started to abate, I was forced to face the blues of my own culpability. It wasn't like Jonathan wanted to dump me; he could barely stand himself knowing how badly he'd hurt me. It was that I had left him no choice. It was, in fact, my fault. My critical, judgmental carping and complaining, coupled with my intense interest in my own needs, and myself, had made it impossible for him to be, and for him to be with me. My faults made it my fault. There was not enough room for Jonathan when he was in a room with me.

Why did I care so much about what he did and why did I think it would somehow reflect badly on me? Wasn't being loved enough to make up for someone's bad taste in clothing? Wasn't a rare intellectual connection more important than the position of the toilet seat? What was wrong with me? If I couldn't figure it out, how could I ever expect to have a real relationship—something as good as what I'd just lost—ever again?

More than anything else, I just plain missed Jonathan.

I've never thought of myself as a broken-wing person. Hardly. But in my dumpee state, I attracted those who are attracted to those with broken wings. Many saw me fall; a surprising number were on hand to put me back together again. Maybe there is something to the myth of the helpless female. Maybe, for those who knew me whole, it was the draw of a different and unexpected state of being. Maybe it was just so apparent that I was a wreck and needed help. Whatever the reason, help was offered. Men I barely knew wanted to feed me. Guys who'd met Jonathan, and thought he was a great fellow, said what an idiot he was and did I want to go out Saturday night? How odd, to be attracted to frailty.

Even after being treated to my incendiary flame-mails, Jonathan had persisted in contacting me, wanting to make sure that I was okay. It finally dawned on me, in a mirroring of my lack of perspicacity during our relationship, how profoundly difficult this breakup must have been for him. How scary it was for him to tell me how he felt; how painful for him to know that he was inflicting pain. And, with awful clarity, it occurred to me how confident he must have been in his own decision to end things to be able to be so stalwart.

Hannah walked around the house, seeking Jonathan in his home office, nosing among his musical instruments, looking. She waited by the door at the night, ears pricked large for the sound of his car on the gravel driveway. She clearly missed him in a way she had not missed Patrick. And she clearly worried about me. She cleaved close, following me into the bathroom, checking, sitting at my feet, shooting love at me with her eyes, while I cried curled up in my chair.

Jonathan moved out just as I started an intense summer-session physics course. Since he wasn't around to help me, and I needed help, I contacted a professor I knew and asked, humbled, if he could suggest a tutor. He gave me the e-mail address of a graduate student in physics and assured me the guy would do a good job.

I imagined that he would look like Vince, smell like Jonathan did when I first met him, and be socially inept. When a six-foot-two stud muffin wearing khaki cargo shorts, a sweaty T-shirt, and basketball shoes knocked on the door of the Love Nest, I almost fell off my kitchen chair.

Hannah barked, as she always barked when someone knocked, and then, when I let him in, she growled.

"Mike?" I said.

"Yep," he said.

"You're my physics tutor?"

"Guess so."

"But you're a stud muffin."

I was shocked. By saying so, I shocked him: a chain reaction of shock.

He blushed red over a face already made ruddy by heat and exercise.

We got started. It was good to have a distraction and besides, I liked physics, was fascinated by the ideas. I wasn't, however, so compelled by algebraic equations. My math was fast, sloppy, and inaccurate. I didn't appreciate units, didn't like to bother with them. I wanted to talk about the concepts.

Mike looked down at my work, messy to the point of illegibility. Steps skipped, units left off—he grew frustrated with me.

"You have to slow down and be more careful."

"Yeah, yeah. But tell me this: when the Earth's gravitational field . . ."

He couldn't help but answer. Then he'd try to get us back on track, back to the problems. I wasn't interested in the problems.

We met once a week. Each time he drove up, Hannah would announce his arrival with sharp barks. Mike would glare at Hannah when he came inside. She'd growl. She wasn't sure about him. Usually he was fresh from a basketball game—the physics grad students had a good team and competed in a university-wide intramural league. He never smelled like stinky man sweat; his hair was tousled appealingly. He was, no doubt about it, a stud muffin.

We'd work for a while, and then I'd start to ask questions. "How old are you?"

"Twenty-five. Now look, you forgot that this is a vector."

"Geez—you're seven years younger than I am. A baby. A whippersnapper. A munchkin. A tot."

"And here, look, you left off the units. The units are part of the answer. If you don't include the units, you're going to get the problem wrong."

"Where are you from?"

"Minnesota. You added five and seventeen and got twenty-three."

"Minneapolis?"

"Long Lake. It's a town of about two hundred people, about two hours from the Twin Cities. You have to concentrate."

"Got a girlfriend?"

He looked at me. "No."

I could focus on physics for the first thirty minutes. And then I'd get distracted. Start to think about Jonathan, start to get sad. Mike rarely spoke off topic, except to say once, when Hannah continued to bark after he'd entered the house, "Where I come from, dogs live outside."

He also wondered why the plants were all dying.

"Because I don't water them."

"Why do you have plants if you're not going to water them?"

"They aren't mine. They belonged to Jonathan, my ex-boyfriend, who moved out. They're his stupid plants, and I'm not going to water them."

When I came back from a bathroom break, Mike was watering the plants.

Toward the end of the summer, the lease for the Love Nest ran out, and I had to find a new place. I moved into a rattletrap of a house, a two-story duplex. I began to call it the Hovel. My college roommate Val came down from New York to help me move. She did most of the packing while I sat and told her stories of the funny/smart/sweet/fascinating things Jonathan had done and said. Moving out of the

Love Nest made the end of the relationship seem more final. Val would nod, cluck, and then ask if I wanted to take the extension cord for the TV. She made fun of my collection of shoes. Okay, so there were a lot of them—she stopped her loud counting when she got to the forty-seventh pair—they were all black, and could appear, at a cursory glance, to be all the same style, but there were differences. Really, there were.

"I miss him, Val," I'd say, and start crying again, packing tape in one hand, desk lamp in the other.

"I know you do, Rach," she'd say, patting me on the shoulder and putting in another Lyle Lovett CD.

"Do you really need three leashes for Hannah?"

On the other end, Val unpacked while I told her how angry I was that Jonathan had never said anything about his discontent.

"If he'd only told me how unhappy he was, maybe I could have changed."

I stopped myself.

She continued to put away a now limited supply of mugs with drug company logos on them, freebies given to my doctor boyfriend.

"I could have *tried* to change," I corrected.

"I'm putting the glasses in the cabinet next to the sink, okay?"

"Okay."

"Do you really need thirty-four"—she'd counted them—"pens that say Prozac, Wellbutrin, and Tegretol on them?"

"No, but you can't throw any of them out. Don't throw them out. Okay? Don't throw them out."

"Okay, okay."

"Why didn't he want me, Val?"

She held me while I cried.

Hannah walked aimlessly around the new place, circling me, looking at the door, waiting for Jonathan.

When I stopped crying, Val went back to unpacking books, and Hannah lay down on her L.L. Bean dog bed.

* * *

I calmed down. I began to eat more, to run less obsessively, to go out occasionally with the broken-wing fixers.

I e-mailed Jonathan and asked if he wanted to have dinner with me. He answered with a cautious yes. To reassure him, I confessed that I needed help with my physics homework. I had fired the stud muffin physics tutor, couldn't afford him anymore.

I had thrown Jonathan the hook I knew he needed.

"I can help you," he said.

"I know you can."

Over a dinner with no tears, no recriminations, a newfound well of patience on my part, and no talk of what had happened, I let him help me.

Over the rest of the summer and early fall, Jonathan and I began to see each other. Not romantically—there was never a hint of trying to get back together—but as friends. Our breakup had put an end to our physical relationship. We never once slipped into old patterns of bodily intimacy; the toll of ending that part of our lives together was so great that neither of us wanted to risk a rerun. Instead we carried on as the friends we had been and wanted, both of us, to continue to be. Best friends.

For a short time I dated a philosophy professor, one of the broken-wing fixer guys, but he bored the shit out of me. He was serious, ponderous. He wanted to talk about The Future, while I wanted only to talk about what we were going to have for dinner. He was old—about twelve years my senior—and saggy. He'd been married and wanted to be married again. I was ready to have some fun. That's another positive thing about being dumped: selfish as it sounds, you feel entitled to do whatever you want to try to make yourself feel better.

I was tiring of the old philosopher and began to seek some young blood, someone who was both more firm and more fun. I sent an e-mail to the stud muffin physics tutor and asked if he wanted to go out for a drink. This guy had *plaything* written all over him. He wasn't at all my type (if I even had a type); he was way younger than me, and he was hot.

He wrote back and said yes.

Unfortunately, hours before I was supposed to meet him, I sailed through a stop sign right into another car. No one was hurt, but I was upset and angry and miserable. Sitting in the cab of the tow truck, I whispered obscenities under my breath and threw myself an all-consuming pity party. When I got home, I called the stud muffin and told him I couldn't meet him—my car was dead, and I was a wreck.

"I'll come pick you up. It's on my way."

"I moved," I said.

"Then I'll pick you up where you moved to."

I thought about it for about five seconds, and I decided that, yes, if anything would help to ease my pain, it was alcoholic beverages and a hot physics grad student.

He was surprised to see the Hovel.

"I know, I know," I said.

When we got our drinks, he wanted to know why I had fired him. Had he done something wrong?

I assured him that he had been great, but that I didn't have the money to pay him.

"But you lived in that big house in that fancy neighborhood. I just assumed . . ."

"I paid only a fraction of the rent."

"I would have continued to tutor you, even if you didn't pay me."

I was flattered and encouraged, but Mike also seemed like a nice guy who might tutor anyone in need. I smiled and touched his arm. "Jonathan," I said. "He helped me."

"The guy whose plants you let die? Your ex-boyfriend?"

"We're friends again."

"Wow," he said. "That's odd."

He drove me back to the Hovel. It was a brisk night in early November. It had been his birthday a few days before, on Halloween—he was now twenty-six. I was thirty-two. I was freezing, as I often am, and the stud muffin cranked the heat in the car. Soon it was like a sauna. I was content, but I noticed rivulets of sweat falling from his temples. We continued to talk; he seemed nervous.

"So," I said. "Can I give you a birthday kiss?"

"Okay," he said.

Not very enthusiastic.

I was bundled up in my black leather jacket; the temperature of the car was surely in triple digits.

I kissed him.

We kissed for a while. He seemed to be into it. But he kept his arms stiff straight at his sides. I couldn't tell whether or not he really wanted to be here, doing this. Maybe this is the way boys usually feel, not sure how to read the signals, pursuing anyway. I knew that no means no, but does yes sometimes mean no? Was I on the road to date rape? I worried that he was bored, that maybe he wasn't into it after all. But he did seem interested in everything I said over drinks. Maybe he was gay. Maybe he wasn't attracted to me. But, he was smiling the whole time. Was this what men went through? The second-guessing, the not knowing, the mixed signals? No wonder they were such basket cases. Was I to him what the philosophy professor was to me—old, boring, saggy?

I was starting to freak out. Was I going where I was not invited? I had to know.

I did the only thing I could think of.

I grabbed his dooker.

I heard a short, sharp intake of air.

And then, there it was in my hand. The dooker, nice and hard. I felt an overwhelming sense of relief.

We saw each other a few more times, and then I brought him into the Hovel, past the appraising glance and throaty growl of Hannah, up to my bedroom. I undressed him, exposing strong, well-defined muscles and lots of hair.

"Here's the deal," I said. "You are completely inappropriate for me as relationship material. And I don't want a relationship, anyway. But I do think you are one studly stud muffin of a physics tutor, and I think we could have a lot of fun. Just as long as there's no mushy stuff. I'll have lots and lots of sex with you, but no falling in love. Okay?"

Silence.

What? Wasn't this every young man's fantasy? No strings, no commitments, lots of athletic, recreational sex. What's not to love?

"I don't know," he said slowly. "I'll have to think about it. I don't work that way."

"WHAT? Are you saying you don't want to have sex with me?"

He reconsidered and, at least for the moment, changed his twenty-six-year-old mind.

I got a new toy.

Jonathan had missed Hannah. When they saw each other again, the strains of reunion music issuing from the two of them nearly made me start crying. Hannah rejoiced to see him. As soon as Jonathan entered the house, she would sing and bark and twirl around him. Jonathan would bang bang bang at her with fingers from both hands, and she, caught between wanting to get as close to him as possible and also to do as he requested, would finally squirm down to her side, and he would give her a belly rub.

We had been seeing each other more and more frequently and had gone back to talking on the phone every day. I told him that I was seeing Mike, and he seemed genuinely happy, relieved, perhaps, of a smidgen of guilt. We continued a ritual that we had started while living in the Love Nest. Every Monday night at eight, we would watch *Melrose Place*, the worst of the early nineties prime-time soaps. We loved it—the bad acting, the embarrassing writing, the over-the-top plot twists. It was divine.

Jonathan would bring take-out burritos, and we'd sit and watch. Or I'd watch, and he'd issue a running commentary.

"Oh, that's just ridiculous."

"Duh. Now keep quiet or we won't hear the dialogue."

"The dialogue. Of course. Can't miss the dialogue."

"Quiet."

"Why would he do that? No real person would ever do that!"

"It's not real life, it's TV. Now shut the fuck up, you *Melrose*-dissing bozo!"

"Sor-ry," he'd sing out, in the world's loudest stage whisper.

Mike was adamantly respectful of not intruding on this special time that Jonathan and I shared each week, even though I invited him to watch with us. He'd work even later than usual on Monday and come over, for the night—he'd begun to come over most nights—well after the last backstabbing, beyond-belief, insanely complicated narrative contortion had taken place. Well after Jonathan had already left.

Mike, like Jonathan, was a geek. But unlike Jonathan, Mike had a narrow view of the world. He came from Sinclair Lewis's *Main Street*—literally. He grew up no more than thirty minutes from the small town on which the classic book is based, the town that signified small-town provincialism. He knew what was right: the way things were done where he came from. That's the way it was. Anything different was wrong. I worked to put a stop to that.

He would make a blanket statement like, "Affirmative action isn't fair." From me he'd get a lecture that started with the history of slavery, reminding him that he currently lived in a place that was segregated when his own father was his age, and asking him hard questions about the meaning of fairness. I'd go on and on, ranting, raving. He'd argue, but without information or knowledge. We covered race, gender, politics, regionalism, philosophy, and popular culture. I introduced him to Indian food, gender-neutral language, and his first lesbians. Mary said she thought I may have gone too far when she heard Mike referring to "person-hole covers" in the street.

Mike stopped asserting, stopped assuming, and began to ask questions. He realized how much he didn't know and, like a true geek, wanted truly to learn. Reason was his god; things needed to make sense to him. From spending time with his graduate student friends (he lived with several of them in a huge but run-down house), I learned that he spoke the brusque language of physics geeks. Someone makes an argument. You listen and understand. Then, if you don't agree, you say, "No. That's wrong." You point out the flaws and fallacies with force, both blunt and incisive. No one's feelings ever get hurt. You just want it to be right, to make sense. Being around a gaggle of physics geeks is a lesson in how to destroy someone's arguments while maintaining close friendships. You attack the ideas, not the person.

This ability not to take things personally made it easy for Mike to become friends with Jonathan. Instead of seeing an ex-boyfriend, Mike looked at Jonathan and saw a fellow traveler. The first time they met, they spent a couple of hours talking about general relativity. I sat back, watched, listened, and was filled with delight. Hannah sat at Jonathan's feet and gazed up at him. When he left, Mike said, "What a great guy. I love that guy. Why did you two ever break up?"

Mike had grown up with a strong mother, a smart and competent woman who had always worked. As the eldest of four children, Mike knew how to cook and clean, and he did. He did what was expected, anticipated what might be needed, and then did that, as well. He'd grown up tall, handsome, smart, respected by friends, teachers, parents, coaches. He had the confidence of someone who had been well loved. The combination of his unthreatened personality and his training in physics made it easy for him to ask questions. And I was happy to mold him in my image. He had refused to be squished into two dimensions, to be a plaything. He demanded that I take him seriously, as a person and, yes, as relationship material. He was proving to me why this, Us, was right.

Despite the progress I'd made in reshaping his views of the world, I was having a hard time changing the way he spoke to and viewed Hannah. He ordered her; he commanded her.

"Hannah, no," he said, firmly, when she came over to the coffee table to check out a slice of pizza, sniffing around the edges.

"Don't yell at her."

"She was going to eat the pizza."

"She absolutely was not going to eat the pizza. In her entire seven years on this earth, she has never taken anything off the table. She was just investigating. Do you really think she doesn't know better?

Do you think she's stupid? And don't ever use that tone of voice with her."

I looked at Hannah. She wagged and beamed love and understanding at me.

"Little dude," I said, just above a whisper, "go lie down on your bed."

She shot Mike a glance and walked quietly to her bed.

"She knows the words, not the tone."

He saw the proof of it.

"Okay," he said, tail between his legs. Despite his remorse, I knew he was still skeptical.

As Mike spent more time with Hannah, he paid attention, he watched her. He began to learn about Hannah, from Hannah. He began to see her.

One morning I woke up to the two of them staring at each other in bed.

"I can't sleep with someone watching me," Mike said.

"What are you talking about?"

"Hannah. She was watching me. Like a person. Watching me sleep."

"Don't you get it? She is like a person."

Mike began to bring Hannah an assortment of dog treats. He figured out which ones she liked best, and brought more of those. He decided she needed a bed downstairs, for when we were watching TV and she wasn't lying on the couch. He got her a bed. His voice softened when he spoke to her. After a while, I didn't have to tell him not to order her around; he saw that she understood his words.

Mike came to the Hovel around six each night and made dinner. I'd been toying with the idea for a while of becoming a vegetarian. There were plenty of good reasons to do it; the only question for me was where you draw the line, how you decided what's okay for you to eat. While taking my premed biology course the answer came to me: you don't eat your relatives. I decided not to eat anyone in my own phylum. No vertebrates. I became, as Jonathan quipped, an invertebraterian. Which meant mostly expensive seafood: lobster, crab, shrimp, scallops. Mike brought over a cookbook given to him by his mother, *Betty Crocker's New Favorites*. I made fun of him for that: How Midwestern! How middle American! How middle brow! I backed off once he started cooking delicious vegetarian meals of soba noodles and peanut sauce, Southwestern vegetarian rice and beans, meatless meatloaf, which I called "neat loaf." He made enough for both of our dinners, and for my lunch the following day. Our deal was simple. If he made the food, I would pay for it. If he cooked, I'd clean up.

When Mike cooked, Hannah stood right behind him, sometimes too close. He was always afraid he'd step on her. She was always hoping that he would drop something on the floor. He never did—Mike was the anti-Jonathan in terms of sloppiness—though he'd occasionally toss her a tidbit, because he was beginning not to be able to resist her charms.

Mike was as easy to train as Hannah had been. He paid attention, and he wanted to please. If I even so much as asked him where he'd gotten that shirt—"What, you don't like it?"—I'd never see it again. He was ever-vigilant, making sure every thing was exactly right, or, exactly as I wanted it to be. I tried to refrain from criticizing him. It wasn't hard. Nothing he did ever bothered me. He was, if anything, overly attentive and grown-up, taking care of me in ways I hadn't even realized I needed. He was husbanding me. And also acting like the wife. I loved to sit in the kitchen and watch him work his magic over the stove.

"This would be even better if you weren't wearing a shirt."

He took off his shirt.

Over dinner we'd sit on the living room couch and watch *Star Trek*, a concession on my part. Like many geeks, Mike loved his science fiction. Like many a literary snob, I never went for it. But I'd watch *Star Trek* with him and came to appreciate the sterling qualities of Captain Picard, even as I railed and decried against Number One, who I thought was more like "number two," if you get my drift. Mike watched with a generous spirit and appreciated each character's nuances, recognizing the role they had to play in the narrative. Mike was nothing if not a generous and astute watcher. In many

ways, physics is about observation and attention to detail. Mike was a
true physicist.

After two years of dating, I went home with Mike for Christmas,
to a place where my eyeballs froze and you could drive across the lake.
We took a snowmobile out to the heated ice houses where Mike's relatives spent their days fishing. His family welcomed me, even though
they didn't understand why I didn't want to go to church with them.
A few weeks before I flew up to Minnesota, Mike had told his mother
that she should know that if we were ever to get married, it wouldn't
be in a church.

"Why not?" asked his mother.

"Because Rachel's Jewish."

"Well, it's just one day. Can't she go for just one day?"

We visited the hotel on Main Street in Sauk Center, the town
where Sinclair Lewis lived and which served as the basis for Gopher
Prairie. Copies of the book were everywhere; I had to wonder if any
of the residents of the maligned town had ever read it. Why would
they celebrate a book that was an indictment of small-town values, a
laying plain of the supposed hypocrisies and untruths? It seemed odd
that they would proudly display it, but this was not my world; I was
clearly out of my element. They were Main Street. This was middle
America.

Mike was torn between wanting to please me and needing to de-
fend his people, his upbringing. He was convinced that I was always
right, yet he knew, deep down, that this was who he was.

In the meantime, his family had set up a Christmas tree, and under it were scattered more presents than I'd ever seen. An incredible
number of them were for me. They bundled me up—the temperature
dropped to numbers that, even if they weren't preceded by a minus
sign, would have been too cold—and warmly welcomed me. They
took me to family dairy farms, and I happily visited with the cows.
Mike's parents each had something like a dozen siblings, and many of

them lived nearby. It was a big change from the small nuclear family I was used to.

We went to see his two grandmothers, one of whom had just been moved into a nursing home. She was a tough old bird. The other, Grandma C., cheerfully received us into the home where she still lived, alone. She was eighty-something years old and put out a feast of Christmas cookies for us, many of which she had baked. We all discovered that I loved "divinity" cookies. I'd never had them before, having never had much truck with the Divine. But these sugary confections were right up my alley, and Grandma C. gave me an extra box to take home.

Though his parents knew that Mike was staying at my house every night back in Durham, on their turf, we were not allowed to share a room. I slept in his boyhood bedroom in the cozily finished basement, football and basketball trophies on the shelves, old textbooks, dog-eared and heavily lined, stacked up in the corner. In the middle of the night I sneaked into the guest room where Mike lay sleeping and crawled into bed with him.

"No," he said. "It's not right. It's my parents' house, and we have to respect that."

Dejected, I went back to my single bed.

On Christmas Eve, the family went to church and I stayed back, reading a novel. They got home after midnight and had their traditional Christmas Eve breakfast of scrambled eggs. I'd gone to bed, but I could hear them upstairs. I heard Mike's sisters ask why I always had to be the center of attention, why was I so excited to see the cows, why couldn't I have just gone to church? I heard his mother say that I was too skinny. She thought I seemed "interesting," which, in the coded language of small towns, I knew meant weird, different, unpleasant. And wasn't I a little old for Mike? Was I the right kind of person, with the right values? Mike demurred. I knew this was hard for him. His father said nothing.

Christmas Day, more family members came over. I had heard about Uncle Earl and Aunt Grace. Everyone liked Uncle Earl—he

was a gregarious guy, a hail-fellow-well-met type. No one liked Aunt
Grace. She was opinionated and bossy, overbearing and demanding.
She had a lot to say, and she said it, tactlessly, unasked. Everyone
dreaded getting together with her. She and I hit it off as soon as we
said hello.

Back in Durham, Mike and I continued to spend almost all our
free time together. He seemed to find everything I did funny and delightful. Even when I whined.

"I can't help it," he'd say, when I was moaning and complaining
about something—about nothing—"I think everything you do is
adorable."

I knew what he meant. I felt that way about Hannah.

And I felt that way about Mike. Like Hannah, he was the perfect
reflection of what I hoped and wanted to be. Kind and soft where I
was hard and harsh, generous of spirit, eager to help, to be of use.
Uncritical and accepting. Yielding. Having Mike around was like
knowing there was a soft pillow on which you could land, from any
height, and never risk injury. I'd never felt so safe, so comfortable in
a relationship. It was as easy, as relaxed, as it had been with Patrick,
but more stimulating. Mike not only paid attention, but he made me
the center of his world, as well.

Mike read what I gave him to read. I loved trying to figure out
which books he'd like. Richard Ford's *The Sportswriter,* a book about
modern manhood, would be, I knew, a winner. As would *The Angel
Killers,* a book by Michael Shaara set during the Civil War. And
Patrick Suskind's *Perfume,* whose protagonist is an eighteenth-century
French murderer. He read closely and carefully, and he picked up on
things I'd missed. We went to the movies I wanted to see, and he'd enjoy them, always trusting that I knew what was good. The few times he
picked out things to do or see, if I didn't like them, he would apologize
and feel terribly, horribly guilty. "It's not your fault," I'd say, but he'd
feel like it was, that he'd disappointed me.

Mike thought about me, about what I needed. For instance, it had never occurred to me that it was stupid to drive a couple of miles late in the night so I could go to my office to staple my lab reports. It never occurred to me to go out and buy a stapler. For Valentine's Day, Mike gave me a stapler. With extra staples. He also realized that the gift might have been lacking a bit in the romance department. So he made me a pair of earrings out of electronics components. They were delicate and beautiful and the combination of the presents—the pragmatic and the purely fun—almost broke my heart. While Jonathan was who he was, Mike wanted to be who I wanted him to be. He was the perfect boyfriend. I was a lucky girl.

Six

A cat will look down on a man. A dog will look up to a man.
But a pig will look you straight in the eye and see his equal.

—Winston Churchill

Mike and I continued to date, Jonathan and I continued to be best friends, and the three of us began to carry on as three. The weekly *Melrose* date turned into a ménage-à-trois: three burritos, one hour of really good (bad) TV, and a happy, happy dog.

Mike developed a huge soft spot for Jonathan; he thought everything he did was funny and delightful and couldn't understand how and why I'd found so many things about him annoying. Jonathan was most himself around Mike—not so surprising, since they were both good men. In both cases, I'd chosen well—the two of them really hit it off.

While he never participated in Jonathan's and my verbal frenzies, Mike became an enthusiastic spectator. He delighted in watching Jonathan and me go off on each other, or go on about a particular topic. He never joined us when we made up songs; he was, as we discovered, tone deaf. But he appreciated us. When I'd told friends over the phone that we were all hanging out together—Jonathan, Mike, and me—at first they thought it strange.

"Doesn't it bother Mike?" Val asked. "Isn't he threatened to have your ex-boyfriend around?"

"Nope."

When she came to town for a visit and saw us all together, she saw for herself. "It does sound strange," she said, "but it works."

Mike, Jonathan, and I began spending a lot of time together, a comfortable if perhaps odd triumvirate.

After Mike and I had been dating for quite some time, I tried to nudge Jonathan into putting himself back out on the market, to find himself a nice Jewish girl. But, he told me over and over, he wasn't quite ready.

Jonathan had moved out of the soulless but clean apartment he had been living in and found another place, a better fit for him. He rented a small shabby shack, overflowing with character, sandwiched between a horse pasture in the front and a riding stable behind. He loved having horses in his front yard, and he stocked up on carrots and apples, and on special horse cookies from the feed store, as well. In his house, Jonathan also kept a supply of treats and bones for Hannah, and a cabinet provisioned especially for me, chock-full of sweets that I loved but could not bear to keep in my own house, the risk of eating to the point of injury being too great. When we would visit, Hannah would get her Pup-Peroni, and I would feast on Tootsie Rolls and Oreos.

But Jonathan, to me, seemed lonely. If he wasn't ready for a new girlfriend, I thought maybe he was ready for something else.

"Why don't you get a pet of your own?" I'd ask Jonathan relentlessly.

"I'm allergic."

"You lived with Hannah."

"I love Hannah."

Jonathan had embarked on a series of weekly allergy shots before we moved in together. I always forgot about his allergies. I forgot about a lot of things, it seemed.

"What about a poodle? They're supposed to be hypoallergenic."

"I don't want a poodle."

"How about a hairless cat?" Trying to appeal to Jonathan's fondness for the unusual.

"No cats."

It took a few months, maybe more like a year, but I finally figured it out. "Jonathan, I have just the pet for you."

"I don't want a pet."

"I know you. You need a pet."

"I don't want a pet."

"Maybe. But could you resist a Vietnamese potbellied pig?"

"A pig?"

"A pig."

He was practically living on a farm already.

The woman who owned the stable said that if he got a pig and didn't want it, she'd take it. Another friend of ours with a farm made the same offer. And finally, to push Jonathan over the edge, I told him that I would act as pig coparent—for better or for worse. I was able and ready to take on this unconditional commitment, a big step for me.

Jonathan thought about it for a while. A researcher, he did research. He even went to the flea market at the state fairgrounds where, among the puppies, kittens, chinchillas, and hedgehogs, a man, Howard the Pig Man, sold pigs. Piglets, actually.

"I'm going to get a pig," Jonathan finally announced.

* * *

We started fighting over the pig even before she entered our lives. Jonathan wanted to name her Emma.

Emma is a fine name, the title of a fine book. Jonathan had never read Jane Austen. His desire had more to do with Emma Thompson. My problem with it was simple: It was too close in sound to Hannah. And if we were going to be coparenting this pig, the little pipsqueak would often be in close quarters with Hannah. I didn't know enough about pigs to know if she'd hear Emma and Hannah differently enough to know when she was being called, and so I said that while I thought it was a great name, we should pick another.

Jonathan said no.

"What?"

"No. I want to name her Emma."

"But I told you why it wasn't a good idea."

"I don't care. I want to name her Emma."

"But it's too close to Hannah—they may get confused."

"I want to name her Emma."

I looked at this man, who now opposed me with a steeliness I'd never before seen. I flashed back to our car trip through New England, where he'd told me that he felt like he couldn't say no to me; more, that I couldn't hear no from him. He never cared enough about what we did to insist we do what he wanted to do, so we always did what I wanted. I thought about the fact that we never fought, ever. He always gave in, always agreed with me. I thought about how awful it had been to feel my heart breaking, and how much worse to under-stand that it had been my own fault.

"Okay, then," I said, chipper. "Emma it is."

Mike and Hannah, who'd been watching us like a tennis match, both let out a long, exhausted, sigh.

The appointed day came. Jonathan and I went to buy pig sup-plies: bedding, bowls, harness and leash, and a number of toys, in-cluding a stuffed penguin and a ball. (Who knew what a pig would want to play with?) Then we dashed over to meet Howard. The adoption was to take place in the flea market parking lot. We walked over to his truck and there, in a box, was a tiny black piglet.

We brought her back to Jonathan's and let her out, thinking she might have to pee. She didn't have to pee, but she did have to run— away. She bolted, faster than I could believe, faster than me. We chased her across the lawn as she made quick turns and sudden stops; we were less fleet of feet, and far more clumsy, than the little squealer. Finally I grabbed her and picked her up.

Jet engines generally produce about 112 decibels of sound. Pigs have been recorded at 116. That a creature so small could scream so loud is still astonishing to me.

She had been born, according to Howard the Pig Man, right around Christmas. We picked her up on Super Bowl Sunday. She was five weeks old. She weighed five pounds and was the size of Mike's hiking boot.

Her hair and her skin were black, she had teeny little hooves— soft fleshy insides surrounded by a hard nail—six white hairs in the middle of her forehead, and on her snout, right between her two prodigious nostrils, she had a heart-shaped pink spot.

She was the ugliest baby animal I'd ever seen.

When I expressed this, Jonathan was outraged. "She's beautiful," he countered.

"She's fast," I offered.

"Beautiful."

"She's loud."

"She's beautiful," he said, cuddling next to her.

"Beautiful," I said, and he shifted his eye-beam of adoration from the pig to me.

Jonathan and I were still working on developing and deepening a language for our friendship. I tried to be mindful of my control-freak tendencies. He was more aware of not giving in to me, not feeding the cycle of capitulation and resentment that fueled the demise of our romantic love.

Mike was a moderating, peacemaking influence. The three of us fit comfortably together. The only conflict centered around the pig.

There is no Dr. Spock of the porcine world. Knowing how to raise a five-week-old, five-pound squealer of an uncommon species was a mystery. While I was fairly confident in my ability to raise a young animal, regardless of genus or species, I was less sure of Jonathan's. He'd never had a pet as a grown-up.

"Jennifer/Juniper doesn't count," I'd argue, when talking about his pet parenting inexperience.

"Yes, she does."

"No, she doesn't."

"Yes, she does."

"NO, SHE DOESN'T. You weren't the primary caretaker. You weren't responsible for feeding her and training her and cleaning up pee, poop, and throwup."

As my voice rose into breathless debate, I noticed that Jonathan was getting that steely, dug-in look.

"Come on, you guys," Mike said, pleading, placating.

Sometimes, I was learning, it is better to be kind than to be right.

"You're right, I'm sorry. She was your dog."

I didn't want to argue with Jonathan. I certainly didn't want to try to overpower him. I thought hard—about him, about me, about our collective lack of knowledge in the arena of pig parenting. The way to reach Jonathan, a true and curious and information-seeking geek, the way to help him in his pet noviatehood, was to get a manual.

I found what we came to call the Pig Book. It was the source of All Pig Knowledge. It was specific to Vietnamese potbellied pigs raised as members of the household. After I got the book, Jonathan cited it during many of our conversations: "Yeah, but, it says in the Pig Book . . ."

Never mind that the author of the Pig Book was someone whose qualifications to write on pigs were never clear to me. The subtitle of the book said it all, though: *A Complete Pet Owner's Manual, with a Special Chapter: Understanding Miniature Pigs.* We consulted the Pig Book regularly, and each used it in our own image. Me, I skimmed it, looking for what I needed at the time. I read the index. Jonathan, always more thorough, more methodical, read the whole thing through. Repeatedly.

"It's time to do away with the paper," I said to Jonathan when, after four days, Emma had learned to go outside to do her business.

"She needs to pee outside."

"She needs the paper."

"No, she doesn't."

"Yes, she does."

"No, she doesn't."

"Yes, she does."

It struck me that Jonathan's house was Emma's primary residence. I shut up, and the paper stayed on the floor of the laundry room. It was easier to wean Emma from the paper than it was Jonathan. Finally, after about three months, he was persuaded to get rid of it. All seemed well. And then.

In his ratty house, Jonathan had a study that was rarely used. Rarely used by humans. One day he called me.

"There's a high-water line in the study," he said, giddy.

"What are you talking about? Was it flooded?"

"In a way," he said.

Emma had been sneaking into the study when no one was around and emptying, under the desk, her prodigious bladder. The study had a semipermanent lake of pig pee, stank to high hell of porcine urine, and it was possible, to see on the wall, the water line.

I was horrified. She knew better than this, and at my house, such a transgression would not be tolerated. But Jonathan was enchanted by her ingenuity, by her sneakiness, by the copious amount of liquid that passed through her, and by the fact that he had identified a "high-water line."

Were we living together, based on historical, empirical evidence, I would have gone ballistic. His joking about this would have made me want to shove his face right down there in the soggy carpet. But it was different now. I got it. Every time he said "high-water line," I laughed with him.

Things that used to drive me nuts about Jonathan I now found endearing. If we arranged to meet somewhere for dinner and I ended up waiting at a table, alone, for twenty minutes before he blew in and said, "I had a really interesting case," now I simply put down the book I'd learned always to have with me and would be eager, happy, to hear what had delayed him. If it took him forty times longer to tell the tale—if his word-to-content ratio seemed excessively high, if the *ums* he used as pauses to gather his thoughts were long enough for me to have knit three sweaters, well, that was just Jonathan. I waited. I even felt a wave of tenderness pass over me as I sat on his toilet and stared down at the small patches of hardened pee on the floor.

Emma grew quickly, and her personality announced itself immediately, loud and clear. There was no mistaking who was Number One. What the little pig wanted, the little pig got. Emma had a lot of wants.

She wanted to be warm. Like me, Emma was always cold. Like me, her body radiated heat—she was hot to the touch, just as I am, but was always shivering and complaining. Her hair was long and black and lustrous. More hair, with roots, than fur. It didn't seem to be very good insulation.

She wanted to be close. She didn't like to lie on the floor at your feet like a dog. No, she wanted to be in your lap, preferably under a piece of clothing. She liked to wear clothes. I discovered this after coming home from a run, throwing my stinky T-shirt on the floor, and having it land, instead, on the pig. Emma stood there, happy as a pig in a shirt. She oinked. She walked around all morning with the shirt draped over her. When I went to take it off, she let her displeasure be known. Emma was never reticent about showing displeasure. When she suffered, the world heard about it and suffered with her. She was her mother's pig.

She wanted quiet. Emma did not like loud noises, too much talking, or music. From someone who was so noisy, who, when bored, would walk around the house oinking, who, when roused from a sleep and told that it was time to go for a walk would emit long, loud groans as if she were being tortured, who, if it was five minutes past her usual breakfast or dinner time would issue staccato grunts that sounded like a duck with sinus problems, it was hard to take. Indeed, the pig could dish it out, but she couldn't take it.

She wanted to be clean and dry. The idea of a pig in mud makes no sense to me, when I think about the fact that Emma would refuse—refuse—to go outside to pee if it was raining. She avoided dirt and puddles, taking a long way around if necessary in order to maintain her pristine porcine state.

She wanted only me and Jonathan. No one else even entered into her universe. She hated Mike. As soon as he opened the door and walked into the house, she began to complain. Loudly. If he came near her, she complained. When we were in bed together, Hannah at the foot, Emma glued to my side, separating me from my boyfriend, she would groan if Mike got too close. When she got up, she stepped on his head. Or more delicate parts.

Mike was not enchanted with the pig. He thought she was selfish and annoying. He'd never say so, though, knowing how Jonathan and I doted on her, but she offended his sensibilities, his belief that everyone should strive to be good, charitable, and industrious. Mike thought Emma should have a job, that she should have something to do.

We'd read in the Pig Book that porkers sometimes liked to poke around in things, rummaging, rooting. "That girl needs a box of rocks," Mike said. "Something to root in, something to keep her occupied." Mike made Emma a box of rocks. She preferred to root under the covers, though, and ignored the rocks, unless we put bits of food in there.

Emma was happy to live in a circumscribed world. She was not interested in strangers; she greeted them with haughty disdain. Strangers were, of course, interested in her. It's not every day you see a pig walking down the street on a leash. Double and triple takes were commonplace. Cars would stop, and people would exclaim: "That's a pig!" I never quite figured out how to respond to that. They'd come over to check her out, and she'd ignore them, stopping to graze on lawn clover or worse (I had to keep her away from flower beds) while questions, many questions, were fired at me, the answers to which were usually the following:

At the flea market at the State Fair.

Because she's hypoallergenic.

It took four days (to housebreak her).

About sixty pounds, unless you overfeed them.

Pig chow.

On a leash.

In the house.

In the bed.

Yes, in the bed.

About as smart as a three-year-old child.

About a dozen years. (When they asked about life expectancy, it always unnerved me.)

Yes, she gets along with the dog.

Actually, Emma loved being with Hannah. If she couldn't curl up against Jonathan or me, Hannah was the next best choice. Hannah, tolerant as always, was nevertheless less than thrilled at having to share our bed with Emma. At my house, Emma had a hard time getting a purchase on the hardwood floors—it's not easy when you're hoofed. So in order to get onto the bed, Emma needed a pillow strategically placed as a launching pad. She'd sit on the pillow, wiggling her butt like a golfer addressing a ball, and then, in a burst of unexpected athleticism, she'd fly through the air, stiff—pigs are stiff, not floppy like cats—front legs tucked under like a champion show-jumping horse, and landing, unlike a horse, butt end first. She maintained her head-up posture throughout the flight. It was an uncanny sight.

Hannah understood that Emma needed the launching pad to get onto the bed. Each time she walked by, she'd casually kick it. Soon, the pillow on the floor would be too far from the bed for Emma to make her ascent. Emma oinked and wailed, and Hannah gazed down at her from the bed, with a what-am-I-supposed-to-do look on her patient, tolerant face.

Once in our bed, Emma wanted to be under the covers, between the sheets. If she got into bed before me, which she often did, and managed to get herself under only the comforter, when I slipped in between the sheets she squealed in displeasure and had to get out and back in, so that she could glue herself to my side. Unmediated proximity was important to the pig.

Mostly, though, what Emma wanted was food.

Jonathan mail-ordered special fancy Vietnamese potbellied pig food for her. One of the points emphasized in the Pig Book was the piggy eating behavior of pigs, and their tendency to put on weight. A fat pig is an unhealthy pig. Knowing that Jonathan, a Jewish mother's son, loved to show his love with food, we had serious discussions about keeping Emma's weight under control. Jonathan said he understood. But he also had a hard time denying Emma anything she wanted. Just as he had with me. Emma was a selfish, demanding, noisy little pig. Just like me. But she was adorable.

It's no coincidence that the cliché is to "eat like a pig." Until you've shared a meal with a pig, you can't do proper justice when conjuring the phrase. Mealtimes with Emma were an event. As soon as you hinted, even in a whisper, that it was almost time to eat, Emma was up and frothing. She spewed enormous quantities of bubbly white fizz from her mouth when she started even to think about eating. It would blanket her mouth and become so itchy that she'd strike at it with a hoof, or shake her head. When she shook her head, the froth went forth—spattering anything in its orbit. Hannah always got her food first. She wouldn't eat it, but instead stood guard while the pig circled, provoking from my sweet and gentle girl an occasional bark or growl that made me proud. She wasn't allowed to harm the porcine princess, but she could discipline her.

Emma loved her pig chow. If I put other, seemingly more appealing food in her bowl, like fresh vegetables or fruit or even meat, she would still go first for the pig chow. I wondered what it would be like to be so content with the quotidian, not to hunger after the thrill of the new but to be happy with what you have in front of you. Hannah, the more human Hannah, finds anything that is not her own food (including other dogs' food) infinitely more appealing. After she'd scarfed down her pig food, Emma would prowl, looking for that one pellet she may have missed, convinced that there was always something hiding under her bowl. Once she'd found every morsel, she'd sidle over to Hannah's bowl. Hannah, well aware of the porcine pattern, would have taken a few unenthusiastic bites, but remained on guard. Emma would approach, slowly, tentatively. Hannah would shoot her a dirty look, maybe utter a growl.

Emma would walk back to her bowl and nose it several feet around the kitchen. But then she'd come sneaking back. Sometimes kneeling on her front legs, trying to stay low, keeping her nose to the ground. Hannah would look at her, Emma would retreat. Occasionally Hannah would give up. She'd leave her food and go lie down. Emma took this as tacit permission and beelined for the dog food. Even if you know your place, if you're clever and patient and persistent, sometimes you can circumvent it.

Emma had an inordinate interest in food. Jonathan and I began to spell, but Emma quickly learned what *E-A-T* means. We had to resort to complicated synonyms, and we couldn't use them too frequently: "Have you already given the porkchop her grub?" "Should we present the Porcine Princess her comestibles?"

Emma was quick, and she was clever. Diabolically clever. She had no moral center. She would do what she could get away with, and she never showed remorse when caught.

Emma's high level of motivation when it came to making a connection with a potential food source, coupled with her resourcefulness, made her extremely easy to teach. I exploited certain behaviors I'd observed in her to get her to do the things I wanted her to do. If you're a pig, your line of vision tends to be floorward. Thus, if a piece of food is waved above your nose, you tend to raise your head, and drop your butt. Voilà—you're sitting. Pigs generally don't sit.

But Emma would, for food. Or she'd approximate a sit, crouching above the ground.

"All the way," I'd say.

She'd put her butt down on the floor for a carrot.

It was an obvious next step to ask for a hoof. Not having a lot of fine motor control or lateral flexibility, she often ended up waving the hoof up and down, a Nazi swine pleasing her two Jewish parents.

Kneeling is peculiar to pigs. Dogs don't bend that way. Not only would Emma kneel, but she'd also crawl around kneeling.

But, by far, her best trick was twirling.

She'd start facing you.

She'd oink.

Stiffly (don't forget, pigs are stiff) she'd twirl in a circle.

Face you again.

Oink again.

This was her favorite trick. In the presence of food, she would spontaneously begin to twirl. It's almost impossible to resist feeding a twirling pig.

One weekend, we five set off, bound for Hanging Rock. One car, three humans, one dog, one small black pig. No Victorian-era Australian schoolgirls out for a picnic were we. No crazed Rachel Roberts headmistress whose hair came undone as the movie eerily progressed. No, this was wholesome, healthy, outdoor fun. This was no *Picnic at Hanging Rock*.

The ride there was uneventful. Jonathan and Mike in the front, Jonathan driving. (Poorly, as usual. Talking, as usual. Not looking at the road, but at least he was looking at Mike and not at me.) I shared the backseat with Hannah, all tolerance and forgiveness, and Emma, who was happy as long as she was nestled in my lap. Any movements in my legs caused great wails of complaint. It was easier to try to remain still than to risk the wrath of the pig.

We got to our destination midday, set up camp, and then drove the quarter-mile or so to the trailhead. We'd just spent three hours in the car. Nothing happened. But during the three minutes it took to drive down the windy road to the trail, Emma pooped. In the car. And not just a little poop, but big huge poop. A projectile poop. A truly gross-me-out-I-never-want-to-ride-in-this-car-or-wear-these-clothes-again poop. Fortunately, I had another pair of shorts with me. But it was Jonathan's car. I threatened to hold the pig hostage if he didn't clean it before the trip home. He cleaned.

We began the hike up Hanging Rock. At first the pig was a trooper. She trooped right up the trail, stopping only occasionally to snatch a bite to eat. We walked a couple of miles, a long way to go on short little piggy legs. Then we turned around.

Emma got tired and refused to walk another step.

She also refused to be carried.

You will remember that Emma had lungs, even when she was a baby. Everyone within a hundred miles of Hanging Rock heard Emma that day. Finally we were able to coax her—pushing, pulling, and making promises of food—back down the trail.

We got back and settled into camp. Mike cooked a delicious, invertebraterian dinner that night over the campfire. We sat around eating good food and drinking nice wine.

Emma was exhausted. She was very, very quiet. Unnaturally quiet.

But she wouldn't lie down in the dirt.

As tired as she was, she was still herself and was unwilling to get dirty. She dozed unsteadily on her hooves.

Finally she noticed that I had stretched my legs out in front of me. She walked over, dazed, and nudged me with her snout, poking at my legs. Then she climbed up, wedging herself between them, lying lengthwise, snout in my crotch, her butt barely reaching my knees. And she went to sleep.

A short while later, Jonathan went into his tent to fetch something. Emma woke. Watched Jonathan go over to the tent. He came out. She got up. Nosed through the opening and discovered the sleeping bag.

For someone who likes to sleep completely covered by covers, the sleeping bag is mecca. She traveled down to the foot of the bag, and there she stayed until morning.

The next day we struck camp, packed up our belongings, and piled once more into the car. Emma was crankier now, and each time I moved her, she oinked.

It was one of those Eureka! moments. I discovered that I could play the pig.

By gently squeezing her sides, I could produce, almost effortlessly, an oink. Even Emma seemed amused by this, her lips pursed in something resembling a piggy little smile.

Eager to share my discovery with the other members of the car, I began a ditty. I started humming the chorus of the theme song to *The Addams Family*. *Duh duh duh duh*—*oink oink*. *Duh duh duh duh*—*oink oink*. *Duh duh duh duh, duh duh duh duh, duh duh duh duh*—*oink oink*. Oinks beautifully replaced finger snaps. Glorious sound. Wonderful music. It was a revelation.

Jonathan began to get agitated. What he found funny at first quickly became a source of vexation—he thought I was torturing the pig. So I did the only thing I could think of to do. I began to play the *Green Acres* refrain: *Do do do do do*—*oink oink*. *Do do do do do*—*oink oink*. I got ambitious and tried the "Happy Birthday to You" song. Not quite as successful, but not bad.

Mike was chuckling quietly. I was giggling maniacally. Jonathan was becoming hysterical, screaming at me to stop torturing the pig. But I wasn't torturing her. I was barely touching her—she certainly didn't seem to be in any pain or discomfort. And just as she couldn't stop oinking in response to a gentle squeeze, I couldn't stop playing the pig.

Mike finally called a halt to the madness. "Can't you see you're upsetting Jonathan, Rach? Stop it."

I stopped.

You couldn't pull the pig. If she didn't want to go, your only option was to pick her up and risk eardrum-bursting sounds of protest. If she wanted something and you wouldn't respond, she'd keep trying to figure out how to make you comply. Emma was clever enough to read the situation, to shift her behaviors in order to best meet her needs. She was always herself, always the cynosure of wherever she was, but with me, the martinet mother, she goosestepped her way to getting me to do what she wanted, and with Jonathan, the doting dad, she was cute and cuddly, at least as cuddly as it was possible for her to be.

Children seem to have a similar ability, to know how to read and work their parents. When do we lose it? When had I become so much myself, so entrenched, that I could not adapt to behaving differently with different people? I loved Jonathan, I had wanted to be with him, but I couldn't adapt to keeping my mouth shut about the little things—the tiny, trivial, picayune things that lord knows why bothered me so much.

Nothing Mike did, on the other hand, ever bothered me. In fact, like Hannah, he was so quiet and innocuous that in the mix of me, Jonathan, and the pig, you almost forgot he was there. Like Hannah, he watched and waited. He worried. After three years together, I wanted Mike to officially move in. He had almost all his stuff at the Hovel, but continued to pay rent for the room in the house he shared with the other physics geeks. The only time we spent at his place, was, for the most part, to watch Duke basketball games and *Sex and the City* with his pals; they welcomed Hannah and eventually warmed up to having a pig around for TV shows. But Mike wouldn't give up his place in that house.

"Why won't you just move in?" I began to ask more and more frequently. Even if we didn't have the same kind of conversations that I had with Jonathan, no relationship had ever been easier, been more satisfying.

When I finally issued an ultimatum, Mike had his say: He was devoted to his career. Every moment he spent with me was time away from work, and his work was, in most respects, his life. I demanded a lot of time and attention. If we were to have kids, he'd be at work all day and then would have to come home and cook, and deal with pee, poop, and throwup, too. He knew I wasn't going to do it, he knew I didn't care as much as he did about having a family. We'd discussed this, vaguely. He didn't want to have to do it all. We never had any arguments, because he anticipated my needs before I even knew what they were. He was even more focused on pleasing me than Jonathan had been, and was better at it. I didn't even realize it.

In a tragically familiar mode, I realized that Mike and I had reached the same impasse I'd come to with Jonathan. Once again, it was a case of complementary pathologies. I do so love the pleasure-givers. Flowers, candy, clothing, fancy dinners, elegant trips—I could convince myself to believe what they said: that giving to me gave them pleasure. And receiving gives me lots of pleasure. I'm a good receiver. I love presents and express gratitude vociferously and with squeals of delight.

What this translates to is that I am a selfish person. That's a well-worn pathology. We know how that story goes. But the pathology of the giver is something quite else. It's less easily identifiable as a real problem, because it's a useful social adaptation. But there is a strong and personal downside, this unwillingness to let the focus be on one's own self. The effacement of needs doesn't mean they don't exist. They go underground. Like moles, they lose the ability to see what's right there in front of them. Sure, subterranean creatures find their way, using other senses to negotiate tunnels and holes. But once they surface, they're screwed.

Like Jonathan, Mike never said what he needed, but unlike Jonathan, he didn't realize it was a problem—until he started seriously imagining our future together. He'd been happy to let me take the lead, to determine everything about his life, happy not only to be with Hannah, but also to be like her. But no one wants to be treated like a dog, even a profoundly well-loved dog.

Both Jonathan and Mike loved me, but I was too much work to make a real commitment to. Plus, Mike knew that even if we broke up, he wouldn't necessarily lose me. He'd seen the evidence of my broken relationship every Monday night.

I told him not to count on it, buddy boy. Just because I was still friends with Jonathan didn't mean he'd get to stick around. I was hurt and disappointed and ultimately not surprised. As much as I loved him, and I did really and truly love him, in the same and different ways from the ways I loved Jonathan, I knew that we were not going to be romantic partners for life. He'd grown and changed so much in the time we'd been together. I found him more interesting now, but also he bore the prints of my making. I'd molded and shaped him. It wasn't right. He had to continue to grow, but on his own.

We were apart for about a week. I called him to check in, remembering how hard it had been for Jonathan when he dumped me and worrying about Mike. He said that he was thinking about quitting graduate school.

"Are you fucking crazy? You have like, what, two months to go before you're finished? You've never quit anything in your life!"

I realized that this may not have been the loving support he needed and changed tacks: "I'll pick you up at the lab in half an hour."

"I can't leave now—I'm in the middle of something." It was a reflexive answer, and he realized it.

"I'll meet you outside."

We went to the beach. In the car, for the two-hour drive, I let him talk. He wasn't sure his work was any good, didn't think it meant anything. He wasn't cut out to be an academic. He was sick of school.

I drove and then parked, and we walked on the beach. He continued to talk. I asked him to think about what he'd like to do instead of finishing. He didn't know. He didn't want to do anything. He was, for the first time, acting like a child.

He just needed a day at the beach. A chance to consider other options. He was feeling stuck, trapped, not unlike how he'd felt with me, he told me in a burst of candor that was, I knew, hard for him. The more he talked about his options, though, and realized that he didn't have to get a PhD, the more he realized that he wanted to. He decided that he would continue on that course.

Our conversation drifted, and we began talking about Us. He tried to review our relationship with the same open-mindedness as he had his career path. But the more we talked, the more he became convinced, once and for all, that being with me would be its own kind of trap. He simply couldn't go on being my partner. He wanted me in his life, yes, but not as a wife, not as the mother of his (notional) children.

I saw it all: the many mistakes I'd made. Those who do not remember the past are condemned to repeat it. Again and again and again. At least I'd chosen well these past two times. I'd picked men who were good for me, even if I wasn't good for them. They were doglike men, both of them. Eager to please, accepting, generally happy. A good complement to my own piggy tendencies.

With Jonathan, I was so busy noticing his flaws and imperfections that I paid no attention to my own, until he was forced, gently, lovingly, to point them out. With Mike, I created, *Pygamalion*-like, the perfect boyfriend. I trained him with treats and caresses. I molded him into exactly what I wanted. He was happy to be molded. But what I tried to ignore—the root of Mikeness, the soil from which he had sprouted—was still there, and was important. Mike was who he was; he wasn't a tabula rasa, not a lump of clay. I now saw this. I hadn't allowed him to grow on his own.

The move from ignorance to recognition did poor Oedipus in: Once you realize that you've fucked your mother and killed your father, how can you not put out your own eyes? How could you ever want again to see? How can you continue to live "at home," in a place that is yours? Banishment is the only option for the tragic sop. I was going to have to stay away from men until I could straighten myself out.

As I had with Jonathan, I would need to find a new way to be with Mike, to be a better, less selfish friend. As coparents of the pig, Jonathan and I became much closer than what we had as lovers. Channels of communication were opened; we shared a common interest that was intense (and often noisy). Maybe this is what happens when people have children together. Another thing that happens, perhaps, is that you see yourself in your kids. I saw myself in the pig, for better and, often, for worse. Her selfishness, her lack of tolerance (even for things she was herself continually guilty of), her bullheadedness, her unconcern for others. I found Emma infinitely amusing and delightful. I loved her, but I couldn't connect with her the way I could with Hannah. I didn't see her shooting love at me with her eyes. I just saw her asking for what she wanted. I wondered if Jonathan and Mike ever saw me shooting love at them with my eyes, or did they see only a litany of requests, complaints, needs. Did they see only me, me, me?

In Emma I saw myself. Saw my selfish ways, my me-centric worldview, my insistence on my own pleasure, my own way. Unlike my other animals, Emma didn't need me; she used me. I still loved her, but I saw that she was limited in her ability to love back. In the pig, I saw, too, my own limitations. I finally recognized what kind of animal I was. The pig and I. What a pair.

Seven

Never eat more than you can lift. —Miss Piggy

WHAT A PIG WON'T EAT

> Parsley
> Onions
> Cilantro

WHAT A PIG WILL EAT

> Everything else (including, but not limited to):
>> Rubber bands
>> Green tea (in bags)
>> Acorns

A Coach leather wallet
Lipstick (Estée Lauder All Day)
Watermelon rinds
Banana peels
Carefully tended flowers planted by grumpy neighbors
Tums (tropical fruit flavored)
Pork

They formed a club. A union, really, they said. The Fraternal Brotherhood of Rachel's Ex-Boyfriends, which they shortened to the REBs. I was the raison d'être, otherwise known as "the Raisin." Over a dinner at the Hovel that would turn out to be the opening, plenary session of this new organization, Mike and Jonathan decided they would come up with bylaws and new membership criteria. All potential future ex-boyfriends would require their approval; merely being an ex-boyfriend would by no means guarantee membership in this elite club. Jonathan wondered if they should use parliamentary procedure. There would be REB meetings once a week over a dose of *Melrose Place* and now *Ally McBeal*, which followed it. I didn't get to vote and could speak only if asked, directly, for my opinion. Sometimes, they threatened, I might not even be invited to meetings. They could get along just fine without me. Though they preferred not to.

After a year of taking premed classes and shadowing Jonathan's colleagues, and another year spent applying, I got into medical school. But, with a shock of recognition, I realized that I no longer wanted to go. I was still interested in thinking about medicine, but I frankly didn't want to practice. And I sure didn't want to incur the kind of debt burden that medical school would lead to. So I decided not to go after all. It wasn't a hard decision. Like the process of marrying Patrick, I loved the idea of applying (asking, accepting, being engaged) but not the reality of the commitment. I didn't want to be a doctor.

Nor did I want to continue in publishing. This was not a surprise, since I had come to this same conclusion almost six years prior, as I prepared to leave New York. I was tired of working on other people's work, of honing other's ideas. I was tired of working, actually. Having gone straight from college to a career, I never took time to play, never just messed around. I wanted to play. If I scrimped and saved, did freelance editing and odds-and-ends kind of work, I calculated that I could take about a year off.

I quit my publishing job once and for all, and was suddenly free. Nothing to do. No real responsibilities. With days at home, I often had the pig at my house. Jonathan worked long and late, and he went out of town on frequent business trips. Hannah, Emma, and I spent our days together. I read all the novels I'd been meaning to read, real books, good books, and a bunch of fun, trashy ones, as well. I read the entire *Raleigh News and Observer* each morning over coffee and then skimmed the *New York Times* on the Web. I went for long runs in the middle of the day in the middle of the week. I sometimes spent a couple of hours having coffee with friends. You'd think, since I had the time, I would have cooked and cleaned. You'd think. But you'd be wrong.

I ran errands for Mike and Jonathan. When Mike finished his dissertation it was not only good, it was prize-winning. He got a high-paying job in the nearby Research Triangle Park developing new laser technologies. He loved his work and spent a ridiculous number of hours in the lab. Jonathan still worked like a madman. So I took their cars in for oil changes. I brought their packages to the post office and picked up their dry cleaning.

Ever since Jonathan and I had first started dating, he'd talked about getting a new car. Five years later, after I went with him for hundreds of miles of test drives, he bought, finally, the exact same black Honda Accord he thought he'd buy five years before when he first started looking. He no longer had to drive with his arm out the window holding the door closed. (His driving, unfortunately, did not improve, but I learned to keep my mouth shut.)

He had also spent years looking for a house. He started looking when we were together, and continued, in fits and starts, for the next half-decade. For someone who was so accepting of my flaws for so long, Jonathan was surprisingly picky when it came to major decisions. None of the homes we looked at were ever quite perfect enough for him.

Until I saw the FOR SALE sign at the end of the gravel road and followed it to a passive solar house in the woods, in a prime location, midway between Durham and Chapel Hill. I told Jonathan that he had to check it out. He resisted. I persisted. When he saw it, he bought it. With a new car and a new house, Jonathan was beginning to have the trappings of a grown-up life.

What we came to call "the Lodge" was set a quarter of a mile back from the road. It had high ceilings and a big green yard. It had an upstairs, a fireplace, and a deck with a hot tub. It had a screened-in porch. Jonathan and Emma moved in.

Just as he was planning to move, one of Jonathan's colleagues put his mother into a nursing home. This colleague then refurnished his home with his mother's fancy antiques and got rid of his nice, fairly new Scandinavian stuff. Jonathan bought all the furniture in one fell swoop and thereby tastefully decorated the Lodge, all creamy white, nubby, natural-fiber fabric, and blond wood. I couldn't get over how grown-up his new place looked, how unlike him.

While Jonathan was at work, I waited at the Lodge and let in the cable guy, the phone guy, the water company guy. I read thick paperback novels in the hot tub and ate the treats that Jonathan stocked for me in his new cabinets. I tossed Dentabones to Hannah and what we called "pig steak"—bunches of broccoli—to Emma while we spent our days playing.

Because he was the proud owner of acres of hardwood floors, Jonathan went on an Oriental rug buying spree, covering much, though by no means all, of the floor. This meant that little pigs had to zig and zag their way through the house, using carpet wherever possible to avoid skidding, sliding, and slipping. Watching Emma navigate Jonathan's home provided me with hours of entertainment. Never had there been a more adorable pig.

Jonathan encouraged Emma to get in touch with her barnyard essence and allowed her to spend time outside. He'd fenced in a portion of the yard that connected to the screened-in porch. But that wasn't enough for his little Oochins. (Jonathan had as many names for Emma as most cultures do for God.) She needed a Pig House. Jonathan enlisted the help of Mike, and engineers both by training and by temperament, they designed a Pig House. Jonathan spent about three hundred dollars on materials at Home Depot, and together they built the world's most glorious piece of porcine furniture.

From the outside, the Pig House looked like a large bench. It had a slanted back, so you could, as a human, recline comfortably while sitting on it. It was basically a long rectangular box. The seat lifted up, but that's not how Emma entered—she went through a doggy door flap into the comfy living space, which was piled high with soft blankets. There was a long, rectangular Plexiglas window so that she could look out. On the far right was the furnace room. The REBs had installed a heater, with a thermostat, and had insulated the whole house so the little darling would never be chilly. It could get hot in there, very hot. For Emma, too hot was just about perfect.

Emma loved the Pig House. You'd enter the Lodge. You'd walk the entire length of the house and then open the door to the porch. You would look out. You would see no pig. You'd call her.

"Emma."

"Mhhhhhhh."

She couldn't help it. She always had to answer.

"Em?"

"Ehhhhhh."

It was a good thing, actually, her inability not to respond. When she'd go out exploring in the lawn, which at Jonathan's house often meant she'd be walking through grass that came well over Emma's head (he wasn't big on lawn-mowing, our boy), you couldn't see her. You didn't know where she was, or if she'd wandered (again) up to the horse barn, an eighth of a mile away, an excursion she loved.

So you called her. She answered. And then you knew where she was. If you needed to reel her in, you used food—or the promise of food—as bait.

You'd stand at the porch, talking to the Pig House, and the Pig House would grunt back at you. Then you'd see that doggy door flap move. Out would bolt the pig. Usually her hair would be a bit disheveled. She would be warm to the touch. She'd shake herself off and come inside.

I loved that making the Pig House had been a labor of love, that Mike and Jonathan had designed, planned, and built it together—a material, physical manifestation of the collaboration of the REBs. While they worked I'd sung "Geek Boys," to the tune of "Bad Boys" (thus revealing my own geekiness). Soon we were all singing. After a while, Jonathan and I told Mike not to sing.

With time on my side, I devoted energy to speculating on what Emma might need, what might make her happy, knowing that the physical fact of her was stretching my knowledge of animal behavior. After yet another incident of Emma wearing my sweaty running shirt around the house for an entire afternoon, it hit me: Emma needed some clothes of her own.

I announced this to Jonathan and Mike, and off we went, the REBs and me, to the fabric store. I'd suggested making her a coat modeled on horse blankets. This made perfect sense to me, since, as a little girl, I'd blanketed a fair number of horses. Jonathan and Mike, however, had no idea how horse blankets worked, fastened, or looked, but from hearing my description, they deemed the construction inadequate for Emma. She needed a tighter fit, Jonathan said. She'll get all tangled in it, Mike said. We came to an agreement: I would pick out the fabric and make aesthetic decisions, but I would leave the design— the engineering of the swine suit—up to the REBs.

We went over to the Hovel, loaded down with supplies: two different kinds of thermal fleece material, Velcro, needles and thread, and a new pair of scissors. We needed to make a prototype first, so Jonathan cut out a beta-version from an old sheet. It took a number of tries and much arguing to get it right.

Jonathan and I argued about how and where it should close, how long it should be, how tight it should fit. Every time we cut out a model, there was something tragically wrong with it: it left her lower half uncovered; it was baggy around her neck (Emma was either all neck or had no neck at all, depending on how you looked at it). Finally Mike took the scissors away from us, harrumphing like a frustrated father, and cut a perfect pattern.

We then used it to cut out the two real versions.

That went fine; since fleece does not fray, there were no hemming issues. We did, however, have to sew on the Velcro fasteners. Here Uncle Mike was undone: the guy didn't know how to sew. A PhD in physics, a knack for cooking, and a first-rate cleaner of bathrooms— he couldn't sew. Jonathan and I sewed, and then there they were: two stylin' polar fleeces for the pig.

One was for everyday wear: it was a textured dark gray, very natural and crunchy granola looking. Would have gone well with a pair of Birkenstocks. The other was to die for. It was the evening fleece. Leopard print. Very glam.

The pig loved wearing her clothes. She began to wear them all the time. She stood uncharacteristically still and uncomplaining while being dressed.

One of the compelling features of the Lodge was that it had, at the far end, a great stone fireplace, in which often lay a great stone fire. There were no logs, just stony loglike things through which the gas-fueled flame flickered. It produced good fire-watching visions and, more important for Emma and me, it produced heat. Especially if you sat right up next to it, which is where we liked to sit.

Jonathan made a nest of brightly colored blankets on the floor directly in front of the fire, and Emma, claiming every physical comfort, would plant herself right there, close to the fire, on top of the mound of blankets. And she'd bask. She'd bake.

The fire was so hot that her long, lustrous black hair would begin to smoke. Jonathan claims it once caught fire, but I never saw any evidence of that.

There was, however, plenty of evidence of heat damage on the little pig: it came in the form of split ends.

Emma didn't have little split ends that gave her body of lustrous hair the appearance of frizziness. Oh no, Emma had big-time split ends. Her hair was so coarse that when it split, each strand was the texture of a normal human hair. Sometimes she even had ends that split into three parts. Now these looked frizzy.

Most mammals groom themselves. A number groom each other. There's a good reason for this: grooming is a calming, bonding kind of activity. Emma was not an autogroomer. She didn't like to be dirty, but once she was, there was nothing for her to do about it. She couldn't reach her mouth around her thick neck to do any meaningful licking, and her hooves were inadequate for fine motor coordination. She did, however, like to be groomed. She loved to be brushed, especially with a stiff boar's-bristle brush that went all the way down to her itchy scaly black skin and brought up gigantic flakes of piggy dandruff. She liked to be picked over during a tick hunt. (The girl was a veritable tick magnet—her soft underbelly was essentially hairless, so it was easy for them to get and stay on board.) And she particularly liked it when I split her ends.

She'd lie there, either in front of the fire, or on the couch, and I'd go through her hair strand by strand, find a tatty end, take the pieces in each hand, and split it. Sometimes I could get them to go inches before one end would break off. Then I'd find another and split away. After a while I had a big pile of ends and a lazy, relaxed, sleeping pig. I drew sustenance from the hypnotic nature of this undertaking. Plus, it was a way for me to feel close to her, to pair-bond.

Jonathan and Mike would catch me in the act: "Are you splitting Emma's ends again?" They realized it was an obsessive behavior on my part. And, sometimes, at Jonathan's, I neglected to clean up the split ends. Now that he had a grown-up house, my formerly slovenly ex-boyfriend, who, let's not forget, shared his bed with a pig, was getting prissy about having clean digs.

"You just never mind."

* * *

The REBs and I, plus Emma and of course Hannah, logged quality hours at the Lodge. Jonathan had a big TV, and a satellite dish. A year or two after we'd broken up, Jonathan had started cooking. Instead of the peanut butter and jelly sandwiches and Frosted Flakes we used to eat for dinner, Jonathan now made Sri Lankan chickpeas, grilled salmon steaks, and sushi. He'd always use the best, freshest ingredients, and always made too much food. During basketball season (when you live a couple of miles away from a school where basketball is a religion, it's hard to resist conversion) we'd all cram into the smallest, darkest room where Jonathan kept the TV, and jam together on the scratchy wool couch (one of the few, original pieces of tatty old furniture he'd been reluctant to part with). Hannah would lie in front of the TV, watching us. Emma, of course, had to be on the couch. Usually she'd jump up and settle on my lap, or Jonathan's. She still avoided Mike.

When she was on my lap, Jonathan would lean over to cuddle with her. He often got in my space, got in my face, and got way, way too close to my boobs. Sometimes as he petted her he elbowed me in a boob. Or accidentally petted my boob along with Emma. It wasn't at all sexual. (Although it probably doesn't need to be said again, those days were long gone.) But I felt invaded, and when I could take it no more, I often found myself screaming: "Stay away from my boobs!"

Not to be overly graphic, but . . . I have enormous breasts. You would not think so, to look at me. But trust me, I'm stacked: small rib cage, humongous honkers. Tits on a toothpick. It's been a bane since high school. Once I went into the extensive lingerie department of Macy's flagship store on Thirty-fourth Street. I told the woman my bra size. She laughed at me. She actually laughed and said, "Why, dear, that's a ridiculous size."

(I know you're curious so I'll tell you. 32D. Yes, Really.)

All my life I've lusted after tiny, frilly bras. I have to wear the old lady kind that usually comes only in black and white and straps you in so you can hardly breathe. It sucks.

"How can I avoid your boobs?" Jonathan would ask. "They're so big."

"Try."

Every time he'd come close, I'd start to fuss.

"Oh no," he'd say. "I'm nearing the breast cylinder."

He decided that there was an invisible cylinder that surrounded my breasts. If he came too close, an alarm went off.

"Just stay away from my boobs."

It was like playing with preschool buddies. There was no sexual tension, just play.

While I often feel like my breasts don't even belong to me, Emma lived so entirely in her body that it was a joy to watch her. My neighbor once said to me that she thought of Emma as a feminist: she went after what she wanted, said my neighbor, and damn it, she got it. She was more of an Emmanist. She was out for Number One.

Aside from catering to me, the REBs also spent a lot of time making fun of me. No one can tease you like an ex-boyfriend, especially when there's another one there to egg him on. They know your foibles; they expect that after you drink your sixth mug of hot chocolate you may fart a little. (And they know that you secretly enjoy bestowing these gaseous gifts because you like to torture them and witness their reactions.) They expect you to be upset after every haircut and wait until you wash your hair yourself before they comment. They try to remember to comment if your hair has been cut. They are not surprised when you refuse to eat an avocado knowing your dislike of slimy foods. When you go to restaurants they understand, and help to convey, your immediate need for a cup of hot water with lemon, even in the summer. They know never to ask you if it's cold outside. They ask your mile splits after a race and applaud, loudly, for anything in the low sevens. They cheer wildly for anything in the sixes.

Jonathan was like a fun, funny version of the pesky younger brother I already had, and Mike was the serious, babysitting elder child. In my unemployed state, they took it on themselves to take care of me. "It takes a village to raise a Rachel," Mike would say.

"The REBs are here to serve and protect," Jonathan would announce, as they came to the Hovel laden with food and stocked the refrigerator and cabinets. They were truly happy, and eager, to serve me—as long as they weren't serving as my boyfriend.

I came home from a quick trip to New York in the summer to find an air conditioner installed in my bedroom window. Given my tendency to always feel cold, I'd insisted that I was fine without one, for years—except for a few nights in the summer when I had to sleep in the bathtub. I didn't want an air conditioner. But I got one, courtesy of the REBs. A new Zip drive to back up my computer appeared mysteriously, as did a laser printer. Mike concentrated on what I needed. Jonathan, on the other hand, thought it was important for me to have a new outfit to wear when I was asked to give a talk. He took me shopping. Jonathan had become interested in clothing, both for me and for himself. He'd come a long way from the man whose every shirt boasted an ink stain.

I won't lie—it was a darned good life. I saw the weariness of career-driven friends, and I basked in my freedom. In my mid-thirties, with no job, no responsibilities, and no money, I needed surprisingly little to live on and was well cared for by my ex-lovers, who collectively showered me with an excess of affection and attention. My only dependents were Hannah and Emma.

In keeping with my childlike reversion to a life of few responsibilities, Hannah, Emma, and I traveled to my mother's home in upstate New York a number of times. We drove the ten hours to visit my mom and George. Jonathan missed Emma's company while she was away, but he also encouraged me to bring her along—he always felt guilty when he left her home alone while he was at work, and he was happy for her to seek adventure. Emma was a good car traveler, though she would often stand for hours on end, her snout nuzzled up against a part of poor, tolerant Hannah's body. Occasionally she would lie down, but mostly she slept standing.

We'd stop at highway rest areas to pee and have some water. It always took a long time: we'd barely be out of the car when our little trio would be stopped by people bored with highway driving and

surprised and ecstatic to see a pig. There'd be the usual questions—
how old is she, what does she eat, where does she poop, and so on. I
tried to keep the rest stops to a minimum.

When we arrived at my mother's home, Emma was delighted to
find that the entire house was carpeted—even the kitchen! What
bliss for a hooved little pig! Not long after we settled in, Emma squat-
ted and peed on that very kitchen carpet.

You can try, but it's hard to stay mad at your grandpig when you're
sitting on the couch watching TV, and she comes over, nudges the edge
of the couch a few times, nudges (hard) your leg, leaps onto the couch
and then, with all sixty pounds of her resting on pointy little hooves,
steps on you and crawls into your lap. My mother forgave the pig for
peeing in the kitchen.

She was less forgiving the next day, when Emma had broken into
a food closet and snacked on crackers, making a huge mess.

I was upstairs when I heard peals of laughter. I came down to find
my mother doubled over giggling and Emma looking frazzled.

"What's going on?"

"She kept breaking into the closet, even after I tied the door shut.
So I used this. . . ."

She held up a small plastic box, a toy meant to look like an old-
fashioned steamer trunk. It was noise activated. When set off, the
box would rattle back and forth, and a little voice would say, "Excuse
me, excuse me, excuse me, would you let me out of here please?"

My mother had set the box against a bread machine on the closet
floor. As soon as Emma neared the door, ready for a jackpot of food,
she couldn't help herself and had to oink. As soon as she oinked, the
box started in: "Excuse me, excuse me, excuse me, would you let me
out of here, please?" and banged repeatedly against the bread machine, making a racket louder even than the pig, who would be
scared off and run away into the living room.

Emma—being, don't forget, pigheaded—would come back later
and try again. And again there would be the voice, the rattling noise,
and the frightened pig bolting into the other room. It was one of those
times when the solution may ultimately have been more irritating

than the original problem. But my mother—and soon George and I—found it hysterical. The pig ate no more crackers.

It had been almost a year since I'd quit my job, and I was still having fun playing. But, as I'd learned when I left Oxford University Press, left Patrick, wanted to leave New York, people often freak out if you say you don't know what you're going to do. They get upset. They want to pin you down. Especially after a year.

"What do you mean you have no idea what you're going to do?" they'd say.

"I don't know," I'd answer. "I'll see what comes up."

It disturbed them.

At first their distress bothered me, made me feel like a slacker. But eventually I realized that this was not about me; their anxiety was not on my behalf, but rather a projection (or so I told myself to make myself feel better). They were troubled because they couldn't picture themselves in my place, and they couldn't help but read themselves into my life. I have never been driven by fear—of the unknown, of financial insecurity, of taking risk; I was, however, ill equipped to deal with boredom. I knew when I quit my job that, eventually, I would tire of having so much freedom, and then I'd figure out what to do next. I wasn't at all scared. But I liked to toy with those who worried on my behalf:

"Maybe I'll go live in Cambodia," I'd say.

"Maybe I'll flip burgers in Stockton."

"Maybe I'll join the Marines."

In fact, I had been offered, for the month of August, a house in California. It wasn't Cambodia, but it would present a nice change from Durham. Jim, a friend, was going out of town and wanted someone to stay in his suburban rancher in an affluent community outside of the funkiness of Santa Cruz. I loved Northern California—I love the differences in culture, the freshness of the food, and the geography, the sunburnt hills of gold, dotted with green shrubbery. Jim rented me his extra car, explained how to adjust the chemicals in the hot tub, and showed me some local running trails. I was set.

The house was about a mile from the ocean. Each morning it was cold and foggy, the sun finally coming out midday. This worked. I'd get up around six, read the *New York Times* via the Internet, and then get to work. I'd taken on various freelance editing jobs, and could do them from wherever I was.

At noon I'd go for a run, usually in the redwood-studded hills. I'd eat some lunch (more cereal), spend the afternoon reading, and then, each night, I'd walk along the beach.

My biggest fear about leaving home had always centered on being away from Hannah. On this trip, though, I didn't have much to worry about—she was safely and happily staying with Mike. It never occurred to me that Emma, three-and-a-half-year-old Emma, the tank girl, the unstoppable force of nature, might get sick.

I hadn't heard much from Jonathan since I'd been in California. While it was unusual, it wasn't particularly worrying. I'd sent him an e-mail or two, left a couple of messages, but he tended to get busy, so I didn't think much of it. I asked Mike if he'd spoken with the other half of the REBs, and he said no, he hadn't heard from him. Finally, after almost a week, I got Jonathan on the phone.

I heard in his voice that something was wrong. Emma had been sluggish. She hadn't been eating.

The world tilted.

Jonathan had been dealing with this alone for a few days, and now I was there with him. He'd taken her to the vet, and it looked like there was a kidney issue. She wasn't peeing.

I got daily—sometimes two or three a day—updates from Jonathan. It wasn't looking good, and he wasn't sounding good. He was driving her back and forth to Raleigh to her vet, staying up all night with her, not going in to work. We were praying for pee. She had started to drink a little, but still, no pee. After we had taken such delight in her prodigious abilities to empty her bladder for many minutes, the pee watch was excruciating. She continued to be sluggish and sleepy, which Jonathan, as a doc, knew was what happened with kidney failure. I was so far away, living in a foreign, suburban house, where I was cold all the time. I was alone. I knew no one in Santa Cruz. Saw no one. My longest conversations were "Thanks very much, you have a nice day, too." I could no longer concentrate on the books I'd been reading—all I could think about was Emma. I felt terrified, and trapped.

I had been training for several months for a trail race up Mount Hood, in Oregon, and despite my Emma-related anxiety, I decided to go as planned. I met up with a group of friends from home who had traveled across the country to run, and I shared a hotel room with my buddy Ralph. In the middle of the night, I heard my cell phone ring. I had given the number to only a few people. I didn't answer it.

The race began before dawn the next morning. I was fueled by anxiety and went out fast until I reached the turnaround point halfway up the mountain; then I began to slow. On the way back down, I started to think. I thought about the late-night phone call. I thought about the fact that Emma still hadn't peed, that it had been almost a week. Jonathan had called the vet school; he'd talked to nephrologists he knew at Duke, to find out if she could go on dialysis. There was no dialysis for pigs. Her kidneys weren't working, and there was nothing to be done.

Toward the end of the race, I began to suffer. It wasn't so much that my body hurt, but that place in my heart, that same broken place, was throbbing, aching. Several women passed me before I got to the finish line, but I didn't care.

There was no way that I could tell the guys I was with that I was worried about the pet pig that I coparented with my ex-boyfriend. Mine wasn't a world that they could comprehend, and I didn't want to take the predictable jokes that would come.

When I got back to California later that day, I called Jonathan. I knew the minute he answered the phone. He could barely speak, and I broke down in tears. Still a doctor, he told me what had happened, that they had been able to keep her comfortable, peaceful. The idea of the spoiled-rotten-little-pig being peaceful, the twirling dervish, the heat-seeking missile lying quietly, broke my heart. We stayed on the phone, listening to each other cry.

Dylan Thomas came to mind: It's not that after the first death there is no other. It's that after the first death, each death brings back every other.

Eight

I don't even like old cars . . . I'd rather have a goddam horse.
A horse is at least human, for God's sake.

—J. D. Salinger

Having known only one pig, I didn't know how much of Emma's pushy little self was pig, and how much was personality. Was she representative of her species, or did we raise her to be a porcine tyrant? Nature or nurture? Did nosology even matter? She was who she was. We loved her both for and despite her narcissism. But it did make me wonder, How do we become the little piggies we are? Jonathan the shrink said that it was sometimes hard to draw a line between mental illness and personality, that one sometimes ran into the other.

Thinking about Emma, and at the same time mentally shuffling through the deck of my failed relationships, I couldn't help but reflect on my own pathological tendencies.

Growing up a skinny little girl, with a controlling, demanding father, I wanted throughout my childhood what any reasonable person would want: to control others. Why a sense of impuissance would lead to a desire to dominate, rather than merely to be left alone, isn't entirely clear to me, but it worked for Napoléon. And as a little girl, it worked for me, though I suppose my conquests—taunting poor Bobby Jones down the street, learning to shoot a BB gun—were slightly more modest.

Girls and horses. Perhaps it's about power. Perhaps it's about fearlessness. There are some who say that it has to do with unacknowledged, inchoate preadolescent female sexuality. Whatever it is, it is a thing. How obviously compelling is the notion of controlling a half-ton beast when you are a small girl child, when you have no real power in the world?

Of course, I didn't think about it that way when I was a little girl. I just wanted a horse. I began wanting one when I was about five, and my desire for equine companionship grew exponentially with each passing year. My room was filled with horse pictures, both hand-drawn and purchased. My head was filled with fantasies of galloping away. I knew all the breeds, could name the parts of horse, bridle, and saddle. But, there was no money for a horse. And I only rarely got to ride.

For my father, the best part of being a college professor (other than getting to call himself "Doctor") was having summers off. Unlike the authors whose books I had published, my father's nonteaching time was not spent doing academic work; he was a teacher, not a scholar. My parents managed to buy a rustic one-room cabin at the foot of a small mountain in an unglamorous part of Maine to which my family—two parents, two kids, one dog, two cats, a rabbit, and my brother's pet mouse—decamped each summer.

My father would spend the hot months building additions onto the house, fishing, and working on a novel that would never be published.

My beautiful and artistic mother did beautiful and artistic things—painting, spinning and dying yarn, weaving. My brother rode bikes, and later motorcycles, with the farm boys up the dirt road. I read great piles of books.

Until, for one month in my twelfth summer, my parents got me what I'd always wished for: a horse.

Not exactly a horse, but a pony, and mine only for one leased month; but still, it was a wish come true, a fantasy made horse-flesh.

My father constructed a makeshift corral in the backyard out of thin alder branches he'd cut with a handsaw. I prepared by daydreaming and anticipating, waiting the days that seemed like months for my steed to be delivered. Nothing more exciting had ever happened to anyone in the history of the world: I was finally going to have a horse.

When the truck came and the owner backed him out of the trailer, I tried not to be disappointed. I tried to see in him all the pictures of all the horses that were imprinted on my brain. I tried not to see what was really there: a skinny, flea-bitten gray nag, with high bony withers, a swayback, and a tangle of mane and tail.

"Oooooh," I cooed. "He's beautiful."

Okay, so he wasn't the perfect physical specimen. It didn't matter, really. He was a horse, sort of. He was mine, briefly. I would be able to ride. I mean, the whole point of horses is that you can ride them, right? The owner gave me a quick lesson on how to assemble the tack—which straps of the bridle went where, how to knot the girth—and then he took off, leaving me with my mount, saddled, and ready to go.

Pepper had stood politely at attention in the presence of his owner, a gruff, overall-wearing horse-trader who said *ain't* a lot and told my father, "If he acts up, smack him upside the head."

As soon as the owner drove off, Pepper put his head down and began to use his long teeth to pull chunks of grass out of the lawn.

I managed to bring his head up after begging, pleading, and tugging on the reins. I held the reins and the saddle horn in one hand, held the stirrup still with the other, gracefully lifted my leg into the stirrup and swung my other leg around. I had studied horse and riding books the way other kids devoured comic books. I sat, shoulders back, tall and straight, on my summer horse.

I gave him a squeeze with my legs.

Pepper continued to stand, statue-still.

Nothing.

I clucked to him and said, with more authority than you could imagine coming from a skinny twelve-year-old girl, "Walk on, Pepper."

A poke with my heels.

He shifted his weight and seemed to sigh.

My father grabbed hold of the reins and pulled him. He yelled at him. He smacked him on the shoulder, and then the butt.

Nope.

Finally, in his own glacial time frame, Pepper moved. He took a couple of steps and then, in what seemed like gentle slow motion from my vantage on his back, he collapsed to the ground, a stubborn pile of pony. I got off, he got up. I got back on, down he went.

It wasn't supposed to be like this. The whole thing was that I was supposed to be able to tell him what to do, and he was supposed to do it. That he didn't comply seemed an unnatural turn in the natural order of things. I was furious. I was frustrated. I was impotent.

When we weren't engaged in the daily power struggle, when Pepper wasn't saddled and I wasn't trying to ride him, things were great. I'd call to him in the corral, and he'd come right over, nosing me to see if I had a carrot, which I usually did.

I brushed his dirty coat until he shone. He would lower his head to me so I could reach around his ears. He positioned himself so that I could brush the places he wanted brushed—the spot just above the tail, the channel under his chin. He was training me.

I tried to teach him to count. I could get him to raise his leg and paw the ground, but we never got the math part right. He'd do a number of hoof strikes, triggerlike, and then he'd get bored and begin to graze.

He wanted to come into the house. I knew this. I could see it in his eyes, in the way he looked into the windows at night from his corral, the way he watched me when I went inside to get him a treat. Two wide, low stone steps led into the kitchen. One uneventful afternoon, Pepper followed me up the steps, encouraged by a carrot and curiosity. With each backwards step I took, farther and farther into the house he came. I thought this was thrilling, and hysterical. I giggled giddily, and whispered for Pepper to follow. He did. Then we ran into my mother. For some reason, she didn't think he needed to come in. Even though he clearly wanted to.

Pepper, like many ponies, was smart and stubborn. As long as I didn't try to ride him, we got along swimmingly. At the end of the month, I was sorry to see him go. He had become more handsome in the time we'd spent together. I'd grown accustomed to his long face, liked the line of his swayback, even grudgingly appreciated his indomitable spirit. Spending time with Pepper did little for my need to exercise control; but by taking him on his own terms, I was able to understand and appreciate his personality and came to understand his, well, his humanness. But it would have been nice to be able to ride.

The next summer my father found another horse trader, who promised horses that were well trained. They were. From then on, each summer, for the entire summer, my parents rented me a horse: big, strong, and tractable. Horses who did exactly as I asked: willing to go, resigned to being ridden.

As it has been throughout history, the horse was a tool of liberation. While I still spent my nights curled around a book, each day I'd saddle up and ride. I'd ride away from my family, away from my beautiful, tractable mother, and far, far away from my father, away from his criticisms and demands and expectations. I came to know the Maine countryside like a well-loved poem.

Each summer I understood more and more about the way horses think: that the same rock they have walked uneventfully by 325 times may, on the 326th pass, become inexplicably terrifying. I experienced the different personalities of different horses, and I recognized the truth behind the stereotyping of breeds—the high-strung Arabs, the stolid quarterhorses. The difference between horses and ponies was more than one of size. Horses offered more promise, more potential. After Pepper, I never again wanted a pony.

I learned to be comfortable alone; I grew accustomed to talking to someone who never talked back. I learned to find solace in my own thoughts, mesmerized by the creak of leather and the clop clop clop clop of the four-beat walk.

I pushed my own limits of fear. If I could get the horse to clear a jump, I raised the bar. I rode bareback, relying on balance and natural athleticism to stay aboard.

I grew to be unintimidated by size or strength. I began to trust the size and strength of my own volition.

Although I spent my childhood maintaining that I loved horses, I now suspect it may have been the idea of the horse, the Platonic equine form that I loved, not the individual critters. I grew attached to each of my summer mounts, but what I loved is that I could make them do what I wanted them to do. Horses were vehicles for my will. Having these huge creatures obey me when nothing else in the world was within my control was like scratching an itch until it bled.

Looking back, though, of all the horses I had over those summers, the only one who sticks with me is Pepper—his uncompromising personality, his quirky ways, his uncharacteristic sense of equine self, his refusal to do as expected. And the fact that he really did want to come in the house, that he had unexpected desires. His unwillingness to accept his lot as beast of burden gave him an integrity that the bigger, better-mannered horses lacked. I did so love to ride, though. I loved moving as one with a horse, becoming a powerful young girl centaur.

Then, as many horse-crazy girls had done before me, after years of loving all things equine, of thrilling to the ability to bend a half-ton animal to the strong will of a small person, I turned my attention—and my desire for control—finally and absorbingly, to boys.

* * *

My infatuation with horses never went away, though, more like into remission.

The scent of saddle leather mixed with the sweet smell of horse sweat can transport me more readily than Proust's muffin.

Decades later, living in North Carolina, I had friends with a farm and too many horses. I'd not ridden since my teenage years, but I'd never lost the desire. Now I had, once again, my childhood fantasy, what amounted to my own mount: complete access to and no real responsibility for a small gray Arabian.

Weasel, in his younger days, had been an endurance guy, competing in long races on the trail. He was a bit past prime, but not so long in the tooth to have lost his edge. He could still compete and liked to. His coat was a flea-bitten gray, the same color as that stubborn old fleabag, Pepper. But his long mane and tail were gorgeous white; when he moved, he held his tail aloft in the characteristic manner of his breed. His face was slightly dished; he had exquisite, small, well-formed ears.

Horses are sticklers for hierarchy. This makes them easy to train. They want to know who's boss and to know their place in the pecking order. Once you establish yourself as the one who tells them what to do, they expect and want you to do just that. It reassures them that all is right in the world. It gives them comfort.

It was a change to be around Weasel after the noisy demands and incessant complaints of the porcine princess; after years of intelligent yet absolute and unqualified devotion from Hannah. Weasel was a horse of a different color. His personality was muted. His needs and affection were more equivocal. He was not warm and cuddly, not someone you'd necessarily invite into the kitchen. My relationship with him was more mechanistic, less joyous.

When I walked into the pasture to get him, halter in hand, and called out, he'd stop eating, raise his head, and prick his elegant ears toward me. He'd wait. He'd wait until I got within a few steps of him. Before I could reach out, he'd trot away. I'd walk after him, and he'd continue to trot, stopping occasionally to look back at me, making sure I was still giving chase. As soon as I got near again, away he went. Finally he gave up and stood still. Sometimes when I neared he'd drop his head so I could slip the halter over it. Sometimes he'd take advantage of the differential in our heights and would raise his head, keeping himself just out of reach. Weasel could be a real ass-hole. If I scolded him verbally, he'd shape up.

Once the halter was on, the lead rope snapped to it, he was trans-formed. He gave himself to me. He followed at a respectful distance. When I slowed, he slowed. I could gesture to him with my hands if I wanted him to move away, and he would, without hesitation, with-out question. It was as if once I'd caught him, he forfeited his sense of self to become one with me.

This only increased when he had a saddle on his back, a bit in his mouth. It took almost nothing for me to ask him to move from a walk to a trot, a trot to a canter. I could ask him (you ask horses, you don't tell them) when we were trotting along the trail to move into a different gait simply by whispering, "Canter, Wease?" I could shift, slightly, almost imperceptibly, the balance of my body weight in the seat of the saddle, and he would slow.

Often I rode him without saddle or bridle, just jumped on his back and controlled him with my voice and weight. Once caught, once he'd realized that I was going to ride him, he was willing to give in. He wanted me to be the one to think for both of us.

Real horse people work on developing a subtle and complex sys-tem of communication with—and control over—their horse. There's constant contact, constant demands. You do something over and over until you get it right. "You" in this case is a unit consisting of person and horse.

I had returned from my less-than-relaxing trip to California, and I was still mourning the recent loss of Emma. I had already read all the books on the list I'd made when I quit my job. I'd rented all the movies I'd wanted to see. I began to spend more time on horseback, taking Weasel into the trails of the Duke forest, leaving the imprints of his fine small hooves on the rich red clay of the Carolina Piedmont. Time on the trail gave me time to think. Would the painful lessons learned from my breakups with Jonathan and Mike sink in enough for me to be able to think differently, to be different? Would I be able to change? Why is the struggle for control so paramount in romantic relationships—does ceding it mean that you will be conquered? What would happen if I gave up a little, loosened a bit? So often it seems that one person in a couple has the upper hand. Could there be a relationship of equals, is it possible to find intimacy and a balance of power? Is it precisely this balance that makes intimacy possible?

I'd been worrying the frayed connections between how I interacted with men and my strained relationship with my father. Riding again made me think about him, made me think about my childhood.

My father's love was conditional. It rested on two pillars: performance and obedience.

My father's field was Shakespeare. He sprinkled quotations into daily conversations. Whenever I answered a question with "nothing," he always responded in the same way, like Lear: "Nothing will come of nothing. Speak again."

Eventually I refused to speak.

A victorious high-jumper will always finish with failure. Each time she clears the bar, it is raised. Even if she beats everyone else, she still wants to beat her best. Even if she beats her best, she keeps trying to improve until she fails. I have never wanted to compete in such an event. It's how I grew up.

In the years after I left home, I internalized the expectations and demands that were put on me and extended them, ungenerously, to others. But I was beginning to realize that, in order to be satisfied in my relationships, I first had to be satisfied with myself.

I was my father's child, but I didn't want to be him. I could choose not to be him: I could see the value of being kind over being right. I'd proved my ability to be successful; I could afford to be generous to others. My relationship troubles would be doomed to repetition if I continued to overdetermine and undermine them. I knew that I had plenty of my own irritating habits and quirks, and that I should be able to put up with those of others. I'd asserted my independence; I didn't have to scream it from the rooftops every moment of every day. I was weary. Maybe, I thought, it was time to let someone else take the reins.

I knew, too, that it was time to grow up. I couldn't rely on my exboyfriends to support me indefinitely. My year of play was ending. I needed money. I needed to get a life.

I got a gig teaching MCAT and SAT prep courses at a local tutoring center. I discovered that I loved teaching, loved the kids; I found it natural and easy to mentor them. Helping them helped me to be more patient; it helped me to be more empathetic. But it wasn't full-time work, and I needed to keep Hannah in her fancy dog chow. I talked to friends within the university, asking for suggestions about jobs that might be fun, might be easy, and might be—important in my unemployed and increasingly destitute state—easy to get.

More than one person suggested working in undergraduate admissions. It made sense: I liked teenagers. I am an enthusiastic public speaker. (Presenting books in front of large groups was always a favorite part of my job in publishing.) And, with twelve years' experience making yes-or-no judgments on seven-hundred-page scholarly manuscripts, it seemed to me that reading college applications would be a snap.

I also knew that such a job would meet my number one criterion for right now: it would be easy to get. No one grows up wanting to be a college admissions officer, and the jobs turn over more quickly than rotisserie chickens.

I met with the director of admissions in his office. He looked at my résumé and asked if I realized that the only available jobs were entry-level.

I did.

There were some hoops to jump through, would I mind going through the process? I'd have to give a short talk to the staff, have to meet with a variety of staff members.

Sounded like fun.

He looked down at my résumé again.

Was I really willing to take an entry-level position?

You bet.

I would have a tiny office.

Fine.

I was trying to give up some of my more Emma-like qualities. I wanted to be easier, less aggressive. I didn't care so much about having a career.

I did care that the women in my new office wore suits—not only pantsuits, but full-out skirt suits with stiff blouses and pearls underneath. It was practically the end of the century. Who wore suits anymore? Women in college admissions, it turned out. It would be a change from when I'd spent my days running around in running shorts and sneakers, or when I was a blue-jeans-clad editor of scholarly books.

I was looking forward to having a fun job and then leaving work at work, getting home well before bedtime and having my identity come from who I was, not what I did.

Just as I was changing my attitude toward work, I decided that I was ready to try again with men. I loved my time with the REBs, but it was time to grow up, to get a real boyfriend. The only problem was, there were no men to be found. Durham's not Manhattan—you can't just head over to the local bar and hope to pick up a cute guy. Especially when you're in your thirties.

I complained about this over dinner with Jonathan and Mike. When Jonathan asked what I wanted for my birthday, I said, "A date."

They thought I was making a joke. They chuckled.

"It's not funny," I said. "I want to go out on a date."

The REBs offered to buy me one.

They decided to put a personal ad in our local, progressive weekly paper. They refused to show it to me before publication, knowing me and my editorial tendencies all too well.

When it came out, I was both embarrassed and inundated with

prospective suitors. Whatever the REBs wrote about me, it was apparently what the men of Durham wanted to hear.

Mike and Jonathan pleaded with me to be open-minded. I was, unfortunately, still me, and crossed scads of prospective suitors off the list—too old, too young, too short, too fat. I was trying to be less critical. I was failing.

One sounded like he might be okay; he sounded even better when we spoke on the phone. We had an easy rapport from the get-go, had many things in common, and appreciated each other's quickness and wit. Our conversation reared and galloped, until it stopped short when we figured out that we already knew each other. Not well, but well enough to know that we did not like each other.

He had used a fake name. He had described himself as a writer, rather than an academic. He had lied about his age and, perhaps, his level of fitness. We had worked together—or had tried to, briefly.

As university press editors, my colleagues and I often enlisted the help and advice of faculty members. Generally they were happy to give it, as generous with their time as they were with their opinions. I loved these academics, valued them for their sharpness and breadth of knowledge. I was able to forgive all manner of social flaws, to sift through the dross to get to the gold. I fawned over them, idealized them.

All except one.

I'd asked him for some advice and, after reluctantly agreeing, he'd blown into my office forty minutes late—straight from a tennis game—for the meeting we'd set up. He was rude, abrupt, and dismissive, and frankly, he stank. We'd had a short, tense conversation. He'd misunderstood what I'd asked him and then got angry with me for not being clear. He'd left in a huff. He was, I thought, a sour, arrogant, narcissistic, self-important little fuck. That he didn't like me, didn't respond to me the way other academics did, pissed me off.

And now he was on the other end of the phone.

We hung up quickly.

* * *

The next day, I took Weasel out for a trail ride. I offered to give him his head, but he stopped. He wanted me to direct him. I wished I knew better what he wanted, wished that he could express his own horsey needs and desires. On the trail I thought about Jonathan, about how when I first met him, there were so many things wrong with him, things I felt needed correction, and how over time, those initial failings were replaced not only by the trivial things I found annoying (because I was a demanding, hypercritical, controlling bitch) but by other traits that now I could not live without. I thought about Mike, about how he always allowed me to take the lead, and how that led me down the path to having no boyfriend. Perhaps my initial reactions to men were too harsh; perhaps I did need to be more open-minded, less demanding, less controlling.

I e-mailed the personal ad guy and asked if we could try a do-over. He called me back in response. There was a certain wackiness to the situation, he had to admit, to the idea of the two of us going out on a date.

So, I asked him. Would you like to go out with me?

At first he was wary.

I asked again.

He said okay.

Over drinks, we were able to recapture the rapport from the phone and managed to forget about our earlier, rancorous business encounter.

He had a mane of white hair and an aloof manner. Like Weasel, he was a bit past prime, but not so long in the tooth as to have lost his edge. Since I'd last seen him, he'd lost about fifty pounds and a wife. Their split was bitter, and he was left with resentment and a daughter. His wit was quick, mordant. He leaned back when he spoke. I leaned in. We drank a little and talked a lot. We knew many of the same people and gossiped, agreeing more often than not. He was far more handsome than I had remembered, his eyes the color of Swiss lakes. I could swim laps in those lakes, I thought.

For the past decade, he'd been working on his second book. His first, which I knew of but had not read, had been a groundbreaking success. It had won all the major awards in his field, had been widely reviewed, and had catapulted him to academic stardom. His next book was almost finished. What I'd taken for arrogance was, I now saw, the confidence of someone who had achieved early success.

He asked about me. I related, with the humor of discomfort, my downwardly mobile spiral from scholarly publishing to getting into medical school but deciding not to go, to my current position in undergraduate admissions. I like it, I told him, because, as it turns out, I love teenagers. He had a teenager of his own at home, he said. He said he thought I'd like her. It seemed that maybe he did like me after all.

I'm smitten, I'd told my friends. This was the kind of man I should be with. I could get serious about this guy. He was smart and successful and confident. He had been around enough blocks. He was who he was.

And, come on, you can't beat the story: Girl meets Boy. Girl hates Boy. Girl's old boys make it possible for Girl to re-meet Boy— and, well, you know how it ends. After our first date, I told the story in a long mass e-mail to friends. The more romantic of them wrote back with a variety of fairy tale–like endings to my story. The more cynical told me to watch out, to make sure I wasn't just attracted to him because of the drama, the tension, surrounding our courtship. After all, when I was in the Girl hates Boy part of the narrative, I did mention that Girl used to think Boy was a sour, arrogant, narcissistic, self-important little fuck.

I sent a copy of the e-mail to him. He said he found it delightful. The only qualifier in the string of adjectives I applied to him to which he could reasonably object was *little*. He signed his e-mail SANSILF (Sour, Arrogant, Narcissistic, Self-Important Little Fuck). Made my heart go pitter-pat.

Our second date was ending. We were walking outside to the parking lot, getting out the keys, getting ready to go to our separate cars. I was chattering away, fast.

"You're talking a lot, but you're not saying anything."
He was right.
"You're nervous."
He was right.
"May I kiss you?"
He did.
It was right.

Resolved: I would be different. Even if he was not perfect, I would be.

I'd get all giddy and giggly and girly thinking about him. He was a grown-up, a real, what? A man. He was not a boy, not a guy. He was a man. He was self-assured, self-contained. He was smart, and funny, and interesting, and, yes, handsome, and he was interested in me. With joy I told Jonathan and Mike about him, about how smart he was, how fabulous and successful and—did I mention?—handsome. Jonathan asked if there'd been any dooker grabbing yet.

"Hey," I said, "don't joke. This could be It."

"It? Are we playing a game of tag?"

"Arrrgggh."

"Before you decide about It," Jonathan said, "I'd grab the dooker."

When he'd call me at work, when his number would pop up on my desk phone, I'd answer with the delicious anticipation of a teenager. It was, more than anything, the Silver Fox's maturity and confidence that made me think that perhaps this, this could be It.

We began to date. When we'd go out to dinner I'd listen to him, rapt. He was an accomplished scholar. He'd speak fluently, with confidence. When the Silver Fox talked, he was controlled, calm. His face was always flushed, but he moved little, only infrequently running his hands through his paper-white hair.

He was seldom wrong, never in doubt. He'd assert. His questions were often rhetorical; he knew the answers. He knew he knew, and I did not question him, even when I suspected that he was not correct. I loved his confidence and self-assurance. I did not want to make my old mistakes of being overly critical and demanding. I paid attention to him.

When I spoke, he didn't look at me. He'd look at the table. At his drink. At the painting to the left of my head.

I found myself speaking less, wondering if I was boring him, a fly-size trespasser on his enormous mental field.

But he'd call me many times a day at work.

Sometimes I was too busy to talk, but I'd talk to him anyway. Or, I'd listen.

I did not call him in the mornings when I knew he was writing. I was trying to be respectful, mindful of boundaries.

I'd ask about his work, and he'd tell me. He rarely asked about mine. I didn't volunteer. I figured that if he wanted to know, he'd ask. When he didn't ask, I said nothing. I was becoming less interested in myself, in my own work. I was becoming less interesting.

The Silver Fox was frequently late, rarely noticing. I made sure I had a book with me when I went to meet him. When he'd finally show up, I'd say nothing—I had learned. The first time he left me waiting, for twenty minutes, I looked at him, looked at my watch, and cocked my head. It made him angry, and he lectured me on why his time was more important than mine. I tried not to get upset with him for this. I must learn patience, he told me. I need to learn patience, I told myself.

I'd rush to be on time for him.

In groups he'd hang back at first, watching silently until the conversation turned, or was turned, to him. Then he'd step up and take it, take the reins and go. He was used to teaching, to professing. With the right prompt, he would, for minutes on end.

I brought him to a gathering of prospective students I was hosting. I introduced him to a few and then went off to do something else. When I returned, I heard laughter and saw only backs: I had to break into the tight circle they had formed around him. He was charming and delightful.

I brought him to the annual banquet of my running club, and he sat among engineers and doctors and investment bankers and techies and charmed them all. He was quick with a quip, though sometimes there was an edge—especially around other men.

I told him about the REBs, told him how a club had been formed by my ex-boyfriends. The Silver Fox said it sounded like a wonderful club that he hoped never to join. So witty! So romantic! He had dinner with us. The Silver Fox talked about Jonathan's work—though his experience with psychiatry had been only on the receiving end—and Jonathan listened politely, never contradicting, though I knew that some of what the Silver Fox was saying was incorrect. I also listened to the Silver Fox, and spoke infrequently. Mike, as usual, was mostly quiet. After the dinner I polled the boys, asking what they thought. Jonathan was curiously reticent, though he did express surprise at my uncharacteristic silence. Mike was more forthcoming and more protective: "I don't like him, and I don't think he gets you."

I was crazy about him. I called him Sweet Pea and while away on a business trip, found a mug with a nineteenth-century drawing of a sweet pea on it. I brought it to him, offered it up like a cat with a mouse. He took it with a chuckle and patted me on the head.

We were lying in his bed, talking.
"Tell me about your father," he said in the dark, out of the blue.
"My father is not a nice person."
"Tell me about him," he said.
"I don't like to talk about him."
"Tell me," he prodded.
Because he asked, because I was trying to be open, I told this successful academic, who went only to the fanciest schools, had taught only at the best places in the country, about my father, an unpublished foot soldier in the scholarly army who spent his career teaching students for whom he had mostly contempt.

I don't like to talk about my father.

I've always longed for the comfort of taxonomy, for a clear and simple explanation, the ability to say that he was a bad father because he—what? Drank? Left? Hit me? Sexually abused me? He didn't, and I'm grateful for that. All he did was be himself, angry and frustrated and third-rate and bitter. Like King Lear, he was "a foolish fond old man."

When I got to college, I began to break away. I shook off the yoke of his control. I quit the circus animal act, stopped jumping through the hoops he put in my path.

When I no longer met my father's necessary conditions for love—performance and obedience—he banished me.

I do not speak to my father; I haven't seen him in years.

The Silver Fox wanted me to meet his thirteen-year-old daughter. I was reluctant. Having only recently discovered that I fit in comfortably with college-aged people, I didn't know if I knew how to talk to someone five years younger; I didn't know what to expect.

Didn't matter.

Kate was sharp and funny. We sat on the couch looking at catalogs and reading to each other from *Jane* and *Seventeen*, agreeing that getting jiggy with Will Smith might not be such a bad thing, while the Silver Fox cooked dinner, trying with limited success to break into our conversations.

My anxiety about meeting Kate had been compounded by what I knew. She'd been a chubby kid, the Silver Fox said. He'd pointed this out to her and suggested she start to watch her weight.

She watched it all right.

All the way to the hospital.

We women are met everywhere we turn with images of how we are supposed to be, act, and especially, look. We encounter the expectations of men and internalize them. The first men, our fathers, can utter one sentence that will stop us from eating; if we give them the power, and we do, we good girls, we overachieving aiming-to-please girls, they can send us down the path to self-abnegation and intentional inanition. When we are vulnerable to feeling out of control, that which we can control—our bodies, our own fragile selves—we do. In punishing and terrifying ways. For the rest of our lives.

It's not like drugs or alcohol, where you can simply abstain. You can't give up food. The disease goes into remission, rather than responds to a cure. For me, the only major flare-up was in college. Since then, I've been able to keep the demons away. Leaving the daily mealtime company of others with disordered eating helps. So does living with men. I made a conditional peace with my body. If I started to gain weight, I'd cut back on sweets. My Achilles heel is made of chocolate.

Once I started running, I began, for the first time, to think of my body as me, rather than something other, something to be vanquished. I learned, viscerally, physically, that you have to be strong to be fast, that you have to fuel yourself in order to run. I didn't worry about my weight and instead marveled at how my body reshaped itself. Now I am lean and strong—thin and muscular rather than thin and weak. When I am training, I am hungry all the time, so I eat. But I will never not think about my weight. I hate the truth: that a pound of flesh can make such a difference.

Hearing about Kate's battle brought me back. It is not just a fall into sexuality that marks the end of childhood innocence; for women, we fall into a consciousness of the power of and around food.

The tree of knowledge bears fruit that has calories.

The Silver Fox didn't go easy on his young daughter. Though he no longer commented on her eating or her body, he rode her hard on everything else. I saw Kate working to please him, wanting to do the right things in the right way. I saw the way she saw him: how she felt powerless to question him, how she believed he so clearly knew. Knew everything.

I watched Kate trying to clear the ever-rising hurdles.

* * *

She came home one night while we were eating dinner.

Before she even took off her coat, she planted a noisy kiss on the Silver Fox's head and waved—one of those cute frenetic girl waves—to me.

"Did you get your English paper back?" he asked.

"I have to tell you the most awesome thing that happened," she blurted out, bursting.

"What about the English paper?"

"No, listen to this: I got voted the—"

He stopped her with a raised hand, palm out, and a look. "Kate. Tell me about the English paper."

She looked away.

Her whole body went quiet.

She walked to the front door, where she'd dropped her heavy backpack. We could hear her shuffling through it.

She came back to the table, slowly, head down. I could see dull lines of mascara mapping her face.

"I'm sorry," she said, placing the paper on the table and running from the room.

He turned to the last page.

She'd gotten a B+.

The Silver Fox talked about the future. He told me that it was likely he was going to be offered another job, at another university.

"It's in a place you'd like to live," he said.

I wondered how he knew what I'd like. I wasn't even sure myself.

He seemed so certain about what I should and should not do. It was right, he said, that I hadn't gone to medical school. He was the son of a doctor, so I wasn't surprised that he was anti-medicine. But he thought my low-level university position was beneath me; I should be doing something that required me to engage more of my brain.

I agreed, but I didn't know what it should be. I was using this time to do some soul-searching, I told him. To figure out what it really was that I wanted. And, I pointed out, it was fun to have a fun job.

He said I wasn't pushing myself hard enough, and challenged me to think harder about what I wanted to do. It mattered less where I did it, he said. Certainly I wasn't so committed to my silly job that I wouldn't consider moving to be with him. Right?

There had yet to be a job offer, I reminded him.

I began to consider.

The thought of pulling up stakes to follow, not having to decide where to live or what to do, is undeniably attractive. It's not unlike the hospital fantasy that has haunted me at various, overwhelmed times in my life.

This is how it goes:

You have to be hospitalized. For something silly, and not painful, not embarrassing. A leg broken while skiing, say. In the fantasy, you get to lie around in bed all day, reading beach novels and tabloid magazines, watching daytime TV, having your meals brought to you and being occasionally visited—at just the right moments—by friends bearing gifts and candy. Lots and lots of candy. You are not expected to work. You don't have to get dressed or even take a shower. Someone else washes your hair. You don't have to make any decisions. You are cared for around the clock, retreating from the slings and arrows of daily life.

Or, there's the truck driver version: someone tells you where you need to go and all you have to do is go. You have maps to show you the way, truck stops to refuel yourself and your big vehicle. You can pass the hours listening to the radio, or not. Talking on your CB, or not. Thinking, or not.

Medical school was, for me, a more serious enactment of this same fantasy of giving up agency, of being stripped of having to make hard choices and decisions. It had seemed like a clear and direct course to follow with a clear and obvious endpoint.

Being a trailing spouse might be like that. Following the Silver Fox to another place, not having to decide when and where and how and why. Maybe I could just be a follower.

* * *

I ran my first marathon.

Not as quickly as I would have liked, but fast enough to qualify for Boston, the holy grail of 26.2-milers. I had discovered, to my surprise, that I was a good runner. I loved the discipline of training and exploited the joys of being in a physical body. Sometimes I thought of Prudence, running madly on her wheel. Now I got it.

Breathless from the exertion and excitement of the race, I tried to call the Silver Fox, but he was neither at home nor in his office.

I phoned Jonathan, the person who had started me running. He whooped and hollered and let me read him my mile split times from my watch, cheering for each segment faster than eight minutes and offering excited suggestions—That must have been a hill! You probably walked through a water stop, then!—for mile times that were less impressive.

I called Mike, who congratulated me and said he knew how important it was to me. All the training had paid off, he said.

I finally reached the Silver Fox. He told me about his class, his work, Kate.

"I ran the marathon today, remember?" I finally broke in to relay my news.

"Did you win?"

Any sense of accomplishment was blotted out by those three little words.

The fact that I had run what most people would consider a long distance, that I had enjoyed every single mile and felt strong and proud and powerful, that I was first in my age group—meaningless against his statement, an edgy and rhetorical question, posed to put me in my place.

I said nothing.

We were lying in bed. I was drifting in his arms.

"You know what I wonder?" the Silver Fox said, in that soft talking-in-the-dark voice that made me quiver.

"Hmmmm?" It was warm under the covers, his hands were on me; it was good.

"How someone who runs so much can still have such a mushy ass."

I sat up. I hadn't heard him correctly, surely.

"Well, I mean, it's not fat, your ass, but it's, well, mushy."

I thought of his daughter, of her life-threatening eating disorder, of the Silver Fox's complicity in telling her that she needed to lose weight, his ignition of what I knew would be for her a lifelong struggle, a fiery tempest of self-hatred. I wondered if she would be okay: a controlling and demanding father and a self-imposed will to excel. Would she turn out all right? Had I?

I thought of many women I know—smart, confident, successful women, who, in the presence of their male partner are transformed to unrecognizable docility like a well-trained horse resigned to being ridden. I recognize a look behind their eyes, a place they go that takes them from the dinner table to somewhere inaccessible. I grew up seeing this look. I would ask my mother a question and, if my father was around, I'd have to ask twice, or three times, before she'd start and say, "What? Sorry." She wasn't there. It was easier to check out than it was to interact. She'd ceded the reins long ago. I swore I would never do this. And then I did it with Vince. A mistake I thought I'd learned from, a mistake I thought I'd never again repeat.

I thought of Weasel. I loved that he listened to me so acutely when I rode him, that he did exactly as I asked. But I wondered, Does he have no desires? No preferences? Can it be enough for him merely to serve? Weasel was not like Hannah, who had thoughts, thoughts I could read in a subtle shift of her nose, a twitch of an eyebrow, or by simply looking into her eyes. Not like the pig who demanded connection and closeness and comfort. I didn't feel the same tug of tenderness with Weasel as I had with Hester and Prudence, where just being with them filled me with overflowing softness. Perhaps it was because Weasel did not live with me. I couldn't watch him while he slept, couldn't witness the naked vulnerability of his dreams. Perhaps it was because he was but a reflection of my own desires. His obedience was dull. Weasel was too blank to be interesting. How can you love someone you do not find interesting?

Being with the Silver Fox made me feel blank. I had gone from the greedy, pushy piggishness of Emma to the docile, unthinking obedience of Weasel. I was to the Silver Fox as Mike (qua boyfriend) was to me, as my mother had been to my father. And like her, like Mike, I checked out; I had lost my self, was bored by myself. I wondered what the Silver Fox saw in me, other than a magnifying mirror of his own ego. I had become a child again, dependent on the need for approval.

I traveled into the heart of my own darkness and I saw it: the horror, the horror.

I had been dating my father.

Nine

*"Can you tell me, please, which way I ought to go from here," asked Alice.
"That depends a good deal on where you want to get to," said the cat.*

—Lewis Carroll

It was the problem of the excluded middle. I couldn't continue being like Emma, but neither could I allow someone to take the reins and control me like Weasel. I needed to find the Zen stream that trickled between.

After the Silver Fox, I spent the next few years going out with men who were either older or younger, but were, like him, immersed in the culture of the university. There were good things about them. If you were stranded at their house, there were always lots of books to read. They tended not to be overly materialistic. They generally weren't overtly sexist or racist: we shared, for the most part, cultural knowledge, values, and a reasonably flexible schedule. They gave good e-mail. True, some of them had to be gently coached in arenas of personal hygiene, and most of them made unfortunate—but remediable—choices in clothing.

They appreciated me, these weedy academic men. They adored me and brought me gifts. They laughed at my jokes and listened to my ideas. Sometimes too well—sometimes I saw my ideas—even whole sentences of mine—appear in their writing. None of them tried to control me: they let be and appreciated me for being me. The ones who lasted more than a few weeks accepted Jonathan and Mike and appreciated them, appreciated what my relationships with them said about me. But once talk started about moving in together, or getting married, or—gasp—having children, I packed up my toothbrush and went home. I just wasn't that interested.

Nor was I that interested in my admissions job. The learning curve flattened out after the first year. When I arrived at work in the morning, I put my head down and did what needed to be done; then I spent hours at my desk playing Spider Solitaire. One afternoon, my game was interrupted by an out-of-the-blue e-mail. (I check my messages—voice mail, e-mail, snail mail—with an obsessiveness that borders on the pathological. The way I see it, you never know when something's going to come that's going to change your life, and when it does, you want to get it as soon as possible.) A few years earlier, I'd written an article for *The Chronicle of Higher Education*, a national trade weekly for the academic set. The article was a "Dear John" letter to scholarly publishing about the intense, important, and odd relationships between editors and authors of academic books. I'd written it quickly, easily, and then forgotten about it.

Here was an e-mail from a different editor at the same publication who wanted to know if I would write for them again.

I never seemed to get any better at Spider Solitaire; this would be a good diversion. And they were offering to pay me money.

The editor wanted me to write something—anything—about scholarly publishing. I thought I could do that.

But there was something else I wanted to write about, too.

"How about an essay on dating academics?"

She laughed. "Do both."

Just like that.

That's why I check my e-mail.

After years of being midwife to other people's books and ideas, after a lifetime as a reader, now I was writing.

After the article on academics came out, I got something better than money. I got attention.

Women e-mailed to say that my story reminded them of theirs and that they'd laughed out loud when they read the piece.

Men e-mailed to say that if they weren't married, they'd want to date me.

One lonely lesbian wrote that I seemed like "a nice lady."

It was intoxicating. The idea that people were reading my work thrilled me. That they would take the time to seek me out, to tell me what they liked about it, was more than thrilling. It was energizing and gratifying and addictive.

So I wrote more.

I wrote about admissions, about the college kids I knew (I had formed a large circle of college-aged buddies), about books, about love, about scholarly publishing, about running.

For years, when people asked me if, like many editors, I had a manuscript of my own stowed away in a desk drawer, in answer I'd hold up my two forefingers, crossed to ward off the devil.

"I don't want to write," I told them honestly.

Much to my surprise, this was no longer true.

Perhaps we do in fact resist the things that attract us most strongly. Or perhaps I simply wasn't ready to really explore my own voice, hadn't had anything I wanted to say, until now.

* * *

For the third time, I quit my job without having another lined up. For the third time, people said I was either brave or crazy. For the first time, however, I knew what I wanted: I wanted a deliberate life. I didn't want to "do nothing"; I didn't want to simply see where life led me. I wanted to write.

I'd learned enough about the intricacies, the oddities, and the injustices of college admissions to know that I had something to say about it. I'd have my say, I decided, in a book.

Within a few days of hatching this idea, I became as committed to the idea of writing about college admissions as I was to leaving my job as an admissions counselor. My plan was to write the manuscript first—trying my hardest to make it good—and then try to get it published. I knew that the way to make money was to tell people how to get into the best colleges. I also knew that doing so would be disingenuous and a load of hooey. I would write the book I wanted to write, I decided, not the one that would make me rich.

With surprise and a shudder of embarrassment, I realized that most of the important decisions of my life had been made not by me but by circumstance; I'd fallen into things—jobs, relationships, hobbies. I landed in publishing because of a failure of imagination, in admissions because I was desperate and needed money. I'd gone from one man to the next, filling the empty space in the bed as quickly as possible. I applied to medical school because I thought I wanted to do what Jonathan did. I was almost ready to pull up stakes and follow the Silver Fox—anywhere but here. I'd hitched my star to the wagons of men. Even as I viewed myself as independent, tough, and unsentimental, I made the same choices many other women make in unthinking, unreflective ways. Frailty, thy name is Rachel.

And so I went to find my Walden. Not a stinky, skanky pond, but a place more suited to me: I went back to California. Thoreau's most quoted insight from the pond was that most of us lead lives of quiet desperation. It is, he says, a characteristic of wisdom not to do desperate things. Instead of going to the forest to suck the marrow of life, I went—to live sturdily and Spartan-like—to the mountains. Instead of finding out what lush woods had to teach me, I went to a sere and shrubby place in need of looking at the sere and shrubby places of my soul.

I was asked to house- and horse-sit for my old friends Dan and Patty, who lived in a tiny miner's cabin in the suburbs of Nevada City, California, a "city" of about three thousand people in the foothills of the Sierra Nevadas. The town was a ghost town. It had been the home of the first long-distance telephone line, and was, during the Gold Rush era, a bustling place. By the time I got there, bustling had long since ceased.

My friends, the owners of the cabin, were spending their summer riding horses from Missouri to California, a different brand of Manifest Destiny. All I had to do was tend to the remaining three horses, a one-eyed dog named Joe, and Chloe, a cat improbably missing the complementary eye. I figured that living isolated in the land of the Cyclops would give me a chance to practice self-reliance, would give me an opportunity to slow down and think, deliberate, about what the next steps should be. It would give me a chance to figure out where I lived, and what I lived for.

On the morning that I set out for the West Coast, I said a teary good-bye to Hannah, who would again be staying with Mike for the summer. The REBs packed me some snacks, drove me to the Raleigh–Durham airport, gave me a tight group hug, and sent me on my way. It was time.

In the mornings I'd sit outside, the sun warm and the air dry. From the porch I'd watch as a group of wild turkeys made their daily trek across the yard. It was a blended family, two mothers and their combined collection of chicks.

I'd been warned about mountain lions. A few years before, a woman had been attacked and killed while trail-running. There were also plenty of bear in the area. I listened to the dire warnings and nodded my head and secretly hoped to see a mountain lion or a bear. I never did.

It took twenty minutes to drive into town. I'd wander around and talk to shopkeepers, hungry for conversation. I spent a lot of time on the phone back at the cabin.

Each time I called Mike to see how Hannah was doing, I'd bark out the same question: "How is she?"

If he hesitated for a nanosecond, I panicked. "What's wrong? Is something wrong?"

"She's fine."

"Fine? Not good? Are you not telling me something?"

"She's good."

We repeated this routine over and over. She was always fine. She was always good. I was always worried.

When I sat on the porch and talked on the phone, Chloe, the cat, would jump into my lap. She'd purr loudly. When she was truly content, she drooled. Not a drop here or there, but copious, pooling amounts of drool. Both Chloe and Joe were outdoors animals. When I drove up in the car, they both ran to greet me. It was hard for me not to allow them in the house, but I'd been strictly instructed.

Chloe waited for me to come outside and then launched herself onto my lap whenever I sat down. She also brought me presents and left them at the door. While I appreciated the gesture, I didn't love waking up to dead critters.

In California, my mind began to feel less cluttered. No TV, no radio, no daily newspaper. Mornings I wrote. Little by little, the book began to unfold—I decided to structure it around the seasons of the admissions cycle. I'd sit at my computer and write for an hour or two, and then I'd be so drained that I'd have to go lie down, or sit outside, drooling cat on lap, to regroup. I never knew writing could be so tiring. In the afternoons, I'd go for a long run on the road out my front door; the foothills of the Sierra seemed mountainous to me. My body became brown and strong.

I realized that there had been little blank space in my life. And then I'd think about the weariness of working mothers and realize that with only my job, a man, and an animal or two, I'd had more time than many. Here in the mountains, all I had was time. Writing led inevitably to reading, so I'd often spend my afternoons on the porch, a sweating glass of cold water and a tall pile of books by my side. I'd go to the library to find copies of the books I needed—not wanted, but needed—to reread. I'd write a line, and it would make me think of another line, by a better writer, and I'd feel compelled to read it. This would lead me to another and another and soon I'd be deep into the thick, rich language of *Paradise Lost,* or the cliché-ridden *Hamlet,* or the squawky, heady poems of Wallace Stevens or the insight and depth of the novels of Margaret Atwood. I felt exhilarated. I read for the pleasure of the words and the thoughts that transported my own further and faster than they could go in the pedestrian ways of working life. I was living deliberately. I was enjoying my company. I was at peace in these beautiful hills.

Sometimes, though, at night, say, when it was dark and the air got colder and I was alone in the small house, I'd wander from the bedroom through the tiny living room area to the kitchen and back, restless, seeking. I'd look in the refrigerator, but there was, of course, nothing there for me. I was hungry for something. I didn't know what. I'd pad back to the bedroom, flop myself on the bed. Lie there for a while, and then tromp back through the living room and open the kitchen cabinets. Nothing.

My speaking voice was used only to greet the horses when I fed them each morning, to chat with Chloe and Joe, and for phone calls with the REBs and other friends far away and in different time zones. While I missed their company, I embraced my solitude.

After a few weeks, I began helping Bud, a neighbor, with his daily work. He was sixty-one, short, with stumpy bowed legs, a tanned and lined face, and startling blue eyes. He always had a cap on his white-haired head. He was a logger and had invested in a bunch of get-rich schemes, none of which seem to have made him more financially comfortable. I liked Bud and his wife, Nancy, liked their connection to the land—they had a ranch, grew their own vegetables, husbanded both animals and crops. Being with them made me feel more connected to the essentials of life, helped me strip away some of the layers of pretension I'd piled on over the years.

Because he thought somehow, someday, that it would be lucrative, Bud bought a bezillion old tires a long time ago and had them dumped—to store—on a piece of land in the diggings, the old gold mining territory. Then the county told him that he must get rid of them. So we spent days loading the tires into forty-five-foot-long trailers to be hauled away. I'd had no idea there were so many sizes and shapes of tires. Cars, trucks, motorcycles, utility vehicles. Some were little and worn down. Many were huge, heavy. Bud drove a loader, a piece of yellow heavy machinery with two long arms. He used these arms as if they were extensions of his hands to pick up individual tires, sometimes scooping up four or five at a time. He'd settle them on a wooden pallet.

Some of the tires were filled with water. All were filthy. It was hot and dusty, and we were quickly covered with a patina of sweat and dirt. I was working hard. I'd look at the gigantic pile of tires and become a little anxious. I wanted to load them quickly, to make the pile smaller. We loaded and loaded, and it was like trying to eat a huge plate of pasta. You keep eating, and the heap doesn't get any smaller, and you get more and more full, and it feels like eating the world.

"Pace yourself," Bud said. "These tires ain't going nowhere."

He loaded them carefully against the back wall of the trailer, stacking them efficiently, figuring out the spatial relations in ways that baffled me. When it came time to make a second tier of huge truck tires on top of the first row, he made a series of steps out of different-size tires and rolled them up. I would not have thought to do that. I watched him stack. My usefulness was in my physical labor and willingness to work. I was no good at figuring out the logistics of this stuff. I loved straining under the weight of the tires, wearing the gloves that protected my uncallused hands. This was hard, invigorating work. But not as hard as writing. Not as hard as typing something meaningful onto the white space of my computer screen.

"That's enough for today," Bud called out.

I was sorry to stop. Tired as I was, this break in my day was a treat. I was trying to resolve that old chestnut of philosophy, the mind–body problem by working each part to exhaustion. I liked spending time with Bud. I liked learning the way his mind worked, so different from mine, and I liked that his world was so unlike any place I'd ever inhabited. I was a comfortable and enthusiastic visitor in the land of manual labor.

"You wanna help me drive cattle tomorrow morning?" he asked. "Be here at five."

Drive cattle? Me? Childhood fantasies of working on a ranch were coming true.

I showed up the next morning, and Bud told me that he was going to put me on the buckskin mustang.

"This fat horse?" I asked, looking at a portly fellow.

"Yeah," he said.

"He's barefoot," I said.

"Yeah. I didn't have time to shoe the Arab, either. We'll do it later."

He showed me how he wanted his horse handled. What I've learned being around horses and horse people is that there are a million different ways to do the same things. The correct way, I've discovered, is the way you are told by the owner of the horse.

He threw an English saddle on the fat mustang, Buck, and we let the girth out to the last hole. It barely fit. He slipped a hackamore over his head; no bit for my cow horse. He put a big western saddle on Moose, an Arab-quarterhorse cross, and we loaded them into the trailer and drove them down the road to where the cows were.

We brought with us Jack, a border collie, and Bob, an Australian cattle dog. Jack was a worker. Bud had given me a demonstration of his abilities earlier when he put Jack into a pen with chickens and ducks. He'd told Jack to separate out the ducks, and Jack did.

I was wearing black Lycra running tights and a long-sleeved crimson Harvard T-shirt. I was to do that old, important, cowboy task: to ride the point, at the head of the herd, and slow down the cars that would be whipping and winding down the road. We had thirty-two head of cattle between us, including three bulls and a long-horned steer, a guy with long horns with a tendency to moo a lot. And then it hit me: I didn't want to date the Marlboro man—I wanted to *be* the Marlboro man.

I rode the mustang out front, and the cars would see me and slow. Some of the drivers acted like it was the most natural thing in the world, to see a woman on horseback riding in the middle of the asphalt road followed by thirty cows being herded by a dog, and they'd ask if they had to wait or if they could pass through the herd.

"Go on through," I'd tell them, parroting what Bud had said to say.

Others expressed surprise and delight when they saw our ragtag group. A number told me that my horse was pretty. I thanked them.

It was still early, and a bit chilly. The cows ambled slowly up the road; it was almost entirely uphill, the four miles we had to travel. They stopped by the side of the road and ate. Each time there was a side road, or a driveway, they tried to turn. Bud would yell to Jack to "get ahead, get ahead" and the dog would zoom into place, keeping them on the right path. I had to stop frequently and wait for them to catch up. I'd try to stop in a sunny spot, so that I could warm myself. But also in a spot where I would be seen by oncoming cars.

A guy came by in a pickup. "Nice way to spend a morning," he said.

I smiled and nodded.

I agreed.

Tires loaded and cattle driven, I got back to my own work. It was going well, but I needed to find some more afternoon diversions. It was time, I decided, to try to find some of the trails that I knew mapped the area. A few miles due south lay Auburn, a small gold-mining town that is also the mecca of long-distance trail running. I had, I realized, gone a little nutty with my athletic endeavors. I had taken to doing ultramarathons, races longer than marathons. Mostly I'd done 50Ks—31 miles—always on trails that involved many thousands of feet of climb. "Why just do it, when you can overdo it?" seemed to be my motto. I'd taken the name of my running shoe,

Asics, and the phrase for which it was created—*Anima Sana in Corpore Sanos*, a sound mind in a sound body—perhaps to the edge of soundness. Despite the admittedly over-the-top nature of my running, with each step I took, I felt my mind becoming a bit less foggy.

I'd learned about a regular Wednesday evening run that left from the Auburn overlook, about forty-five minutes away. Perhaps I was ready for company. I'd been enjoying the sound of my own voice, but was beginning to miss the harmonizing strains of others.

I found the group, and though we all started together, I ended up at the front of the pack with a woman named Lisa. We ran and chatted together comfortably for such a long time that I was surprised when someone else caught up to us. Covered in sweat and dust, the guy was tanned to leathery outdoorsy-ness; he was all lean muscle. He looked like he was in his early forties. Lisa knew him and introduced us. His name was Ed. She was slowing down, she said; we should just go on ahead.

Ed and I did some of the usual—where are you from, what do you do—though, in the way of too many men, Ed asked not many questions. He chatted not so much about himself, but about the trail, running, the geography of the Sierra foothills.

We made it back to the overlook. Ed had another fifteen or so miles to run that day, training, as he was, for a one-hundred-mile race in Utah in early fall. We were both, it turned out, taking part in the Western States hundred-miler, coming up in two weeks, him running fifty miles as part of the safety patrol, me planning on pacing a friend from North Carolina for the last thirty-eight.

The rest of the group finished, and they broke out a cooler with icy cold beers. My running companion asked for my phone number, which I did not provide, because I couldn't, having failed to commit it to memory. I gave him my e-mail address, a preferred mode of communication; he volunteered his, and I drove forty-five minutes back up Highway 49, following the Gold Rush trail back to my miner's cabin. I was looking forward to going back to my solitude. It had been fun to be with other humans, but I itched to get back to writing, to my hours of blank time.

Ed e-mailed the next day and called as soon as I sent him my phone number. He was having some friends over for a run and a barbecue that weekend, would I like to come?

Would I?

Mostly no, I thought. I didn't want to get involved in anyone else's life. I wanted to maintain my monklike state of reflection. What did he want from me? Was he attracted to me, or just being friendly? He seemed interested, but even if he was, I didn't have to be. I'd spent too much of my life responding to the attentions of men. I could turn away, back to my horses, my one-eyed companions.

But. Never having learned to cook, I was getting tired of eating popcorn for dinner. The writing was going well; I was feeling productive. Maybe it would be okay to take a little time off. I said yes.

There were only four of us running. The other two, a man and a woman, were both tapering to run the hundred-mile race, so this was to be an easy ten miles. Easy for them. I struggled to keep up and felt only slightly better when I learned about the running bona fides of my companions. Unwittingly, I had entered the company of Ultrarunning Big Dogs. These are people who do marathons as training runs. People who go out on the trail equipped with food, drink, and toilet paper. People whose body fat percentage is lower than a snake's belly.

For dinner we were joined by more elite ultrarunners. All the talk was of the upcoming race. It was a rare treat for me to be in a conversation where no one found the idea of running thirty-one miles (or one hundred miles, for that matter) in one day as anything other than what you did for fun. Everyone around the table had some connection to this year's Western States, either as a runner, a pacer, or a crew member. It was a fun and easy evening. I detected no solitude-threatening expression of interest from Ed, merely an open and generous spirit, a welcome extended to an out-of-towner. Maybe he was gay. Maybe I wasn't fast enough for him. Wait, shit, I didn't care. I didn't want him to be interested in me in that way. Did I?

A few days later, Ed called inviting me to join him on a weekly Wednesday evening group run, this one leaving from the fire station in Cool, another nearby town. I had been planning on rejoining the folks I'd run with the previous week, but he convinced me that I'd be missing some fine California scenery if I went with that group. I hesitated. I was reluctant to commit, to see him so soon again.

"I promise that this run is much, much more beautiful," he said.

"Okay," I said, reluctantly, unable to resist the prospect of taking in every inch, every mile, of California trail.

When I arrived at the station, a number of folks had brought their horses with them in trailers and were tacking up and getting ready to hit the trails on horseback. Riders and runners passed each other companionably. When Ed showed up, he was alone. When I asked where the other runners were, he said they'd bailed. It was just us. I was immediately suspicious. Had it been planned like this? Was he hitting on me? I felt reassured (yes, I'm still attractive), confused (had the others simply not shown up as planned?), and alarmed (I don't want to get into a relationship!).

So we set out. We ran along a portion of the Western States race course. He pointed out places where the trail forked and reminded me that they would look different in the dark, during my pacing duties. He ran easily, climbing strongly up the hills and flying down with a confidence and surefootedness that took my breath away. I could barely keep up, and I knew he was slowing his pace for me.

"I'm not in a hurry," he said when I offered that he should feel free to go on ahead.

It was a good run, a fifteen-mile loop. We got back, and I collapsed atop the picnic table, leaving a shadow of sweat on it.

"I have a lot of steak and chicken left over from the barbecue," he said.

I had been looking forward to living unfettered by others' desires, others' moods. I'd decided to take a break from always being with a man. I needed to work on myself. I wanted to concentrate on writing. He wasn't my type. Not an intellectual, not a reader. I loved spending my days alone. But nights in my miner's cabin were long and quiet, too quiet.

I agreed to have dinner with him.

It was fine. We were comfortable together, not flirty. I felt no sexual tension. We talked about running, about the differences between the trails on the East and West coasts, the differences in the climates and landscapes. Maybe he was just friendly. Maybe he was gay.

I was getting ready to leave.

He was sitting on the table, Teva-sandaled feet resting on one of the chairs. I thanked him for dinner, told him it was a nice time.

"Come here," he said, extending a hand mapped with veins, a strong, steady hand.

I squirmed, but stepped closer.

He slid his fingers through the belt loops of the jeans I had changed into and drew me close to him. He smelled like soap and fly repellent. I could see the lines around his eyes, from too much sun, from smiling.

I braced myself.

I did not want a boyfriend.

I was here to write.

He was not my type.

I was done with relationships.

He pulled me closer, and I pulled back.

"I can't get involved in a relationship now," I said.

He smiled, the lines around his eyes crinkling. "You're leaving at the end of the summer, right?"

Closer now, I could smell the woods and the scent of him, clean.

He kissed me. His strong arms wrapped around me, and our hard bodies came together.

My mind was whirling. Okay, so he wasn't gay. He was clearly interested. He was suggesting that this just be a summer fling. Would that help or hinder me in my quest? Hinder . . . right? I had to be alone. I had to get at what it's like to be alone. I pushed him away.

He looked at me with those crinkling eyes.

In my mind, I heard lines from the Stevens poems I'd been spending my days reading. I wanted to have a "mind of winter." I wanted to clarify, to simplify. But then I thought of different lines, from another poem: "I have said no to everything to get at myself. I have wiped away moonlight like mud." It felt good to kiss him. I did not want to wipe away moonlight like mud.

When the summer ended, so would this romance, I decided. For the first time, I was content by myself. I didn't need Ed the way I'd needed men in my past, to feel complete and content—but I could still enjoy his company, right? My quest was important, but it was also important not to take myself too seriously. I could do both. I could carve out the time I needed to write, to think, to be. But that didn't mean I shouldn't have a little fun, as well. I wanted to live de-liberately, but there was no reason that meant taking a vow of celibacy. Old Henry David must have gotten mighty horny out there in the woods, beside the skanky pond.

"Gravity is your friend," Ed said as he floated down the steep canyons, pulling ahead of me. When we stopped I'd tell him no, it's more than just gravity. It's about the fundamental laws of physics: momentum. Bodies in motion like to keep going.

We learned that I was good for four hours. After that, I could still run, but I'd lose sentences. I'd get down to single words: "Tired." "Hungry." "Water." "Pee." And some occasional phrases: "How much more?" At that point, I did not want to be touched. If he came too close, I'd bark, threatening to bite.

But before that, when I was good, it was good. During these long runs, we were not in a hurry. We made a practice of stopping. On a large granite rock, alone in the wilderness, we'd strip out of our run-ning clothes and do things I would never consider doing with my usual training partners. We'd frolic in streams—or, rather, beside streams, as the water was icy cold and good mostly for shrinking swollen muscles. I was eager to play, at least during the first four hours. Ed learned the point at which I would no longer be happy to frolic.

We traveled to run. We went to Squaw Valley and ran high above Tahoe. We explored the trails on the Nevada side of the lake. We took a trip to Utah and ran on the Wasatch Front trail.

We went to Yosemite one weeknight. We slept in his car and

early the next morning started at Tuolumne Meadows. We ran down, stopping at Cloud's Rest to have a bite, which I shared with a friendly squirrel.

"Don't feed him," Ed said. "He needs to be able to make it on his own."

Ed was all about self-reliance. He lived by himself, always had, and, at age forty-two, said he always would. Never married, never came close. He traveled to explore, and worked—in some kind of sales job—to be able to travel.

We had agreed that this would be just a summer fling. We both knew that I would be going home in August. Neither of us was interested in a serious relationship; we told this to ourselves and to each other. What we had in common was running. We were just having fun.

Ed expected me to be able to take care of myself. If he saw me struggling—putting up the tent, carrying wood, trying to make coffee—he would not offer to help, though he would take over the task if I asked. I didn't like to ask. He didn't talk about his work, didn't ask about mine. We talked about where we'd like to go, what we'd seen on our runs. Much of the time, we didn't talk at all.

Our angular bodies fit well together. When we were not running, we were either eating or having sex. Ours was a basic, animal connection. The Silver Fox's age and antidepressants depressed his libido. Having gotten used to that, my own had gone dormant. With Ed, it woke up and wanted always to dive into bed. Or onto the couch. Or on the deck. Or by a stream or on a granite rock. We had a lot of sex. Athletic, fun, house-rocking sex.

Afterwards, spent, we'd refresh ourselves with sleep. No talking in the dark, no intimacies revealed or futures imagined. We'd touch each other—bodies, not souls, revealed. Our connection was physical, not emotional.

When Ed went off to work, I drove back to the small cabin, gathering myself again. I'd sit on the front porch, computer in lap, Chloe drooling at my feet, Joe off on his adventures. I could hear the horses behind me and watched the daily parade of wild turkeys strut across the lawn. Hummingbirds buzzed around my head like insects. It was a nice place to write. When enough words had filled my screen, I'd pack up and go back to Ed's.

Sometimes I got to his house first. Though he left his door unlocked, often I sat outside on the deck and looked down into the canyons, and farther, across the gap of the American River to the hills on the other side. Sometimes I saw squirrels, deer, different kinds of birds. I used the time to relax, to space out. Sometimes as I waited for him I thought about our curious, limited connection. It seemed to be working for both of us, a relationship based on a few shared activities and not much else. It wasn't perfect, but it was good summer fun.

One evening, a cat strutted out of the woods. He swaggered like he was king of the jungle, though he didn't look the part. He had a big tomcat head, and big feet, but the parts in between were so emaciated and filthy that you'd have thought he'd be kicked out of the feline club; his ribs were clearly and individually visible beneath a dirty coat of yellow fur. Given his scrawniness, I supposed that cleaning himself in the fastidious way of normal cats was far down on his to-do list.

When he saw me, he stopped dead in his big-footed tracks.

I was just sitting there on the corner of the deck. I didn't move. "Hello."

He arched, sampled the air.

"Where did you come from?"

He came to me.

I was cautious, not wanting to touch him, but he left me no choice. He rubbed his filthy skinny self against my bare legs, dragged his head against my hand. His canine teeth stuck out, and I felt them caress my skin. I stroked down his back, and he pushed his tail against me.

He went in circles. He stepped over my legs, slid his head against my side, against the tops of my thighs. He looked me dead in the eye like he'd known me for years and had been wondering where I'd been.

He shocked me by climbing into my lap and purring. Unlike Chloe, he didn't drool.

The cat closed his eyes while I stroked his matted, dirty fur and felt every bone beneath his skin. He looked like he was literally starving to death.

Carefully I lifted him down and went into the kitchen to get him some of the cream Ed used in his coffee. I poured a generous amount into a bowl and put it down in front of him.

The cat looked at it, looked up at me, and didn't eat. Instead he came back to my legs and twirled and arched and rubbed and waited until I sat down, when he circled his head around my hand, purring louder now and climbed back into my lap.

I dipped a finger into the cream. He licked it off—a favor to me. When it was gone, he kept licking. I guided his head toward the bowl. He knew it was there. It wasn't his priority.

Ed came home to find us together. The cat jumped off my lap at Ed's approach, like a guilty lover caught by a jealous husband.

"Do you know this guy?"

"Oh, he's a feral cat. I've seen him around for years."

"Feral?"

I watched the cat at my legs as he contorted his body to get maximum physical attention.

"Do you feed him?"

"Hell no. He can take care of himself. He's been doing it forever."

I decided to call the cat Sam.

When we went to sleep that night, I left the cream outside. In the morning, it was gone.

Whenever I drove up to Ed's house I called out: "I do not like green eggs and ham, I do not like them Sam-I-Am."

From wherever he'd been, doing whatever he did, Sam-I-Am came running.

Ed wouldn't allow him in the house, not that Sam wanted to go. The two of us sat on the deck while Ed cooked. We'd look out into the valley below, him purring, me sighing contentedly, each with our own thoughts.

Thoreau said, "If you have built castles in the air your work need not be lost; that is where they should be. Now put foundations under them." I was working on my foundations, my essential self. I had tried to go from one extreme—round-the-clock companionship with the REBs and other friends—to total isolation. Perhaps being with Ed offered a kind of transition on my road to complete self-reliance. Perhaps this was the happy medium, the middle path.

Sam embodied independence. He took care of himself. He would barely allow me to feed him. I tried tuna; I tried chicken. He would never take food when we first saw each other. Instead, it was all about rubbing and purring. Eventually, he'd have a few bites. I continued to leave food for him at night, never sure if it was he who was eating it or a raccoon, or maybe a mountain lion. What he wanted was the company, having someone to sit beside and look down at the valley.

Ed liked to say that he had "work years" and "training years," alternating his focus from making money to preparing for big events. He prided himself on not having a TV; it was, for him, a badge of honor. I have grown to love TV. I miss it when I don't have access to it, and I don't think this enjoyment makes me seem stupid. Ed did— he teased me about it, and his teasing got old.

He paid attention, and he had a good memory. Memory can pass for intelligence. When I mentioned things he didn't know or hadn't heard of, he never asked questions. He'd say "yes," and "uh-huh" and "of course," until I realized that he didn't know. But he didn't ask. When he did ask, it was to offer up his own knowledge first and formulate a question by asking, "right?" Often, I felt compelled to point out, he wasn't.

It's not that he wasn't smart. More that his mind didn't move in ways that moved me. That he wouldn't ask questions bugged me; it trapped him in the prison of his ignorance. My old snobby habits died hard, and when I got e-mail from him, it always contained embarrassing mistakes in grammar. Embarrassing to me, anyway. Sometimes the grammatical mistakes we make provide windows into our lives: Ed had no clue about possessives.

Ed wanted only to have fun. If he wasn't running, he was biking. Or kayaking, mountain climbing, diving, or spelunking. Work was what he did to make it possible to play. He didn't care about finding a meaning in life; it wasn't something he thought about. He didn't want to get married and certainly didn't want kids. He'd been in a relationship for ten years with a woman who didn't believe him. Finally she broke up with him and soon after married someone else. Ed wanted no dependents, no strings. He didn't expect anyone to take care of him and didn't want to care for anyone else. It worked for him.

And, for a summer, it worked for me, most of the time.

When I yearned for a greater emotional connection, I knew where to find it: Sam. I had tried not to get too attached to him; he was not a settling-down kind of guy, and besides, he was old and still, despite my efforts, horridly thin. But still, I knew—it was easy to see—that Sam loved me. I began to look forward as much to seeing him as spending time with Ed.

I bought a bag of dry cat food and left piles of it in bowls on Ed's deck. I regularly left out saucers of cream, cans of tuna. I bought Sam catnip toys (no interest). But he knew the sound of my car and raced from the woods to greet me when I arrived.

Until one day I drove up and he wasn't there. I called out, Sam-I-Am, Sam-I-Am, and waited in vain. He didn't show. I imagined the worst, the unthinkinable.

A few days later, Sam came bounding when he heard my car. I picked him up—he didn't mind being picked up, which always surprised me, it seemed so out of character—and I hugged him close. His disappearance was an episode that repeated over the course of the summer. He had things to do, places to go. Sometimes it took more than a day. And I was not at Ed's every day. I tried to make peace with the fact that Sam might not always be there.

* * *

It should have ended when my friends returned to their cabin, when I left California for my own home, my books, my friends, my life. I'd been cut off from the world.

"What's Enron?" I asked Val during one phone conversation, realizing I'd been living in a news blackout. "And why is everyone talking about the president choking to death on a pretzel?" She filled me in on the world, and I gave her the latest on Ed. It should have ended at the end of the summer, I told her. He and I knew this. We'd talked about it. It was clear and obvious.

But he kept calling me. He wanted to talk about making plans to go places, getting together for races. He, too, it seemed, longed for some other kind of connection.

When we'd go onto a trail that may or may not have crossed private property, Ed would say, for the 1,290th time, "It's easier to beg forgiveness than to ask permission." He was forever "swinging for the fences." "Fool me once, shame on you. Fool me twice, shame on me," he'd say, more than twice. He was a "no pain, no gain," guy. He was always saying, "As I always say." And he'd always say something that he'd never said in the first place.

While I noticed his recycled language during our summer of physical exertions, it began to grate on me more during long transcontinental phone conversations than it did over long runs. When we weren't running together, it was hard to connect. The physical was our realm.

About six weeks after I returned home, I went back to California for the wedding of friends of his—now friends of mine—and things with Ed felt very different. Since I'd resumed my life in North Carolina, I'd gone back to reading the paper and being involved with the world. My Walden-like summer was receding fast into memory.

Sam-I-Am, still dirty, still bony, came zooming out of the woods when I called him, twirling and swirling around my legs, purring like

a well-oiled machine when I picked him up. Ed was typically non-
chalant. After I dressed for the wedding, in nice clothes and makeup, things I hadn't had with me in the summer, I waited for him to
comment.

I never thought of myself as someone who relied on compliments
about my looks, never put much stock in them. I was never even gracious about accepting praise because as good as someone thought I
was, I could tell you fifteen ways in which they were wrong. I realized
only then that Ed never said anything "nice" to me, and realized, too,
a bit surprised, that when all the other men had, I'd taken it for
granted and now missed it.

"You're a tough little runner." This was all he'd ever said. He valued my ability to withstand physical challenges, to be on my own, to
make it through. When we'd finished a hard run, he noted how strong
and able I was. How I looked, what I wore, my wit, my wisdom—
nothing. It all went by without comment. And he'd never asked to
read anything I'd written.

We went to the wedding, and I watched him interact with others.
He had the quick laugh of a salesman. Conversations skimmed
along. I remembered Swift's devastating lines from A Tale of a Tub:
"Last week I saw a woman flayed and you would not believe how
much it altered her appearance for the worse." The surfaces of things
were certainly more attractive.

I knew that this wasn't going to work for me. I had finished my
book. It had been accepted by a publisher, and was scheduled for
quick publication. I was intellectually and emotionally committed
to my work for the first time in a long time. I had the freedom to
travel and good friends to visit. I had little money, but few needs.
The REBs and my female friends gave my life a richness and fullness
that made it less important to have a committed relationship with a
man. It should have been enough, this dalliance with Ed. Why
wasn't it?

The great sex would have been greater if, occasionally, it was
tempered by tenderness. Our physical connection was all that kept us
together. Without it, there was no Us. Babies who are not touched

enough can suffer—can even die from—"failure to thrive." I had hoped that touch would be enough. But it wasn't. I thought of E. M. Forster's famous line from *Howard's End*: "Only connect," and I knew that you need both, the prose and the passion.

As fall turned into winter, I decided that I wanted to celebrate my fortieth birthday by running the gnarliest, nastiest race I could find on my own turf, to regain a sense of myself as a tough runner of trails. And there it was: the Black Mountain Marathon and Mount Mitchell Forty-Mile Challenge. It seemed a perfect combination of ancient eastern mountains, and vibrant intellectual and cultural life.

Western North Carolina combines the best of the Northeast and the West. The tiny town that hosted the marathon had also been the home of Black Mountain College, which, in the years of its existence—1933 to 1956—was a hotbed of alternative education in America, a Greenwich Village in the mountain range they call The Blacks. In a pastoral setting, culture bubbled; it still does.

The mountains themselves are surprising, with an ecosystem that is as diverse as you will find outside a tropical rain forest, and a climate more like Canada's than that of the South. The variety of plant and animal species is mind-boggling due to peculiarities of glacial movements in the past. Mount Mitchell, at 6,684 feet is, to the astonishment of many, in fact the highest peak east of the Mississippi.

This was the place for me. This is where I wanted to turn into a masters runner, joining the ranks of the forty-and-over set, and I didn't want to do it alone. Despite my ambivalence toward our relationship, I invited Ed to come with me. I wanted him to see the difference in trails, to experience the zeitgeist of the eastern trail runner, to dabble in both the natural and cultural wonderland of southern Appalachia.

I began talking to Ed about the race and once again, in the context of running, it was fun. He wanted to celebrate my birthday with me, to come East. We would spend a weekend in the Black Mountains, dining in nearby Asheville, one of the truly groovy towns of the United

States, where dreadlocked, hemp-wearing, rainbow-flag-stickered twenty-somethings peacefully coexist with followers of Billy Graham, rural mountain people, reclusive artists, and ritzy tourists. We would each run our own race, the forty-miler for him, the marathon for me. We would soak romantically together in a post-race bath.

Like many of the best-laid plans, this one went, naturally, to hell.

Our phone conversations had been getting strained. Yes, we had the race to talk about, but you can have only so many variations of the same conversation before you get bored, and frustrated. I got impatient with him, with us. About a month before the race, I told Ed not to come. There was no point in dragging this out. He took it in stride, and said I should call him if I changed my mind. I did, he pointed out, have a habit of changing my mind. He had often said that he felt he had to poll me on an issue. If he asked ten times, I might answer the same way six or seven and that would be the answer. He did know me a little. He was used to waiting me out. He waited, called again two days before the race, offered to come out.

"I already told you no."

"Yeah," he said, "but that was only a few times. I haven't cancelled my reservations. It's not too late."

"It is too late, Ed. It's too late."

Enough was finally enough. At a certain point, you just know.

I checked into the hotel Ed had reserved for us, a family-run place of tattered elegance, faded glory. No phone, no TV—it seemed perfect for us. But there was no Us. There was just me, a bag of Tootsie Rolls, a two-liter bottle of diet root beer, and a mystery novel. It was just me, on my birthday, turning forty. All by myself. I enjoyed my mystery novel. I enjoyed my own company. I ate myself sick on candy, hydrated on soda, and then stretched diagonally across the bed. There was no one with me, but I didn't feel alone.

Had my Walden experience been mired by getting stuck with Ed? Should I feel that I'd failed because I'd hooked up with yet another man?

No.

I wanted to become a writer, and I ended the summer with a completed book. I'd learned to load tires, drive cattle, poop in the woods, and be content with myself. Absent Ed, I would have had more lonely nights, but it would have been fine. It would have been good. I may have read more books. I may have cultivated a garden. I may have learned how to cook. Well, no, I probably wouldn't have cooked. But it would have been fine, it would have been good, to be without a man.

Ed was not a man that I should have been with for longer than a summer. Unlike with the Silver Fox, I wasn't rewriting some tired old narrative from my childhood. Unlike Mike, I didn't find him easier to be with than being alone. Unlike Jonathan, we didn't have anything to talk about. Patrick at least had made jokes and gotten mine. Had I learned nothing? Shouldn't there be some positivistic progression of relationships, where each one builds on what you've learned from the previous one? Is it, perhaps, that there is a system instead of bonds and debts—the next person gets to trade in the goodies you've learned before and, unfortunately, has to compensate for what you've been missing? Had the attraction of Ed been his hard body, in contrast to the aging sagginess of the Silver Fox? Had it been that I just wanted to be touched?

Forty years old. I couldn't tell if that was really old—it seemed like a big number—or midway through an exciting adventure. Was I losing parts of myself—my personality, my quirks—or getting stronger and more wise? Was I becoming less myself or more—and was that a good or a bad thing? Had my trail of failed relationships given me insight into myself and my needs, or was I continually making the same mistakes? Had I wasted time, or had I been building strength?

It was becoming clear to me: to really understand myself, to avoid the risk of losing myself to a man, I would have to be single. For real this time. No more this-isn't-really-a-relationship relationships. I was eager for the next stage of my adventure, and I would need to go it alone. Forty years old. Instead of feeling panic, I saw opportunity. A chance to remake the second part of my life, a desire to understand how to live meaningfully, to figure out who I was and what I wanted to do. Scary, yes, but more, exciting.

Race morning. I trotted down the hill to the start, only to realize that I'd neglected to pin my number onto my shirt. I jogged back to the hotel, thinking that this was not an auspicious beginning. When I got back, I was warmed up, even though it was quite chilly out. Chilly, but not cold, not freezing. No snow. What I knew was that there was only one hill. We'd go up to the turnaround, and then come back down. I was worried. I was not feeling fit. It had been many months since I was running on the dusty California trails, months since I did training runs of twenty-five miles with only a few days' rest in between.

The race started. I took it easy. I walked when I got tired. During my time in California, I learned the energetic efficiency of walking, rather than running, steep uphills. Compared with the runs I had done out West, where the terrain is higher and craggier, and where there is less ambient oxygen, this did not seem all that hard. Hell, I did a race at Lake Tahoe that started at the elevation of the peak of Mount Mitchell. But still, I walked. I did not want to feel uncomfortable; I didn't want to suffer.

I chatted with the other runners. I tried to relax into the race. At times I slipped into thinking about my time in the mountains. Had it been as good for me as the pond had been for Thoreau? "I left the woods for as good a reason as I went there," Thoreau wrote. "Perhaps it seemed to me that I had several more lives to live, and could not spare any more time for that one." Perhaps the fact that I had no money, no health insurance, no visible means of support was not so bad: "However mean your life is, meet it and live it; do not shun it and call it hard names. It is not so bad as you are. It looks poorest when you are richest."

The trail was beautiful—lush, rich, varied. Halfway through the race, we turned and headed back down the mountain. Now I was flying. I passed a guy, and he gasped, "Where did you learn to run downhill like that?" I shouted back at him: California. I learned in California.

My summer did me good. I wrote a book. I became a stronger, tougher runner. I explored places I didn't know existed. I experienced the joy of doing something you love with someone who loves it, too, mingling physical pleasures and athletic pain. Maybe it was asking too much for that bond to be enough to make us love one another. Maybe, sometimes, relationships can be like races: discrete moments in time that you capture, experience, enjoy, remember, and move on. I crossed the line that day after my fortieth birthday not only as the first masters—over forty—woman, but as the first woman overall. It seemed a good way to begin middle age.

Ed called to find out how it went. I told him. He didn't congratulate me on the victory, just said that it sounded like fun.

I changed the subject. "How's Sam-I-Am?"

"Oh," he said.

"What?"

"Well, he hadn't come around for a while—a couple of weeks, actually—so I started looking for him."

My stomach clenched.

"I found his body—frozen—under the deck."

No. Not the independent one. Not Sam, my tough guy, who needed affection more than he wanted food. I thought about his big tomcat head and the acrobatic moves he made to be scratched and rubbed. His filthy pelt, his big-footed strut and swagger. The way he gazed into the valley, dominant, serene. He lived his independent life, self-sufficient, self-reliant, he had his work—whatever it was he spent his days doing—but still, still, he was desperate to be loved. At first I had thought Sam mirrored Ed, living out there on his own, taking care of himself. He did. But now I saw that I, too, was like Sam. While we both prized our independence, we both craved affection. Without touch that was affectionate and loving, we failed to thrive.

I said good-bye, again and finally, to Ed.

Ten

And so it came to pass
Titania waked and straightway fell in love with an ass.

—William Shakespeare

Back in Durham, I showed up at the farm, ready to ride, to find that Weasel had thrown a shoe and was unavailable for a spin on the trails. So I scooped up a sloppy handful of grain, sweetened sticky with molasses, and went into the "critter pen," a crazed nativity scene of miscellaneous fauna. I was mugged by goats. They climbed on each other and on me to get to the feed. They are not respecters of personal space, goats. Sal, the llama, walked over, haughty, disdainful, keeping a distance but unable to conceal his interest in the food.

Tess, the bumptious sheep, also drew near. Anyone who believes in the meekness of the lamb has never spent time with one. Tess was given to head butts and pushy power plays. She would, on occasion, race around the pen, leaping joyously like a cartoon character, and then come to a skidding stop. She was an odd duck, that Tess. The ducks themselves mostly stayed away from the four-legged critters, while the geese attacked us two-leggers. They had announced my arrival with vicious honks and snapping beaks. Chickens wandered, pecking, squawking. Sometimes one would fly up and perch on Tess's woolly back.

Out of the fray stood Stevie, a Sicilian and, therefore, by definition, miniature, donkey; his back was no higher than my hip. I elbowed through the multispecies crowd, having saved some of the grain for him. He waited for me to reach him, and when I lowered my hand with the grain, he took it gently. We were surrounded and accosted by greedy goats, who stopped at nothing, walked over anything, for a bite to eat.

Once the grain was gone, so, too, were the goats. Sal strutted away, long eyelashes flashing on a tiny head atop his improbably long neck. Tess moved off as soon as I looked at her. She is periodically shorn, a process she does not enjoy, and didn't chance coming near, in case I had knitting in mind. Only Stevie remained.

He stood next to me, close, so close that his furry shoulder leaned against my thigh. I reached down to scratch his ears, and he dropped his head, raising it again when I stopped. I walked across the pen, gingerly through mud and poop, and sat down on a stump. The other animals were oblivious, on to sorting through the hay and looking for tender morsels, but Stevie watched and, after a few short minutes, followed. He came right up to me, his head even with my own.

"I have no more."

I held up my hands, palms toward him, empty.

He sniffed my shoes, sniffed along my legs, and then stood stock-still. He wasn't looking at me. But he was right there with me. I rubbed his ears more vigorously, up and down their long length, and he stretched his neck out. He settled his head in my lap. When I stopped rubbing, he did not move.

Stevie was, I noticed, an attractive specimen of donkey-flesh. He was also shaggy and filthy. I got a stiff rubber currycomb and a brush. I groomed him, and clouds of dust erupted. Chunks of dried whatever fell off. His coat was a rich gray. He sported a cross, a stripe that went down his back and across his shoulders. His dark brown mane stuck straight up, like an eighties punk rocker. He had a modest tail, just a stick with a tuft at the end.

When my friends, Weasel's owners, came home and found me in the barnyard, I realized I had spent the last hour communing with this ass. I asked about him. I learned that they took him in after he had gotten "sour," having been used for too much little kid entertainment, pulling carts, and allowing children to grab his ears. He'd been bottle-raised, I was told, and—despite his aversion to kindergarteners' birthday parties—he liked people. That much was clear to me. He was in ripe middle-age, no longer young, but not yet old.

After that, each time I went to the farm to ride, I stopped in first to grab a handful of grain and entered the critter pen to be mobbed, again and again, by goats.

"You people just need to back off," I said to them.

It's a horrid, rude construction, "you people." It should be deployed sparingly, used righteously against smokers, Californians proffering avocadoes, and mobs. The critters too often acted like a mob, and they deserved a you-peopling every now and then. Valiantly I fought off goats, threatened the sheep with a shake of my shoe, and made sure that the little donkey got the lion's share of treats. The llama kept his supercilious, if not respectful, distance.

Stevie stayed with me. He wanted only proximity. Like a cat, he worked his head under my hand. He was a love-starved little ass.

His life was too constrained, I decided.

In the barn I found an old red halter for him, crusty and dusty from disuse. I slipped it on him, and he minded not at all, stood quietly while I fussed with the buckle. I attached a rope and led him around the pen. When I took off the lead rope, he continued to follow me, stopping when I stopped.

I asked if I could take him out for a walk.

"Donkeys don't like changes in substrate," my friend the farmer warned.

"Changes in what?"

This is the kind of farmer you find in the overeducated town of Durham, North Carolina: one who will never opt for a good old Anglo-Saxon word when there's a Latinate version available. My farmer friend was also a professor. He often used arcane language simply because he could.

Apparently, what he was trying to say is that donkeys don't like walking on different kinds of surfaces.

With a harrumph, I pointed out that the "substrate" was the same—the same concrete from the barn paved the way to the paddock.

"Try it," he said, and went off to muck a stall.

I was convinced the little long-eared guy would follow me anywhere. He rested his head against me when I stood in the pen with him. Why wouldn't he welcome a chance to change his venue, break his routine?

I opened the gate and tried to lead him out.

He would not move.

"Come on little man."

His ears, always turned toward me, swiveled back.

I was shocked.

He was a pissed-off ass.

"Stevie, come on, let's go for a walk."

No.

I pulled on the lead rope, and he planted himself more firmly than you could believe. He locked his front legs, shifted his weight back, and would not budge.

"It's me, Rachel. Your buddy. I'm going to take you for a walk."

Surely he wanted to be out in the world, to graze on fresh grass, to run.

No.

He would not move.

I tried a bribe of grain, holding it in front of him. He stood firm, and again I was mobbed by goats.

Frustrated, I stripped him of his halter and sat down on my stump. Stevie followed and put his big head in my lap. Devotion was not enough to overcome his fear. Being stuck in a mucky pen with critters unlike himself was his rut.

My rut—my man rut—is over.

I do not want another boyfriend. Not now. Not for a while.

I know I've said it before. Like, in the last chapter. But at this moment, right now, I know it's true.

When I watch couples, I rarely find myself thinking, "I want that." The viscera of most relationships is, thankfully, not visible to outsiders. If you get too close, you risk seeing the squabbling, the spats, the splattering of feelings like bugs on a windshield. It doesn't make you want to enlist.

I know that this is not always, of course, the case. I know that there are couples who teach by just being themselves together—who listen to each other and don't get impatient hearing the same story for the 473rd time, who don't think they can always predict the thoughts, actions, or feelings of their partner. And I know that there are couples who see each other and nurture each other and are equal and loving partners. I have a few friendships where I am delighted to have the spouse answer the phone when I call to talk.

I observed, with delight and awe, how my mother, after years of being squelched by my angry and controlling father, found George, her match, in middle age. They have been together now for nearly two decades. She left the prison-house of a frightening and stultifying marriage and grew into a strong and forceful person, without ever losing a sense of gentleness or play. When I visit, I sometimes catch them dancing together in the kitchen. I will walk into joyful and noisy water fights; sometimes I'll come across billets-a-deux, poems and drawings (often hysterically obscene) that they've left around the house for one another.

Sometimes I think of couples like these and feel a sense of longing.

But mostly, well, I have had my share of romance. I realize that, at least for now, I am happiest on my own: less moody, less critical, more free and capable.

I realize I have invested in my love affairs with animals and men, preferring intensity of focus to the warm glow of a broader spectrum. Now I look up from the narrow gaze to see that you get not only the families you were born into, but those you create.

I have—and have made—a big and perhaps eccentric family.

Growing up, my mother was my best friend. We withstood the tempest that my adolescence brought to the relationship and have worked hard over the years to form a mature and mutually respectful bond, no less close but more realistic. Sometimes, even, I don't get pissy when she worries about me, asks if I'm eating enough or if I'm sleeping okay. I've watched her grow and have tried to learn from her mistakes, and from her courage and strength, too. I've watched as she has reinvented herself, learning new tricks (especially on the computer) and honing and developing her skills as an artist. She inspires me by her accomplishments, sure, but also by her ability to embrace the world. And me. Even when I'm being pissy.

It was my mother, obviously, who brought George into the mix. For years now, I have referred to him as my Honorary Father and called him Hon Fat. He calls me, his honorary daughter, Hon Dot. George provides the paternal love I missed out on by dint of biology, though like everything else about him, his fathering is not typical. He has taught me how to sit at the table of a fancy restaurant and catapult a fork so that it lands neatly in a glass of water. He's walked me around art museums and pointed out things I did not see, did not know, even, how to see. He is a conversational gymnast, full of twists and leaps and a sense of play. He will not offer advice, unless asked. It's easy to ask him. Every day I give silent thanks that my mother brought him into my life, and that he is in hers.

My brother Mark has grown from a pesky pipsqueak into a good man, thoughtful and generous, with a mind I respect and a heart I hold dear. When I told him, some years back, that I had gotten a new black leather motorcycle jacket and joked that now I needed a bike to accessorize it, he bought me one. (It took me three attempts to pass the written motorcycle driver's license test. Don't ask.) I make frequent trips to the huge house he shares with the woman he finally married, Allyn, who has become a sister to me. Mark, an aggressive lawyer by training but a sweet nurturer by inclination, loves nothing more than to cook enormous and elaborate meals. As soon as I arrive at his house, he asks me what I want to eat. I have only to imagine; he can and will provide it. He also provides care and feeding in the less material, more abstract realms.

While I have only one brother, I realize that I've built, in fact, a whole circle of sisters. I've kept in touch with the various female friends I've made throughout my life, and now more than ever, they are my touchstones, telling me what is real about the world and, more, about myself. Some I have known for decades; we have been together through job changes and marriages and divorces and deaths and pets, many pets. Some I have only more recently found. It is a rare gift to make friends in middle age, to find the time to invest in getting to know each other, to hear and learn each other's stories. While the available space in daily life is often so much less than it was in college, say, the quality can, like wine, age finely. Though none of my close women friends live in my time zone, long distance is not so long when there are cheap airline fares, cell phones with lots of free minutes, and e-mail. Thank God for e-mail.

And, of course, I have the REBs: Jonathan and Mike.

When I thank Mike for something—for taking care of Hannah, for doing my taxes, for breaking into my house and "unburgling," as Jonathan calls it, filling the refrigerator and cabinets with food, his response is always the same: "That's what family is for." Mike, with his rational, realist view of the world keeps me steady and stable. His abilities to see with clear, hard eyes combined with his gentleness and sensitivity make him a tender teller of truth. I rely on this more than I can say.

Jonathan is the only human being who can comfort me when I am hurting. He's the one I tell it to. He's also the person who can bring out the silliest, most playful parts of me. With him I can laugh; in front of him I can cry. And think. He makes me think. If I ask Jonathan to read something I have written, he will always claim that he doesn't know anything about it and then will see right through to the core, will penetrate to the root and point out what I have missed.

These are the best men I know, and I know that they are there and will be there, for me and for each other. They are the people I am most at home with; they are my family.

But our triumvirate has perhaps also held each of us back. Mike, the stud muffin, has not had another girlfriend in the eight years since we broke up. He has married his work, despite repeated protests from Jonathan and me. And despite our repeated attempts to set him up on dates. Jonathan has had a number of real relationships with good and smart women. None yet has proved quite good enough or smart enough for him to commit to a longer-term arrangement. And, as for me, perhaps the reason I don't feel the need for a romantic relationship is that I get too many of my emotional goodies from the REBs. That they are my best friends makes it easy for me not to seek out new ones. We have in many ways a wonderful world, but it is circumscribed. We are playing in our own pen.

I am beginning to see that this is not such a good thing.

I see it with Stevie. Even though he is clearly comfortable with the status quo, I still want him to leave his pen.

I put on his red halter and lead him to the gate. He follows and then stops.

No way.

He's a stubborn ass.

He will not even near the gate when he's wearing his halter. He knows what I have in mind.

Then I realize that one of the horse's stalls opens out into the critter pen. I walk around, dodging piles of llama poop and pushing goats out of the way.

Maybe I can get him to jump up the foot and a half rise into the stall and sneak him into the outside, before he realizes it.

He has been following me around the pen, dogging my heels, as I look for a way out. I turn to him and scratch his ears, and he lowers his head, lower, and lower until his nose is resting on my shoes.

"Okay," I say.

"Follow me."

He does.

I open the stall door.

He sniffs.

I jump up into the stall.

"Come to me, my darling boy," I say, arms outstretched.

He sniffs, his ears forward-facing elongated funnels.

Then, with a grace you'd never expect from a wee small ass, Stevie leaps into the stall, like a show horse, like a champion stadium jumper, front legs tucked neatly under his narrow shoulders, into my arms.

Oh frabjous day! Callooh! Callay!

It's easier to make a leap of faith if there's someone you know, someone who knows you, waiting on the other side.

Stevie looks around the stall. He's not left his pen for years. Literally, years. Fearful, he clings to me, attaches himself to my leg. Slowly he follows me through the roomy stall, stopping to sniff at the feed bucket, nibbling up a couple of stray pieces of grain. Slowly, he follows as I walk through the gate.

And then we are on the other side of the looking-glass: the paddock.

Stevie's hooves are tiny, no bigger than the diameter of a small apple. He treads carefully, each step a baby step, making slow forward progress. He stops when he sees one of the big horses cross-tied, being brushed and readied to go out for a ride. Stevie backs up.

I see it in his eyes. Even as he is scared, I see the desire to go over and check out the horse, different from him but more the same than those in his pen.

I take him back to the critters. It was enough for one day. But it was a start.

Now when I drive up to the farm, I get out of the car and immediately bellow: "Stevie!"

It's hard to describe the bray of an amorous donkey. It sounds like a death rattle, painful, gasping, groaning. It sounds eerie, Eeyore-y. Like everything else about my beloved ass, it is a little strange.

Sometimes there's a lag. Sometimes I have to call out again. But always, always the sound, the greeting, comes.

It is only to me that he responds in this way. He has recognized me as his, and while he technically belongs to my friends, I refer to him as mine.

"I have the world's most beautiful ass," I am likely to mention in casual conversation with strangers.

"Would you like to see my ass?" I'll ask friends.

Now when I go into the critter pen, red halter in one hand, a scoop of grain in the other, Stevie lets the goats have the grain and stands by the gate while I get him ready for our walk. If I take too long with the buckle, he nudges me with his nose. He is an impatient ass.

I no longer have to bring him through the stall. He will exit through the narrow concrete passage, but only if I am in front of him. This requires some agility. I have to put the halter on him, open the gate, fend off the goats who want not only more food, but also to go out, and get Stevie past the gate so I can close it after us. Then he just stands there. He will not move ahead if I am behind. Even if I push on his butt, shove him, poke him, implore, he will not move.

I do not have a fat ass. But Stevie is, well, wide. I have to slither past him, not easy, in order to get him to follow me out. It has to be me. He won't follow anyone else out of his pen.

At first he is reluctant to leave the paddock. He likes to go into each of the open, unoccupied stalls and sniff around. He eats the pieces of grain he finds, and spends a lot of time examining poop, which is, apparently, captivating. He wanders from stall to stall, baby steps on tiny hooves.

I sit on the mounting block and brush him. He loves to be brushed and moves around, giving me greatest access to the areas he feels need most attention. Usually they are at the front and the rear: his head and ears and the spot just above his tail. The spot that all animals love to have rubbed. You know, the Spot.

When the big horses come in from the pasture, Stevie hides behind me. He peeks out to look at them, but looking is all he wants to do. At first they are, being horses, spooked by him. They snort and sniff, come close and then back away. Whenever anyone is riding, I am careful to let them know that there's an ass in the vicinity, and to keep Stevie hidden. As much as he would like to join this horsey herd, he is more comfortable in the cloven-hooved, ragtag group that shares his pen.

The next time I visit I am able to get Stevie to agree to leave the barnyard. We go out for a walk on the trail he follows me slowly, looking around, sniffing up and down. When I stop, he stops. He walks at a ridiculously slow pace. No matter how much I encourage him, he will not speed up.

He likes to linger and eat roots. He digs with his front hooves, both hooves, like a dog, energetically making holes that I must refill before the horses come through. He chews the moss off tree trunks.

"What kind of an equine are you?"

Each time I arrive at the farm, I call to him, he answers, and we go for a walk before I ride. When I brought Hannah along for one of our walks, Stevie laid his ears back and lunged for her. I saw it and yelled at him, for the first and only time. He never did it again. For her part, Hannah ducked out of the way, unfazed, and then ignored the ass.

Jonathan lives right next door to the farm and tells me he wants to come for a donkey walk. He visits with me, and spends a lot of time making jokes about little Stevie: he thinks my ass has an oddly shaped ass. He may be right, but still, I protest loudly. The next time we go over, Jonathan decides he wants to take Sal, the llama, with us. Like Stevie, Sal has rarely been out of the critter pen. Jonathan is intrigued by his oddity and thinks it would be funny to take a llama for a walk.

I put a halter on the skittish creature, and we set off: me and Stevie, Jonathan and Sal, and out in front, Hannah leading the way. If Jonathan walks behind Stevie, I can move my ass more quickly. He trots and even breaks into a charming little canter. Sal canters, too, his knobby legs and long neck reaching out ahead, causing Jonathan to struggle to keep up. We stop at the pasture and let them eat some fresh grass. Jonathan thinks Sal needs to eat more and is reluctant to pull him away so that we can go home. Finally I prevail by asserting that the change in diet could upset the llama's stomach (that might well be true—I'm guessing), and it works: we head home, returning the critters to their pen.

They like to be out. But they also love the comfort of their motley crew, the hodgepodge of species that their family comprises.

Have I mentioned that my own odd, eccentric, homemade family has become multigenerational? That's right: I have acquired children, a whole host of them. Did I mention that?

When I started working in admissions, I got to know many of the students whose applications I read. I learned about them on paper, and then, when they showed up on campus the next fall, I tracked down a select few because from what I'd read, I thought I wanted to know them. Usually I was right.

After my first year, I decided to hire a work-study student to help me with recruiting the top applicants, a special assignment I'd been given. When I met the incoming kids, I found my girl. Redheaded, freckled, with a smile that lit up the world, I tapped Lauren to work with me. She did, for three years, and when I quit my job in admissions, we continued to breakfast together every Friday morning at Elmo's, a local coffee shop. Each week she brought with her the excitement and passion of new ideas, always eager to tell me about a lecture she'd heard, a conversation she'd had. I listened and then asked her to think about the assumptions she made, caused her to reflect on her developing self. I saw myself in her, and tried to help sharpen her intellectual edges while she maintained a soft and gregarious personality that I envied and which made me proud.

There were more, others. One was a boy whose permission I'd needed to use his essay in an article. He'd written back, flattered, and asked if he could have coffee with me. He was a handsome frat boy, but also an English major—the kind of guy who'd sit at the end of the bar and not say anything, but whom all the girls would look at and wonder what he was thinking. We set up a regular weekly breakfast. Soon I was having "office hours" over huevos rancheros and endless cups of decaf. I met with premeds, prelaws, and pre-I-have-no-earthly-idea-what-I-want-to dos. Those breakfasts fueled me with intellectual and emotional sustenance.

After I returned from California, I began to write a running column for the local paper, the *Durham Herald-Sun,* and soon after I got an e-mail from the athletic director of a state-funded boarding school for gifted eleventh- and twelfth-graders whose campus was just a mile up the street from the Hovel. Did I know of anyone who might want to be the cross-country coach?

Surprise. I wanted to be the coach; I thought it would be fun. In spite of the fact that I'd never run cross-country, had never before coached or been coached, was scared by the thought of driving a fifteen-person bus, and didn't have the required first aid certification, I told her I was interested. I went in for an interview at 11:45 a.m. and at three the same afternoon I was meeting with the team. I was hired because I met the most important criteria: I was available every afternoon, I was willing and eager to do the job, and no one else had applied and they were desperate.

My runners taught me the facts about how meets are scored—it's complicated, believe me—and gave me the low-down on what was expected from the coach. (They wanted me to tell them what to do.) I told them what my expectations were: I didn't give a hoot about winning. Academics came first, then developing as individuals, then having fun. Only after all that did I care about our record as a team. I told them I never wanted to hear them say "Do we have to run today?" I wanted them to love to run, to realize that we "get" to run, rather than "have" to.

I wanted my kids to understand what it took me a few decades to get, that it was a both/and situation. They could be intellectuals *and* runners, academics *and* athletes. At the ends of practice, we did rudimentary yoga (I had taken a few classes here and there, and yoga-guru Val provided a list of runner-appropriate poses) and SAT vocabulary drills. I had them write essays to earn my old but never-worn race T-shirts.

After the season was over, I took a handful of the kids with me to one of my running club's races. I'd asked them not to call me "Coach" around my friends.

"Why, Coach, are you embarrassed? You shouldn't be embarrassed."

"Can't you call me Rachel? Just for today? Please? Please?"

I'd encouraged them to do this during the season. But most of them—especially the boys—resisted. It felt strange to be called Coach, though I did surprise myself by turning and answering whenever I heard the word.

"But we love you, Coach. We love that you're our coach. We're proud of you."

I couldn't help but smile. These kids were so great, so great for me.

"Humor me. Around my friends, call me by my name."

After the race, when I went up to collect my award—a huge chocolate bar that I was happy to share with the kids—I heard a collective cry go up from my runners:

"Way to go, Mom!"

The next time I take Stevie out alone, I decide to let him off the lead. I walk behind him, and then he moves off at a trot.

"Hey!"

His ears swivel back, he turns his head toward me.

"Stop, you little stinker."

He slows.

As soon as I get near enough to touch him, he kicks up his heels and canters away.

I run after him. I notice that he keeps looking back, making sure I am still following.

"Stevie!"

He stops. I walk up to him.

"You pain in the ass, ass."

He nestles his head under my hand while I reattach the lead rope, and we turn to walk home. I cannot believe how cute he is and how much joy he gives me. I know that he is happier having left his pen. I am proud of him for being brave enough to do it.

Women of my generation were raised with strange and mixed messages. We were told we could be president and then, when bored in school, we scribbled our first names followed by the last names of the cute boys in class. Our mothers began, tentatively, to work outside the home. They attended consciousness-raising sessions; they burned their bras. And then they came back and cooked dinner, cleaned the house, and did the laundry. We could grow up to be anything, they said, and

by the way, what kind of silver pattern would you like? The expectation was meaningful work and marriage and kids.

And yet I know dozens of people—both women and men—in
their thirties, forties, and fifties who have never married. Some have
been in long-term relationships—lived in coupledom—but have not
tied the matrimonial knot. Some have lived their entire adult lives
without having to share a bathroom, kitchen, or, on any kind of regular basis, a bedroom.

Why aren't all of us getting married? Why does it become so
hard, once you're a grown-up, to commit to a relationship? When I'm
in airports, watching people stream by, I often, unconsciously, do a
hand check: I look at the ring fingers and marvel at how many sport
wedding bands. How do they do it? How do they know they've found
the right person? What have they forsaken in order to wear that ring?
Have they somehow avoided forsaking anything? Or at least, anything important? My guess is that a lot of them married young. I married young. There wasn't as much to think about back then, and I
wasn't as fully myself to worry about what I'd be giving up.

There's a reason the age of conscription ends at thirty. No one
wants to join the military when they're old enough to know better,
unless of course there's a good reason to fight. Plus, after thirty, it's
harder to control the recruits. They start questioning everything.
They won't just follow orders.

A friend who is a classical scholar says he doesn't like teaching
Latin to adults. There are some things you just have to take on faith
if you're going to learn another language, particularly an old dead
one. Young people suck up the information blandly and blindly. The
older ones want to know why. Like two-year-olds: Why? Why? Why?
Try getting into a relationship with one of them.

So some of us don't. We live these sometimes happy, sometimes
lonely lives. We have friends. We go out. We take trips together. It's
not a bad way to live. It's just different from what our parents' generation did, and it's unrecognizable to our peers who got married young
and are still, some of them, contentedly coupled. When you've been
single long enough, it's hard to make the necessary compromises that

allow for relationships. But we keep looking. We get into love affairs, and we get out. We are hopefully seeking, hopefully eager. And hopelessly critical.

They don't make a lot of movies about contented singletons. We may have evolved from the time of Shakespeare, when comedies always ended in a marriage, and yet, we do still want movies and novels to end with people going two-by-two onto the ark of the nuclear family.

There can be no doubt: Romantic love adds a richness and excitement to life. What is more delicious than waiting for the phone to ring when you are smitten? What is more riveting than hearing, for the first time, the stories that make your new lover who he is? What is more erotic than a first kiss? The feeling you get in your heart, your stomach—lower—when you see him again after an absence of only a few hours, the way the sound of his voice is enough to make your heart quicken. The tingle of spying him from across a crowded room, knowing that later you will get to unwrap that package; looking under the hood, the thrill of the new is one of the greatest thrills of all. Who doesn't want to fall in love? Like pregnancy, it's a state of expectation, of anticipating a fresh future. It's about hope and glory, about unchartered possibilities, about a new you.

I love falling in love. I want to do it again and again. Maybe someday it will last. Maybe not. I am still hopeful, still hopefully seeking.

I am beginning to realize, though, that what does last, what sustains and grows and completes and nourishes me, is the love I get from being my own friend, from enjoying my own company. And from the families I've made, my own crazy collection of critters, who may or may not be like me, but with whom I share (and have shared) a love that is as real and as important as any I could hope to find with a romantic partner. I don't care if they have four legs, tails, hooves, slow 5K times, neckties with food remnants, make childish mistakes in grammar, leave the toilet seat up, eat books, read bad books, leave me waiting for an extra twenty minutes at Elmo's because they are college students and are too hungover to get up on time. I don't care if they sometimes poop in the house—I love who I love.

Since I quit my job, I have moved down, down, down the financial ladder. I have not cracked into the five-figure income bracket for the last two years. I spend almost no money on food; when I am not fed by my friends, I eat popcorn for dinner with hot chocolate for protein. Like zillions of Americans, I am without health insurance. I do not buy new clothes, though I am frequently clad in hand-me-down Prada from generous girlfriends. I live frugally in my Hovel.

Life, Thoreau tells us, looks poorest when you are richest. I feel filthy rich.

I walk to the gate of the critter pen. Stevie sees me and begins to paw the floor like a raging bull. He bites the top of the gate while I sort through the big horse halters to find his. As I go to open the gate, the goats come over. Tess and Sal follow. They have gotten used to me, are happy to see me. I say hello, and toss them some grain. Stevie nudges one of the goats, shoves, hard, to get her out of the way.

He moves quickly to leave the paddock, to get on the trail, our trail. We go to the sand riding arena and he starts nosing the ground, walking in a circle. I let him. I'm not sure what he's doing, so I watch and wait.

Then his legs buckle beneath him, and he sinks to the ground.

I'm afraid he's sick: horses with colic lie down. My heart is racing. He cannot be ill. I could not bear it.

He lies on the sand. Most horses will not let people near them while they are on the ground: if your only means of defense is to run away, you tend not to laze around in the dirt.

But Stevie is not a horse, and he is not sick. He is rolling. His little hooves are pointed skyward, wiggling as he tosses himself back and forth over his backbone. He is joyfully, playfully, rolling on the ground like a puppy, as Hannah has always done.

He stops, and, still supine, looks up at me. I sit down in the sand next to him and scratch his ears. He places his big ass head in my lap. And then, I see it. Stevie has left his pen. He has discovered a new world, a new self. It was scary at first. But leaving was the right thing. I knew this for him, and now I know it for me. I remembered my Milton: "Space may produce new worlds." Like Stevie, I have been comfortable in my surroundings and have been perhaps afraid to kick up my heels and make big changes. Maybe now it is time.

Eleven

She was growing old now and so was Flush. She bent down over him for a moment. Her face with its wide mouth and its great eyes and its heavy curls was still oddly like his. Broken asunder, yet made in the same mould, each, perhaps, completed what was dormant in the other.
But she was woman; he was dog.

—Virginia Woolf

Hannah has become, unaccountably, inexplicably, shockingly, an old dog. I don't know when it happened. She is seventeen, ancient for someone her size. She is completely deaf. Her eyes have the thin cloud of age on them; her vision is foggy. She walks stiff-legged, shuffling. No

231

longer does she prance on diagonals like a trotting horse—front and back leg on each side of her body move in concert now, not much bend in the joints.

Her muzzle, formerly black, has gone gray, her expression seems less worried, now that her eyebrows have turned white, blending into her face, making it, to those who do not know her well, less expressive. Her cinnamon-and-sugar coat now looks sweeter, more flecked with light. She is frail. She has lost a third of her body mass—her former barrel shape has thinned, and each of her ribs is visible. She's chosen not to eat dried dog food, her staple for the past sixteen years. She's gone on hunger strikes, waiting for hamburger or roasted chicken to appear in her bowl. Before I realized, before I knew it was a choice and not illness, she would go for days without eating. Now I buy roasted chickens and canned dog food for her.

She no longer follows me around the house. Often she will leave my side and lie down in another room, go upstairs while I am downstairs. Sometimes she doesn't want to do as I ask. She will look away, refusing to catch my eye. Since she went deaf, we have worked out a system of sign language, dependent on eye contact. I sometimes see her willfully refusing to look at me, stating clearly her preferences. I respect this. She can read my lips. I mouth to her: I love you. She shoots love at me, thumps her tail a few times, and then closes her eyes.

Many days she is as sprightly as a puppy. She still gets the paper each morning. She goes out to the yard, looks at me, looks at the paper, and waits for me to motion for her to get it. Sometimes she wanders. Sometimes she stops to pee, or sniff. Sometimes I have to beckon repeatedly. But then she pounces on it and comes trotting, head high, paper in mouth to the door, where I wait with a treat.

But she can no longer manage the stairs by herself. While she can, slowly, laboriously go up, coming down frightens her. It's not that she's physically incapable, merely scared by the vulnerability of age. I have to escort her, sometimes touching her reassuringly on the head, other times simply standing by her side. And then she makes her descent. She waits for me. Sometimes she calls me from the top of the stairs, barking—previously she had never barked as a request, only as an announcement—until I am there to walk her down.

One morning she had trouble coming down the stairs. It seemed that her hind end was weak. She struggled to walk. I managed to get her outside so that she could pee and I could watch her gait. I watched her walk, and then I became dizzy. As worried as I was about her, I had to sit down with my head between my knees.

She came back inside, still wobbly. I examined each of her feet. I ran my hands over her legs and body, checking for soreness. As I watched her move, it occurred to me that it seemed she, too, was dizzy.

We went immediately to the veterinarian. We were brought into the examining room by a vet tech who asked me to describe the problem.

"It's going to sound crazy," I said, "but I think she's dizzy."

"Oh, sure," said the young woman. "Geriatric canine vestibulitis. We see it a lot in older dogs."

When the vet came in, she confirmed the diagnosis. An inflammation of the inner ear. What had looked catastrophic to me was just another artifact of aging. Hannah had tilted her head to try to right the world as she saw it. The dizziness had gone away, but she remained slightly tilted.

We have grown up together, Hannah and I. She has been my constant, loving companion for the past seventeen years, through moves, and boyfriends, and jobs, and no jobs, and travels. She is my life. I am now only middle-aged, but she is old. She is very, very old.

After the dizzy spell, I had the conversation with Suzy, my vet, that I never thought I'd be capable of. I asked how many dogs Hannah's age she'd seen.

Suzy shook her head. "Her size? Maybe five. None were as healthy as Hannah is now. But, Rachel," she said, touching my arm, "she's a very old lady. Very, very old."

Thinking of the unthinkable and having to plan for it. To love someone this much is almost unbearable.

* * *

We have adjusted our routines: shorter walks, bowls of water both upstairs and down, softer beds with more padding. It still feels odd to hear a doorbell not followed by the sound of barking. People can come in the house when Hannah is upstairs, and she doesn't realize it. I go up and escort her down, and then she stands and barks. Her voice is hoarse, deeper, her barking less enthusiastic.

She still likes to go. She is expectant in the early evening, waiting to see if I am leaving alone or if we will together be off to Jonathan's or Mike's to hang out. When I motion to her that yes, she is coming, she prances and circles and stands by the door. If I explain that she's in for the night, she goes to her bed and follows me with her eyes. The worst is when I am packing for a trip. If I am not taking her, I pack furtively. I cannot bear to see the disappointment in her cloudy eyes. While I am gone, I never stop worrying.

Vacuuming up the clumps of dog hair that collect in every corner of every room in my house, the way it's been for almost all my adult life, I wonder what it would be like to live without dog hair, without pieces of stray dry dog food on the kitchen floor, to have the backseat of the car be uncovered. I can think about it for a moment, and then I move my mind along. It is unthinkable.

I recently came home late from a night out. Hannah no longer wakes when I enter the house. I must walk upstairs and rouse her. I have tried every way I can think of to wake her without a startle, a jolt, but she is always surprised. She used to be so vigilant. Nothing ever got by her.

I put my hand on her shoulder, touched her softly. She did not wake. I rocked her gently. She lifted her head slowly, not in the jerky normal What? What's happening? Where am I? way. She looked drunk.

"Come on, little dude, let's go out for a pee."

She stood, but she was wobbly. I waited at the top of the stairs, as usual, ready to go down with her, step by step, my hand on her head to give her confidence, assurance.

But she was unsteady.

I scooped her up and carried her downstairs. She has never liked to be carried. Even now, when it is an effort for her to climb the stairs, if I offer to carry her, she tries to move more quickly, proving she neither wants nor needs the extra help.

I carried her downstairs and brought her outside, watching from the door as she took tentative steps into the yard.

She looked around, walked a few steps, and then fell.

She lifted her head, confused. She looked back at me and then— she was flat on the ground, head down as if she were about to roll they way she used to roll, full of play, full of joy, legs kicking in the air.

But there was no joy, no play.

I rushed over to her.

Her head was heavy.

I couldn't wake her.

I bent to pick her up, but her body was floppy, and I couldn't get a purchase.

I continued, frantic now, working to get my arms underneath her, and with a strength that was not mine, I carried her inside.

If she was breathing, I could not tell.

I pleaded with her to wake, wake up, I love you, wake up.

This could not be it. It could not be.

I held her head in my hands.

Wake up, Hannah, I need you. Wake up.

Panic, desperation. I thought about calling the emergency vet service. I thought about calling Jonathan.

And then, she opened her eyes, her glassy, age-veiled eyes, and looked at me.

She shook her head, confused.

I smothered her with kisses, and she shook me off.

She scrambled to her feet, toenails clicking against the hardwood floor.

I offered her water; she didn't drink.

I carried her up the stairs. She settled in to be carried and then settled onto her bed, near my bed, her limbs stiff and creaky buckling uncomfortably under her.

I watched her and dialed Jonathan's number.

As soon as he answered, I began to cry, to sob.

I'd been holding it together, keeping myself together, thought that I might be okay even if she wasn't. I knew this wasn't true.

Hannah fainted, I told him.

He waited.

"She is fine now," I was able to say.

She was watching me crying, watching me talk on the phone.

Jonathan listened to me, and then he spoke, his voice the voice he used when he told me stories to put me to sleep, the voice of a caring doctor, a kind man, a good friend.

It could have been an arrhythmia, he offered. Or it could have been a seizure.

There was nothing to be done, nothing that needed to be done.

I knew that he was concerned about Hannah. And that he was also thinking about Emma.

We hung up, and I watched her from my bed.

I was afraid to go to sleep.

I knew that she was, for the moment, fine, and that I was making her upset by being upset. She watched me, head down, unwilling to close her eyes.

We spent much of the night like this.

Hannah is not—has never been—a pet. The mouse, the rat, the cat, the pig, the horse, the ass—as much as I loved them, they were pets. Hannah is something else entirely. She is my heart, my soul, the most stable and steadying influence I have known for the last seventeen years. I know the time we have now is borrowed. I wonder how I will go on without her.

In order to be good, really good with animals, you have to be able to love them deeply and to think yourself into their world—to step outside yourself, leave behind your ego with its nagging need for attention and respect, and figure out what interests them. What do they like, what do they love? What smells good to a dog? (Sometimes it's cheeseburgers; often it's rank dead things.) Where on a pig's body does she most like to be rubbed? What soothes an anxious mouse?

Food will take you far in terms of reaching into the animal heart, but not all the way. You have to recognize what scares a dog, cat, snake, mouse, horse, or pig, what pleases them, motivates and shames them. (Animals are not immune to shame.) You learn these things by watching and listening, by attending to them. Adam got the task of naming, a task that each of us shares when we bring a new critter into our lives. By naming you make something, someone, yours. Once she's yours, you have the burden of care, which, without love, is simply a burden.

If an animal disappoints you, you have only yourself to blame: a lack of understanding, unrealistic expectations, crossed communications. Perhaps, perhaps the same is true in our relations with two-legged critters. Perhaps the fault lies not in the stars.

To be less disappointed in yourself—well, there's a task. Striving for perfection is as exhausting as it is daunting, but overachieving is a tough habit to break. Suspending disbelief may be easier than suspending judgment.

I look at myself and my friends, my high-achieving, professionally successful, smart, funny, attractive friends. My friends who travel the world, who run the world, who are rewarded in most of the tangible ways of the world. My single friends.

When it comes to our love lives, we are, as I've said, hopefully eager and hopelessly picky. We have made our own beds, and in them we lie, alone.

And you know what? It can be darned nice to have that bed all to yourself.

The animals in my life have not only given me love, unstrained and undiluted, but they have also shown me myself. Perhaps I am drawn to those who reflect what I need to see: the smallness of a

mouse, the angry frustration of a rat misunderstood, the solidity and
security and wisdom of a great dog, the narcissism and self-interest of
a pig, the need for control felt by a horse, the independence and surprising tenderness of a feral cat, and the oddity and *sui generis*ness of
an ass. I have loved both wisely, and too well. None have I loved
more than Hannah, and now I am having to prepare myself for the
fact that she is only getting older and more frail.

Just as Hannah has slowed, so have I. In my youth, I rushed head-
long into a career; now I am content to be without a business card,
that passport to grown-up life. I have gone from being someone who
always had a boyfriend to not even wanting one. I've come to value
my time alone so much that it is hard to make room for anyone else.
My needs are richly fulfilled by the animals, friends, family, and, yes,
ex-boyfriends who sustain me. Instead of thinking about a man, I
have had the intellectual capital to work on my own stuff, my writing
and my life. I travel a lot—to where there are people who love me
and will feed me. I have nothing but freedom and flexibility and answer to no one. I am secure in my friendships, if not my finances. I
am trying to forgive myself for not always being the best—at everything, at anything. I'm working on appreciating what is good about
those I love and forgiving them my trespasses of judgment. I have
made community, found friends. I will not live alone, even if I am
"single."

I have made the decision to go back to school, to pursue a graduate degree in writing. I want this, the writing life, but know that I
have a lot to learn. I want to be in a community of readers and writers, to stretch and bend and glean wisdom from strong voices. When
I am finished with my degree, perhaps I'll teach. Perhaps I'll write.
Certainly, I will be changed.

While some people are fearful of the unknown, I am made antsy
by the familiar. I have chosen to go to Montana, a place as different
and foreign as I can imagine. A place of icy winters and inspired
scenery—lush valleys, glacial lakes, and ragged, jagged mountains. A

place where the buffalo still roam, where bears are grizzlies, and where there are six acres of land for every person. A place of space.

I am preparing to leave. I am preparing to go by myself. No man, no pet.

Hannah will not be making the trip West with me. I know this. I cannot talk about it; I try not to think about it. But I know.

I am going to be on my own, and I am able to do this because I am not alone. Shoring me up, supporting me in every way, I have my family—the one I was born into and the one I made.

After college, I spent seven years living in New York City, and then thirteen years ago, I packed up my dog and left Manhattan for the South. During these past two decades, I have fallen in and out of love with a number of men and have fallen only in love—never out—with a variety of animals.

Why, I wonder, is it so easy to love an animal, so hard to live with a man?

Loving animals allows us to access the most tender, most vulnerable, parts of ourselves. Their needs are relatively simple: good food, clean water, a soft place to sleep, exercise to get their ya-yas out, activities to keep their minds engaged, and love. Animals ask us to love them—different animals in different ways. It is our job to figure out how. And then they love us back, pure and unqualified, devoted and attentive. This is where the goodies lie. We have all seen people— grown up and hardened, high-powered and cutthroat—reduced to giggling, simpering idiots in the presence of their pets. It is impossible not to feel fondness for these people.

I find it uncommonly easy to feel fondness for men. It's not really that hard to live with a man. Romantic relationships with members of our own species are simply more problematic because our complex, convoluted brains make it challenging to know each other and ourselves. The essence of loving is, I think, knowing. Knowing first, and then accepting. Too frequently we end up being with the people we happen to meet; the randomness of the universe works both for and against us. Sometimes we are with the wrong person because we met him at the right moment. Sometimes stars get crossed when we find our true love in a place where the time is out of joint. Sometimes, perhaps often, our expectations, our fantasies—the stories we've been told about what love is and isn't—get in the way of finally finding lasting love.

In Plato's *Symposium,* a group of men spend an evening drinking together and each, in his way, gives a speech in praise of love. When it's Aristophanes' turn, the comic poet tells a creation myth.

Originally, according to Aristophanes, we were all little round blobs, circle people with two sets of arms, two sets of legs, and one head with two faces, facing in different directions. They could walk, but when they really needed to move, they rolled.

At a certain point in prehistory, these roly-pollies got uppity and foolishly tried to launch an attack on the gods. The gods were not pleased. After much thought, mighty Zeus decided to put the human blobs in their place. So he smote them in two. They were split, right down the middle.

Humans were ever after condemned to search the earth, looking for their lost "other half."

The notion that originally we were one, we were whole, and that the desire and pursuit of the whole is called love, has messed us up in profound ways. The idea of looking for someone else to complete you, whose identity can merge with your own, is pernicious. Aristophanes' joke is on us.

Rainer Maria Rilke provides another, more serious account of romantic love in his *Letters to a Young Poet.* Rilke warns that truly loving does not mean surrendering to another person. Young lovers, he explains, mistakenly tend to glom onto one another until "they can no longer tell whose outlines are whose."

Rilke's metaphor for a more evolved—still perhaps unattainable— ideal of romantic love is when "two solitudes protect and border and greet each other." Two solitudes who touch. How infinitely preferable an image to that of two desperate halves trying to smush themselves into one blob.

Two solitudes. How lovely. But really, how many of us, male or female, are truly realized, self-contained units? It's easier to search for someone to fill the gaps, to make up for what we are lacking in ourselves—to abdicate the responsibility to complete ourselves and just find someone who might, we think, do it for us.

This is what we must resist. The ancient Rabbi Tarphon cautioned: "It is not necessary for you to complete the work, but neither are you free to desist from it." Whether it is the work of service to some higher power, perfecting the world, oneself, or a relationship with another person, the admonition is well worth remembering. And repeating to ourselves. Perhaps the key to a good relationship is work, work, work. And then play, play, play. We must not to forget to play. The work makes romantic love manageable, like weeding a garden. The play makes it an earthly delight.

Walking at the end of Mike's driveway on a cold spring day, I turn to see a tiny baby squirrel about ten feet away.

"Hello," I say, crouching down.

The squirrel crawls right to me, crawls right into my outstretched hand.

Now what?

I look around for a nest, a mother, a clue of what to do. I try to shoo him back on his way, but he keeps returning to me. He has the trusting insistence of the very, very young.

I bring him inside Mike's house. He has crawled into the pocket of my fleece vest. I find a shoe box, line it with one of Mike's old T-shirts, and try to put the squirrel in. He will not leave my hand.

I coax him down into the box, and he looks up at me.

"Here," I say, and cover him with a T-shirt. He curls up into a ball while I try to figure out what to do.

After four calls, I find a wildlife rescue operation. The woman on the phone tells me that the squirrel's mother was probably killed, that he may be dehydrated. She tells me how to check, as you would with a horse, by gently pinching the skin. I do, and he is. The woman tells me that I can feed him a solution of water, salt, and sugar. She says I can bring him in, and they will nurse him until he's old enough to be released. She says it is illegal to keep a squirrel captive in the state of North Carolina. When I hesitate, she tells me that if I don't bring him in, he will probably die. She adds that adult squirrels don't make good pets.

This woman on the phone does not know that I am good with animals. She does not know that I have loved a long list of them, loved them for themselves, seen who they really are. Nor does she know that my animals have completed various parts of me and taught me things about myself I couldn't have begun to know if I'd stuck with my own species. She doesn't know that I am about to strike out on my own and a squirrel would be a good companion now.

I tell her I'll think about it. She says they'll be open first thing in the morning.

I take the little guy out of his box and hold him in my hand. I give him a few drops of solution. He licks my fingers dry, looks around for a moment, and then nuzzles in again. He curls up, and I stroke his ears and watch while his eyes get heavy and then close. He is perfect.

I decide to keep him overnight.

But I do not name him.

I know when I wake up the next morning that I cannot claim this wild creature. I know that I must give him up. I know that he must be cared for in ways I cannot provide. He has a squirrel life, a wild destiny of his own to live out.

I bring him to the rescue center and relinquish him into the hands of the veterinarian.

And I am alone, about to embark on a new chapter, wondering hopefully who the next critters to cross my path will be: the next animal, the next man. I am looking to live my own wild destiny, whatever that is. Rattling in my head, I hear the final words of James Joyce's young artist: "I go to encounter for the millionth time the reality of experience."

My own ambitions may be less lofty than those of Stephen Daedalus, after whom, in my youth, I named a six-toed yellow cat, but still, I go forth: optimistic, energetic, hopeful, knowing that the love in my heart will land somewhere and be expressed. It will be expressed.

Acknowledgments

This book was birthed by a quartet of midwives: good, strong, smart women all, animal lovers all.

My deepest appreciation goes to my publishing team, "Laurielle." Danielle Friedman, editorial wunderkind, and Laureen Rowland, gracefully feline publisher, repeatedly and carefully, with good cheer and humor, went over every word of this book more times than I can believe or give thanks for. No author could hope for better and more thoughtful attention.

When my literary agent, Susan Arellano, told me about feeding noodles to Mr. Lucky, her daughter's guinea pig, I knew that she was the one who I could tell it to, the person to help me bring to print my love for animals (and men). Susan has made me think harder, write better, and have more fun with this than I would ever have imagined possible. She is the *ne plus ultra* of agents, the ass-kicking, smart-alecking, cut-through-the-crap cream of the editorial crop. She continues to provide me with tough love and funny lines, and I continue to feel thankful for her every single day.

Candace Karu made it possible for me to write. Simply, without Candace this book would not exist. I respect and admire her more than I can say; my gratitude is as boundless as my love for her.

This book is not about women. But I could have written volumes on these amazing creatures.

About the Author

Rachel Toor graduated *cum laude* from Yale University and spent the following ten-plus years climbing the editorial ladder in the publishing industry, after which she became an admissions counselor at Duke University. She currently lives in Missoula, Montana.